IMPROV FOR DEMOCRACY

SUNY series in New Political Science
_____

Bradley J. Macdonald, editor

IMPROV FOR DEMOCRACY

HOW TO BRIDGE DIFFERENCES AND DEVELOP THE COMMUNICATION AND LEADERSHIP SKILLS OUR WORLD NEEDS

DON WAISANEN

SUNY PRESS

This project was supported by a research sabbatical from the City University of New York

Published by State University of New York Press, Albany

For information, contact State University of New York Press, Albany, NY
www.sunypress.edu

Library of Congress Cataloging-in-Publication Data

Name: Waisanen, Don, author.
Title: Improv for democracy : how to bridge differences and develop the
    communication and leadership skills our world needs / Don Waisanen.
Description: Albany : State University of New York Press, [2020] | Series:
    SUNY series in new political science | Includes bibliographical references and
    index.
Identifiers: LCCN 2020015262 | ISBN 9781438481159 (hardcover : alk. paper) |
    ISBN 9781438481166 (pbk. : alk. paper) | ISBN 9781438481173 (ebook)
Subjects: LCSH: Citizenship—Study and teaching. | Democracy—Study and
    teaching. | Plays—Improvisation.
Classification: LCC LC1091 .W345 2020 | DDC 372.89—dc23
LC record available at https://lccn.loc.gov/2020015262

10 9 8 7 6 5 4 3 2 1

Contents

Acknowledgments

This project came into being through others' generosity. I'd like to thank David Hoffman, Michael Phillips-Anderson, Deborah Dunn, and Greg Spencer for their early feedback on chapter drafts, and my impeccable research assistants Prabin Ranamagar and Shana Kieran-Kaufman. I'm grateful to Cindy Thompson and Raquel Benbunan-Fich for believing that having students up on their feet and playing with one another could make a significant contribution to an executive MBA curriculum. The same thanks go to Jerry Mitchell and Patria de Lancer Julnes, for allowing me the space to run Improv for Democracy as a course with our public administration students. To Dean David Birdsell, his incredible staff, and all of my colleagues and students at the Baruch College, CUNY Marxe School of Public and International Affairs, I owe immense gratitude for the ways that you have supported and inspired my scholarship over the last decade. I'd also like to thank Becky Heino and Beth Yoshida-Fisher at Columbia University's School of Professional Studies, Kim Pearce and friends at the CMM Institute for Personal and Social Evolution, Marian Rich, Carrie Lobman, and many others at the East Side Institute, Michael Seltzer and Gaurav Bawa at the New York Community Trust Leadership Fellows program, and Todd Kelshaw at Montclair State University for providing me with other platforms for this work. My thinking has also been greatly informed by partnerships with many individuals and organizations working in the public interest, especially the Kettering Foundation. From the improv comedy world, I'd like to thank Gary Kramer for years of being able to perform with the National Comedy Theater and run WITS Teambuilding sessions. Without Jill Shely, Glenn Packman, Drew Tarvin, Amelia Fowler, Mike Gregorek, Jason Scott Quinn, and so many others, I wouldn't have had the honor of performing and working with the incredible cast of Comedysportz New York City. To everyone in the Applied Improvisation Network, thank you for the years you've labored to make this work matter around the world (and a second shout out here to the fearless Marian Rich for co-leading AIN-NYC with me and being a continual source of encouragement on this project). To my parents, thanks for your unconditional support and love, every day I'm trying to pay it forward. Last, all my love goes to my spouse, Lauren, and sons, Joel, Sam, and Levi, who every day teach me how to best improvise into the future.

Introduction

The Upward Call

In a small city in the Netherlands, the tensions between police and Dutch-Moroccan youth had reached a crisis point. After a young man robbed a bus driver, officers and youth began clashing on the streets. One young person, Ilias, expressed his anger toward the cops for arresting him several times, beating him violently, and throwing him into some thorn trees. On the other hand, with so many kids standing on street corners engaging in suspicious behaviors or hurling insults, the police felt they were simply doing their jobs. Fueled by media stories about rising crime, the conflict spiraled out into the community when local restaurants began refusing service to the young people. Throughout the city, shouting, hatred, and distrust filled the air. Like so many places in the world, this had become a normal part of life.[1]

For close to a year facilitators tried to bring the two groups together. As part of the intervention, they asked the police and youth to play improvisational games with one another. With much skepticism and little interest in the process, the young people told one another it would be useless to engage with the police. One participant even said that for the first few meetings he wouldn't shake hands with anyone in law enforcement because of how violently he had been treated. From the opposite end, one officer shared how the idea of playing games with the young people originally sounded ridiculous to his squad.

But then something extraordinary happened. After engaging in these exercises, the officers and young people began to move beyond their rigid positions and see the humanity in one another. In one activity, the facilitators asked the police and youth to switch roles for a day, improvising what it might be like to step into the other's shoes. The young people donned police uniforms and traveled through the city on bikes, while the cops acted out the youth standing on street corners and giving the officers a hard time. The shouting and anger turned into laughter and empathy. Both sides enjoyed the activity immensely, and the stage was set for real, solutions-focused conversations.

After these experiences, Marieke Borg, a police officer in the city, shared how she would now greet young men on the street, a previously unthinkable behavior. One young man related that "the two groups became one, and they understood each other better." Another officer shared, "I have been released of my negativity. The negative feeling I had toward these boys." In fact, the project's first year was so successful that the youth and police continued into a second. Jaap Norda, a researcher analyzing the intervention, noted how such "changes begin at a small scale. . . . an atomic reaction starts between two molecules, but the explosion has an enormous effect."[2]

Over twenty years ago, I went to see a live, professional improv comedy performance for the first time. I was stunned by how the performers worked with and trusted one another. They exhibited a level of play and joy seldom seen in everyday life, constantly built on one another's lines and actions rather than negating them, and overall, practiced fearless, seemingly superhuman communication skills. After, I decided to take an improv class, and I have never looked back. Little did I know that what basically started as a fun hobby would go on to have so much application to the rest of life. When I look back at what fields have most informed my thinking, improvisation remains at the core. Beyond its personal and professional benefits, however, the applications of improvisation hold the potential to transform our organizations and societies in ways previously unimagined. As the police and young people in the Netherlands discovered, improvising well matters.

As they also learned, the potential for change begins with us. Our lives mostly hang on the quality of what we say and how we interact with one another.[3] Day by day and moment by moment, we spend our lives affecting one another for better or worse in every encounter. Sometimes strong friendships dissolve from a lack of conversations. Different communication styles or statements interpreted in different ways can create unproductive tensions in the workplace where there were none. These stakes are only raised in our neighborhoods, communities, and nations, with racial and ethnic divisions arising from the ways that people talk about one another. Leaders have collapsed economies with their words, while politicians have traded insults that have brought us to the brink of world wars.[4]

In our increasingly partisan and polarized world, we need to find new ways to educate and train for democracy. Think about how people often approach one another on just about any major political issue, from immigration to the climate crisis, and you'll mostly find monologues rather than dialogues, fixed talking points rather than open and honest inquiry, and entrenched tribal positions and group loyalties rather than listening and attempts to work across differences. As life increasingly goes online, it's also clear that the architectures of social media and other platforms frequently compound these problems by fueling social distrust, informational enclaves, and other forms of isolation and anxiety.[5] If there's one point that even many public leaders agree on, it's that "the partisan discord in our country followed very closely on the heels of schools stopping to teach civic education."[6]

Traditional notions of civic education and training will remain important but inadequate for addressing this challenge, however. The US Department of Education published a report arguing that narrow conceptions of civic education are not enough to tackle these problems, with a call to "expand education for democracy so it reaches all . . . in ever more challenging ways."[7] A host of educators and analysts have pointed out that "requiring students to take civics classes and relying on their volunteerism may be insufficient to prepare them for the life of active citizenship," so we "need to make a more systematic effort to create opportunities for teaching and learning democracy."[8] In essence, all of this "calls for a new movement to revive and reinvent civic education for the twenty-first century."[9] Such a movement would focus on training the high-level skills of bridging differences with others, learning to make important decisions in an engaged and collaborative manner, and ultimately creating the conditions for outstanding individual, organizational, and societal relationships—an education in the art and science of citizenship.

I found myself compelled to write this book in our current moment because there's no other way of educating and training for citizenship that I, and so many others, have found as powerful and liberating in people's lives. This project builds on many initiatives worldwide to reinvent civic education in new and surprising ways and, most importantly, converges with the best ideas and practices from across disciplines in doing so. I came to the point where keeping this story boxed up for much longer just wouldn't do: there's simply too much unrealized potential at stake for our educational systems, organizations, and societies writ large. It's a story that reminds me of how, as William Gibson once said, "the future is already here—it's just not very evenly distributed."[10]

Before we begin this journey, a good starting point is to recognize how all of us face difficulties in our work with other people. To make this real, I want you to think for a moment about who you struggle with in your work.

Educators often struggle to motivate and connect with their students. Scientists can find it difficult to translate complex ideas to potential funders. Doctors with unfriendly bedside manners may find themselves on the receiving end of patients' tempers or lawsuits. Managers may hurt staff performance by providing infrequent or unhelpful feedback. Executive directors and CEOs can forget to collaborate with others up and down their chains of command. And, as the Netherlands case shows, police and young people may even fail to work with one another, creating problems for their communities that threaten to spiral out of control. These examples all raise the question of what kind of teaching and training could help us most in these types of moments. From our everyday interpersonal interactions to the highest echelons of business and policymaking, we desperately need the skills that can help citizens and societies function more productively on our increasingly interconnected planet.

How Can People Develop the Skills
Our World Most Needs?

What kind of teaching and training can show us *how* to achieve so much more in our interactions with others? Not simply at an intellectual level, but with the full engagement of our bodies, minds, and spirits? I have long explored these questions in my professional work, joining others around the world committed to finding ways of improving human relationships at every level. To these efforts, this book contributes a unique, practical approach that builds upon a growing evidence base and global movement: that improv-based teaching and training methods—which originated in improvisational theater but have since been adapted and evolved in many other contexts—can bridge differences and promote the communication and leadership skills our world urgently needs.

For many readers, the idea that "improvisation" and "theater" should have anything to do with improving the world may at first seem strange. Yet it's important to remember that the best ideas sometimes emerge from the unlikeliest of places. Improvisational theater has traditionally involved performances by actors or comedians in short scenes or longer plays entirely made up "without scripts." Figures such as Tina Fey, Wayne Brady, Stephen Colbert, and many others have all come out of extensive backgrounds in improvisation, with television shows like *Whose Line Is It Anyway* and *Curb Your Enthusiasm* popularizing the form. The tools and values of improv are no longer unique to the field of entertainment, however. Individuals and groups in business, government, nonprofits, and other sectors have found that ideas from improv translate directly into professional settings as a way of quickly improving and leaving a lasting imprint for many skills.[11]

These claims aren't speculative. Emerging scholarly research is now replete with findings demonstrating that people who have undergone improvisation training "improved their confidence, effectiveness, ability to adapt, spontaneity and comfort in successfully handling unique situations."[12] With measured success, improvisation has been used to train scientists, medical and pharmacy staff, engineers, state officers, business students and faculty, service employees, managers, social workers, military personnel, and countless others.[13] Half of the world's top business schools now have a course on improvisation.[14] Fortune 500 companies have even embraced an improvisational model in their work, seeing firsthand that sales representatives have become more effective and empathetic with customers as a result, while CEOs of companies have undergone improv training for professional development.[15]

The organizational value of improvisation makes sense since, in study after study of the skills employers most value, several terms that improv training targets now top the competency lists for twenty-first-century workers: adaptability, enthusiasm, initiative, teamwork, resilience, leadership, and outstanding communication with diverse people.[16] With responses from 600 employers across 44 countries, the Graduate Management Admission Council's annual report finds that communication skills continue to be the most sought-after aptitude among new hires, with speaking and listening skills ranked on average "twice as important as managerial skills."[17] In a survey of 349 executives from across the world, 90 percent identified "organizational agility" as a key differentiator in our current environment,[18] and in recent research, 1,500 chief executives from 60 countries highlighted "creativity" as the most important skill for future leaders and organizations.[19]

These skills have become crucial because the world is changing faster than ever, so much so that "a person who gets locked into a set way of doing things finds it difficult or impossible to adjust."[20] In fact, one of the first experiments using improvisational practices to help citizens involved public services in a Canadian city, where fire department chiefs realized that they needed training to become more adaptive during unexpected moments: "they would be under pressure to drag a passenger from a crashed car, only to find that the door was not quite the same door that they had learned about in basic training."[21] The skill with which firefighters could work with surprises became a recognized competency and a counterweight to using unbending principles and strategies.

This type of need will only intensify, according to the American Association of Colleges and Universities' National Leadership Council, so innovative thinking will be an essential learning outcome for our globally connected futures.[22] From Daniel Goleman's groundbreaking work linking "emotional intelligence" with professional success to Richard Florida's argument that "the creative class" is a key to economic development,[23] organizations are increasingly placing value on finding people who can think and act imaginatively in solving problems.[24]

Applied Improvisation

Given improvisation's relevance to organizations, since the early 2000s a global network of practitioners and scholars have come together to formalize and name this movement: "applied improvisation."[25] Applied improvisation is "the use of principles, tools, practices, skills, and mindsets of improvisational theater in non-theatrical settings."[26] Among other outcomes, it seeks to improve peoples' abilities to listen, accept and support others, be flexible and mindful, take risks, innovate, and create positive professional cultures. Inspired by but different from improv for comedy entertainment, applied improvisation seeks to train "individuals or groups who seek personal development, better teamwork, and more thriving communities," with a focus on "directly impacting personal or organizational change."[27]

Contrary to the kinds of associations the term "improv" may bring up, applied improvisation isn't "winging it," but rather "a highly-refined system of observing, connecting and responding,"[28] with "the honed ability to put all your preparation into practice without getting tangled up by your plans."[29] It's about reacting, adapting, and communicating well, all actions that promote active listening.[30] Even key figures in improvisational theater argued that improv comedy was always meant to be founded first in "what is important about being human in a community," improving the ability of people to connect with one another, understand patterns in their lives, and more.[31]

These ideas have a long history. Many ancients argued that improvisation is a skill requiring training, and should be considered one of the most important subjects in an educational curriculum.[32] Given the weight of evidence for applied improv, I believe that every school should have a required course in the subject, while every community should prioritize this way of thinking and acting in its civic programming—and this book will show both why and how to implement these ideals in practice.

I have been a communication professor and consultant, a researcher of civic engagement and public discourse, and an improvisational performer in Los Angeles and New York City across the last two decades. In addition to running applied improvisation workshops all over the world, I teach improv for executive business and public administration students at the City University of New York and incorporate applied improv in my professional workshops and classes at Columbia University's School of Professional Studies and New York University's Wagner Graduate School of Public Service. In my teaching, improv has helped me drop my scripted lesson plans when necessary to meet the needs and interests of my students as they happen. I have also walked into rooms rife with conflict and seen those tensions dissolve within minutes of getting people up on their feet and trying out new, more positive ways of interacting with one another. In countless teams, applied improvisation has helped me listen better and shift more easily between the roles of leader or follower as the situation demands. In my role as an advisor to many organizations, it has also helped me observe where and how institutions could be more adaptive in their work.

I have never carried out any of these practices perfectly, of course, but with its emphasis on process, learning from and moving beyond mistakes, affirming and adapting to others, and embracing a playful attitude, applied improvisation has substantially aided my own and others' journeys toward these ends. In essence, I often feel that I've held on to a secret for too long: *that improv provides some of the best training for life that one can get.* It has helped me become more aware of when I'm failing to be present with other people during a conversation. It has even changed how I teach courses such as public speaking, reversing the typical classroom setup from lecturing to "side-coaching" students.[33] Most importantly, as this book will highlight each step of the way, applied improvisation has helped me understand how communication works and the role it can play in improving society at a more advanced level. Let's turn to these stakes for a moment.

Pulling Ourselves, Our Organizations, and Our Societies Upward

As our scientific and technological knowledge of the world continues to grow, human beings have failed to develop and spread sophisticated communication practices at the same level.[34] Imagine what would be missing from modern life if engineers had been unable to move beyond the most simple of mathematical formulations. We wouldn't have refrigerators or airplanes, that's for sure. In the same way, think about what we miss by relying on only the most basic understandings and practices of communication. In a conflict with a friend, we may stick to only one narrow story about the problem, omitting many important details or options that could create a better future for us both. In a team meeting, we may get so hung up attributing the organization's problems to others' "personalities" that we fail to think at a higher level about the role that the meeting's very structure or organizational policies could be playing in these problems.[35] In the midst of an intense negotiation, we may get so busy trying to claim value for ourselves that we miss opportunities to create value for both parties.[36] Whether it's a lack of listening or longstanding personal habits, the complexities of communication show that it's anything but a "soft skill." No one achieves anything of consequence without the ability to create meaning and productively interact with others.

Barnett Pearce finds that these are urgent matters and that we're all in a race that we need to win. I founded my consultancy, Communication Upward, on Pearce's ideas that—while so much in the world has the potential to pull humanity *backward*, and though forces like technology can certainly pull us *forward*—what's really needed is better insight into what will take us *upward*. Pearce writes,

> The pull upward consists of new ideas, institutions and practices that elevate and enhance human beings and society. . . . But is the evolution of our ability to act wisely keeping pace with technological developments . . . or sufficient to overcome the downward pull of the old, familiar ways of being? . . . If we divided the past 4,000 years of human history into 200-year increments and plotted innovations in this "upward" direction, we'd rightly say that our era is experiencing a dizzyingly rapid rate of social development—very likely faster than advances in technology.[37]

All of this calls for new ways to improve our social skills. No one approach will ever provide a definitive answer for doing so, but this is a mission whose parts can sum to a greater whole—and applied improvisation provides one avenue for getting us further down this path.

Although evidence on improv's benefits for outcomes such as higher productivity, reduced stress, and improved customer service in business have burgeoned in recent years, this book ultimately points readers toward a larger societal possibility: that *applied improvisational training can provide a foundational education in democratic practices.* We need more and better tools for building trustful relationships in a time of civic crisis. By many measures, including political polarization and the erosion of public discourse, many of us are living in a "diminished democracy" and a "democracy at risk."[38] What's needed are new forms of broadly defined civic engagement, "which include all activities aimed at enhancing the quality of life in a community, not just those designed to address social problems."[39] In other words, "Civic engagement means working to make a difference in the civic life of our communities and developing the combination of knowledge, skills, values and motivation to make that difference. It means promoting the quality of life in a community through both political and non-political processes."[40] These definitions of civic engagement highlight a need to think more widely about the practices that put citizens in contact with one another. Not just surface-level interactions, but interactions that manifest the best of free and collaborative exchanges that take into account one's own and others' needs. If the most central resource for any community is "speaking relationships, among neighbors and acquaintances in addition to friends,"[41] then a commitment to new methods for improving that capacity becomes critical to the civic challenges of our time.

From another perspective, many studies bear out that citizens across the planet now have increased expectations for transparency, co-created services, post-bureaucratic flexibility, trust, and robust communication with public organizations,[42] underscoring the need for more improvisational approaches within such institutions. The advance of many forms of divisive, post-truth populism around the planet has also led scholars to bemoan the decline of a "communication commons—a public space characterized by diversity, tolerance, reason, and facts."[43] Citizens need to build "civic muscle," or the strengthening of "people's capacities to shape the world around them,"[44] yet spaces where citizens can meet and grow their civic selves through positive interactions with others appear to be declining almost universally. In essence, our current political environment implores the development of depolarizing people and organizations.

Addressing these concerns, I move previous conversations and connections about improv into the civic realm, especially in forwarding the value of improvisation for education, governments, nonprofits, healthcare, and other organizations working in the public interest. Challenging existing patterns of thought and behavior, this book will show how different our world could look if improvisational teaching and training methods were part of every educational system, professional development program, and community.

Like the police and youth in the Netherlands, with more diverse people and cultures coming into contact than ever before in human history, we need new skills, habits, and ways of thinking.[45] Consistent with civic engagement research, we need to counteract "the narrative of citizens as combatants with preformed and inflexible preferences" as "incompatible with the still-robust democratic faith in a citizen body concerned with the common good and for a political life that display[s] the virtues of civic friendship and social solidarity."[46] Working with some of the best ideas in the communication field, improv-based methods can promote communication excellence among people. Aligned with decades of leadership studies and current trends toward building distributed and adaptive leadership in organizations, improv training can help individuals translate theory into practice, putting a range of supported ideas about democratic leadership within anyone's reach. For our civic capacities, improv training shows us what communal and political engagement can look like at a societal level. From each of these angles, applied improvisation can build democratic commitments by bridging differences and fostering connections. Following Meira Levinson's lead, this project therefore moves from a focus on "education *within* democracy" to "education *for* democracy."[47]

What You Can Do with This Book

This book offers a novel, unconventional way of teaching and training the hard skills of bridging differences, building connections, and improving communities from the ground up. It's primarily for anyone whose work involves civic education or community engagement, including educators of all kinds, advocates for civil discourse, those involved in conflict management and resolution, diplomacy, and negotiation or mediation; training and development specialists; administrators looking to build new curricula or programming; and professional organizations seeking to embed productive, sustainable, and socially responsible forms of interaction in their teams and organizations. At its core, improv for democracy provides a complete framework of field-tested and evidence-based lessons and practices for accomplishing these goals.

In the course of giving presentations and workshops on this subject around the world, I've also discovered secondary audiences who will use this book in other ways. I've met communication and leadership experts who have begun using some of these ideas and practices in their training and consulting interventions. I've met managers trying to find ways to get their technically brilliant teams to become more adaptable to the challenges of dealing with actual human beings. I've met social workers and family therapists who have started using many of the lessons outlined in this book in their sessions with clients, especially in promoting dialogues that accomplish significant work without the somber spirit that these methods sometimes require. I've met teachers and professors seeking to ditch their PowerPoints and teach the same content with more interactive techniques, given research on the need for "democratic classrooms" or the effectiveness of a broader range of performative, affective, and cognitive learning methods for just about any subject.[48] Many people I've met are simply interested in the value of improv as a methodology, form of pedagogy, or way of living. In essence, I never cease to be amazed at how improv-based teachings and practices continue to be taken up and adapted for new contexts.[49]

This book should become a core resource for such individuals and groups, adding a powerful new philosophy (and the many schools of thought that support it) and a hands-on toolkit of exercises to their educational repertoires. Whether your goal is to create an improvisation course as part of your school or other curriculum, to experiment with applied improv exercises in existing teachings and trainings in areas from communication to management, or simply to start using the lessons within in your personal life, this book will show you how. Many ideas about applied improvisation have emerged from different places,[50] but the research findings, interdisciplinary connections, and applications of learning in this way have yet to be threaded together in a systematic manner. Having worked with groups from many different countries, and since applied improvisation is a global network, I also stay attentive to how this work can be applied internationally.

While this text provides an analytic framework for applied improvisation, it also covers specific exercises, games, and thought experiments that trainers, instructors, and others can use to help participants become more creative, heighten awareness, think faster, stretch behavioral flexibility, build confidence, improve expression and governance skills, and, above all, think and act more democratically. While I've worked with many of these exercises hundreds of times, I made sure that each has been field-tested in my teachings and trainings with different audiences.

Data for this project were gathered from nearly two decades of notes I have taken as a participant-observer, former student, and performer at many major improv theaters across the US, as well as thousands of articles, books, and multimedia artifacts on improvisational theater and applied improvisation.[51] I translate concepts from improv theater that are applicable to our public lives (e.g., an insight into how each of us is always shifting between a low, medium, or high "status" in different situations), while leaving behind anything that's irrelevant to that purpose (e.g., tips on how to make a scene or character funnier, which is a goal for improv for comedy entertainment). Since it's an area where practitioners have generally been ahead of scholars, I fill this theory gap by paying attention to interdisciplinary scholarship that supports this work, including communication research on interpersonal and public engagement, educational and leadership research, and more. I also apply lessons from my own experiences teaching applied improvisation in undergraduate, graduate, and executive courses and workshops around the world.

Toward Communication, Leadership, and Civic Excellence

Chapter 1 of this book will provide a framework for developing an improv-for-democracy curriculum, highlighting connections with leading ideas and empirical research supporting its methodology and approach. Chapter 2 will guide readers through how to prepare for and implement applied improvisation, some core ideas about improv that provide a foundation for more advanced applications in the rest of this book, and a sequence of exercises that demonstrate how this can all be structured for best effect. Chapter 3 will focus exclusively on the democratic communication lessons that can be drawn from applied improvisation, with supporting examples and applications. From a larger perspective, chapter 4 dives into connections between applied improv and democratic organizational leadership. Some work highlights how improvisation accounts for 75 to 90 percent of leadership decision making, but "no other leadership skillset that is applied [at least] two-thirds of the time has ever been so underdeveloped."[52] Institutions across the private and public sectors have also increasingly called for ways to train for "interpersonal organizational citizenship behavior (OCB) that is affiliative, co-operative, and directed at other individuals."[53] This chapter addresses these gaps by working with current conceptions of leadership that focus on adaptation and interactivity in the context of contemporary organizational life, including exercises that can be used toward this end.

    Chapter 5 moves to an even higher level, considering the applications that applied improvisation brings to the training of civic skills, ideas for how this work could play out across societies in the future, and accompanying training methods. While drawing useful distinctions between communication, leadership, and civic skills—or individual, organizational, and societal competencies—I position all three of these levels of intervention in terms of their contributions to the building of vibrant democracies. An ability to work responsively with others is as much a concern for individuals in face-to-face conversation as it is for government agencies delivering programs to populations in need. Ultimately, in practice, these three areas blend together, with each informing the other. Applying this perspective, the concluding chapter will focus on the overall contributions of this project and what's next for this emerging movement.

Before diving into the following chapter, it's worth underscoring the core point that runs through this book: whoever you are, if you start using applied improvisation as one way of teaching and training, you are doing the work of democracy. A lot has been written about *what* democracies should look like. Far less has covered *how* to actually train citizens in democratic perspectives and skills. Some exceptions exist, such as the burgeoning fields of dialogue, deliberation, and debate, which are creating new ways to train citizens in how to listen, learn, and become more engaged with their communities.

Unlike many ways of building bridges between diverse citizens, however, applied improvisation advances democratic skills in a playful register. It builds on a deep spring of ancient and contemporary thought about the centrality of meaningful, "serious play" in the public sphere, especially "the ability to play with ideas in such a way that cultivation of those ideas and communicative growth with others in public contexts can occur."[54] In a telling moment, former US Supreme Court Justice Sandra Day O'Connor shared during a hearing how she felt about the traditional civics classes she had taken in her early education: "I well remember having a lot of civics classes, and I got pretty sick and tired of it, to tell you the truth. I thought it was miserable." Looking to build a platform in which young people could feel the excitement of educating and training in democracy, she started iCivics, a curriculum that teaches civics through games.[55]

Following O'Connor's lead, by aiming for societal improvement this project builds on key works such as Joshua Lerner's *Making Democracy Fun: How Game Design Can Empower Citizens and Transform Politics*. Lerner details how "for most people, democratic participation is relatively unappealing. It is boring, painful, and pointless. . . . The demand is there, but attractive democratic processes are in short supply."[56] He makes a compelling case that one way to make public participation more engaging is to learn from an area that people everywhere already volunteer countless hours to: games.[57] From Argentine cities where game design has influenced public policy strategies to Canadian housing projects and assemblies designed like game shows, such experiments in democratic work are moving beyond the status quo.[58] The civic potential for games has also been recognized more broadly, building on the "gamification" movement that is increasingly showing how, for instance, turning regular workplace tasks into game-like activities provides people with the increased motivation and incentives lacking in many organizations.[59]

This project further advances works such as Augusto Boal's *Legislative Theater: Using Performance to Make Politics*. Boal's use of theater-based interventions to turn community concerns into public policies in Brazil remains legendary. As Boal puts it, "in the Legislative Theatre the aim is to bring the theatre back to the heart of the city, to produce not catharsis but dynamisation" by moving beyond traditional methods for transforming each citizen's "desire into law."[60] Many organizations focused on improving public participation continue to ask, "What does it take to make democracy work as it should?"[61] Like these projects, improv education demonstrates that play and games can be a more consequential matter for people's civic lives than has often been recognized.

Indeed, this book builds on current work underscoring the significance of play and performance to human and community development. Human development is active, emergent, social, dialectical, generative, flexible, and always in the process of both being and becoming in created environments that hold the potential to either grow or impede these forces.[62] In this spirit, growth "is the activity of creating who you are by performing who you are not. It is an ensemble—not a solo—performance," centered on the goal of "creating new forms and performances of life."[63] This perspective on development seeks to create maximalist rather than minimalist social and political practices, emphasizing what it means to be a fully public, community-oriented being, moving beyond the reductions of civic life only to voting or holding a few, individualistic political positions that one brings up occasionally within circles of influence.

Along these lines, in an exciting development, applied improvisers have been getting together to raise the stakes for this work on behalf of "humanity." Working with organizations such as the Red Cross and disaster relief workers, they have shown how an improvisational philosophy and techniques can address how people respond to some of the most vexing problems the planet currently faces.[64] After Typhoon Haiyan, groups all around the

Philippines participated in applied improv workshops that "enabled them to feel what it was like, and to practice their responses, to unpredictable situations." The participants rated the experience positively, feeling more ready to handle these situations and act on disaster preparedness principles.[65] Similarly, given how little impact traditional forms of training have had during unimaginable moments of crisis (such as 9/11 or the COVID-19 global pandemic), with its emphases on confident, connected leadership and communication, improv is now being used as an effective means of training government personnel for high-stakes emergencies.[66]

Moreover, the United States Embassy in Cyprus has hired improv teachers to do greater societal work on its behalf. Instructors ran extensive improvisational sessions as "part of the Embassy's ongoing effort to facilitate reunification of the island by fostering dialogue between people with shared interests and goals," with a particular interest in promoting "lessons in agreement to the Greek and Turkish Cypriots, helping them raise the borders and live as one people."[67] In another application, improv was applied with particle physicists at CERN's Large Hadron Collider in Switzerland "to help a disparate group of physicists from all over the world work together . . . [and] avoid disaster."[68] Other scientists are also now deep into research on how improv can create inclusive environments.[69]

These developments show that a next step is to establish higher purposes and practices for applied improvisation, applying a "civic frame" to this work.[70] This book works parallel to these efforts, setting out a challenge to embed and scale applied improvisation as a philosophy and set of concrete lessons and trainings that can affect the level of societies.[71] From the ground up, applied improvisers are looking to change the way human beings relate to one another in every community. For the public good, let's call it "Improv for Democracy."

Chapter 1

A New Curriculum for Training
Engaged, Innovative, and Flexible Citizens

After earning top grades and graduating from an Ivy League university, Natalie found herself fired after only 13 months on her first job. Her academic training had prepared her well for many of life's challenges, but she credited this first big professional failure to something missing in her education: a lack of training in people skills.[1]

Increasingly, we see that stories like Natalie's aren't unique. Schools teach a lot about following authority, learning technical knowledge, and taking tests—all important to do at times—but these don't translate to workplace and societal skills such as listening well, reading a room, and adapting to diverse people's needs.[2] Even for the more social and less academically inclined, practice in a fuller range of people skills helpful to our work and personal lives remains underrepresented in many educational curricula.

This problem isn't just a matter of opinion: a National Bureau for Economic Research report on "The Growing Importance of Social Skills in the Labor Market" recently concluded that "nearly all job growth since 1980 has been in occupations that are relatively social-skill intensive, while jobs that require high levels of analytical and mathematical reasoning, but low levels of social interaction, jobs that are comparatively easy to automate, have fared comparatively poorly."[3] When research from scholars such as Jean Twenge is added to this mix—that the most recent generation (iGen, born 1995–2012) are less skilled socially than any previous generation, with correlations between the advent of smart devices and anxiety in face-to-face social interactions—these findings are only compounded.[4] These trends highlighting the importance of social skills show no signs of abating.

Like Natalie, I remember once yearning for something that might help turn so much theory into practice, especially in areas such as communication. For years I had read books, crammed for exams, and gone through the motions of a typical education. After I graduated from college, a mentor at the time told me something that has long remained on my mind: what most people need to add to their education is a "learning that occurs by the nervous system."[5] This is a type of high-level learning that seeks to get the very best ideas into the body, not just the head. And there's more to it than just "getting experience." After all, people can have a lot of experience practicing the wrong techniques, using unproductive behaviors, or simply never seeking to learn from their experiences.

Take public speaking, for example. There's a lot of value in studying great public speakers and the many established techniques that can greatly increase the chances that a presentation will be effective. There can also be value in just getting up and practicing public speaking to get more comfortable with doing so. Yet in many areas like this, the *best* kind of learning engages both the mind and the body, alternating between important field-tested or evidence-based concepts and opportunities for guided feedback and practice that help the learning sink in deeply. No matter what level a public speaker is at, they will always stand to improve the most by learning about *and* practicing the art and science of speaking. It's about getting on both the "balcony" (where you can get some reflective distance and a good view of what's going on from a higher-level) and the "dance floor" (where you are fully involved in the experience).[6]

We're in good company in thinking this way. From John Dewey forward, leading educators have argued that people, especially adults, learn best from real, immediate experiences, so an ongoing mission has been to find "a methodology that can teach further below the neck."[7] That's the curriculum that this book engages, and it's a curriculum that can be added to anyone's thinking and toolkit.

For improv to improve democracy, we need to first understand how this new curriculum promotes a "learning that occurs by the nervous system," where it comes from, and how it ties into and is supported by interdisciplinary work. Readers of all kinds can use the ideas in this chapter to make a case for the value and support that applied improv can bring to any curriculum. This chapter will establish the educational grounding for applied improv, show its connections with a broad range of thought and practice, and set a foundation for the specific competencies in communication, leadership, and civic skills covered in the rest of this book. I will draw on guidelines from improvisational theater only as they are applicable to professional contexts, translating where certain ideas have emerged, why they are important, and how they can be applied in teaching and training across many sectors. This chapter will also provide some initial exercises that readers can apply to see exactly how this new curriculum supports the development of engaged, innovative, and flexible citizens.

Changing *How* We Educate

Applied improv works with and challenges how we typically learn, addressing one of the biggest problems that educational and similar institutions currently face. I wouldn't be the first to note that the way colleges and universities have always gone about their business has lately come up against tremendous pressures from within and without. From critiques that universities don't place enough value on teaching to objections that many curricula remain irrelevant to students' lives, the value of higher education has come under fire as never before.

Industries from newspapers to mail delivery to marketing have all undergone radical changes in the past several decades, and education will be no different.[8] Linda Weiser Friedman, Hershey Friedman, and Martin Frankel highlight how an increase in work-related certificates, empirical research supporting the effectiveness of the flipped hybrid model (i.e., courses that mix both online and offline teaching), and converging opinion about some of the most in-demand educational competencies (communication, creativity, collaboration, critical thinking, character, and curiosity) show that, "in a nutshell, what matters are skills, not degrees."[9] With almost all of young people involved in education, and nearly half of all adults engaging in some type of formal learning experience every year (classes, professional development workshops, certificate programs, etc.),[10] at the very least, what's become clear is that many longstanding models and habits of instruction need to change as the world around us shifts.

Several years ago Sir Ken Robinson gave a presentation that has become one of the most viewed and praised TED Talks of all time. In his speech "Do Schools Kill Creativity?"[11] he argued that most of the world's educational systems need to move beyond industrial workforce models and flatten their hierarchies (which prioritize subjects like math at the top) so that other subjects focusing on social skills and creativity might have more of an equal standing across curricula. In many places, the arts in particular have been eliminated from educational programming. Robinson underscored how joy, play, and laughter, long thought to be the enemies of "serious" instruction, should now be seen as a means of boosting and achieving educational and training goals. Susan Engel puts it this way: "Adults tend to talk about learning as if it were medicine: unpleasant, but necessary. Why not instead think of learning as if it were food—something so valuable to humans that they have evolved to experience it as a pleasure?"[12] She argues that joy is the very foundation of education. Similarly, others underscore how in improv instruction, "we're often fighting a real battle to help adults recover from having the desire to play—and, by extension, creativity—beaten out of them," so they should be invited "to look at the world with the eyes you had before the world told you what you were supposed to see."[13]

I'm a big proponent for the need to approach education seriously and improve instruction and learning in more technical disciplines, especially in STEM (science, technology, engineering, and math) subjects where there's substantial work to do in training our next generation of scientists, engineers, and more, especially in the US. But it's also worth recognizing how Robinson struck a chord with a global audience because of the number of people who have experienced a lopsided education and limited opportunities for learning in creativity, communication, and similar areas.

Remarkably, the very same concerns motivated those who founded modern improvisational theater. Some of improv's major figures in the last century felt impelled to innovate new methods for teaching because of what they had experienced and observed in the educational systems all around them. Schools all have socialization processes complete with rituals of competition over collaboration (e.g., for grades), authority over discovery (e.g., having a syllabus handed to you), and learning how to not show incompetence or make mistakes, among other issues.[14] Keith Johnstone clued into these trends long ago, seeing improv training as a vehicle for countering some of the largest blind spots in formal education. Growing up in England, Johnstone noticed that a great deal of schooling in his younger years seemed monotonous, controlled, and designed to suppress spontaneity.[15] Not all of life needs to be filled with spontaneity, of course, but when parts so central to the human experience such as play and dealing with the unexpected are so routinely excluded from entire institutions, Johnstone couldn't help but feel that something was awry. In the end, he concluded that his education was making him less responsive to others and less mindful of the world around him.[16]

In the US, several figures identified the same problems and began experimenting with potential theater-based solutions to these issues. One of the founders of modern improv in Chicago, Viola Spolin, originally developed many of her exercises as ways to help refugee and immigrant children to overcome language, adaptation, and connection problems in their new country, while Neva Boyd applied them in military convalescent homes to help wounded veterans feel more confident upon leaving hospitals.[17] From the very start, these figures saw improv as a way to make a difference in the lives of individuals and as crucial contributions to society. This work has been carried forward by academic institutions like the London School of Economics and Political Science, which more recently has been using improvisation to teach language skill development.[18]

Improv teachers note the strange turn many of us take at a certain point in our educations. While young children love to try new activities and generate new ideas, after a number of years we become adults who sit back, assess, and critique our creative abilities at every turn for fear of looking foolish or talentless, or simply failing.[19] For too many people this translates to approaching learning opportunities with anxiety and tension at every turn.[20] In countless trainings, I have entered a room full of adults to run an applied improv or related workshop where rigidity and fear run thick in the air. You can see it all over participants' bodies and facial expressions, which broadcast, "I hope he doesn't make me get out of my seat," "I'm no good in front of people," "I'm not creative," and more. Fast-forward to a workshop with kids and it's the opposite, with every child looking like we've just run through five exercises before we even start: "I want to go first," "I can't wait to jump in," "This'll be fun," etc. One of my favorite parts of running an applied improv curriculum is seeing the protective layers adults learn to build around themselves gradually peel off after years of acting fearfully.

Given the pressures education now faces and the gaps it needs to fill, we need new tools and skills for how we educate. Many have woken up to this reality, but far too many participants still walk into classrooms or workshops that ask them to sit passively while instructors lecture from endless, bullet-point-filled slides. Lectures aren't intrinsically bad, but when they become the only way of teaching and training, we're setting the bar about as low as possible for inclusive and engaging learning processes. As we'll explore further in this chapter, these methods also fly in the face of a great deal of evidence about the ways human beings best comprehend, remember, and apply anything.

Applied improv reverses a typical way of educating by having partic- ipants *experience* a concept being taught before intellectualizing about it. We know that seeing, feeling, and experiencing an idea tends to sink more deeply into long-term memory than simply thinking about and analyzing it.[21] Tangible, relatable information tends to stay with us, so it's surprising that our educational experiences aren't often more like this.

To see firsthand what this kind of teaching and training can look like, read about the two exercises in box 1.1 Please note that for all exercises adapted in this book, I will include in the endnotes links to video demonstrations and other multimedia content similar to what's being described, if they are available online. Although every exercise has many potential meanings and implications (and readers and participants are certainly encouraged to make further connections), I will end each with debrief questions, applications, and possible variations that can be provided to focus the transfer of learning to participants' lives and progress the overall curriculum developed in this book.

Box 1.1
Adapting to Change and Building with Others

Rebecca Stockley provides two effective opening exercises for an improv training that demonstrate the "experience first, let the concepts sink in later" approach.[22] They also provide an introduction to many of applied improv's core lessons, such as building on your partner's ideas, adapting to change, managing failure, and learning not to take things personally by "letting go" more often (see the next chapter for more on these basic background concepts). Try these two initial exercises to get a feel for what this approach offers.

Working with Change

Ask your participants to find a partner. The instructor should demonstrate the exercise with one participant first. For the first round, each pair should smile and make eye contact, then the first partner will say the word "one." The second partner will respond with "two." The first partner will then say "three," then the second will go back to "one" again, and so on. Each person will go back and forth with the next number up to three. Ask the participants to go as fast as possible as they conduct this activity (this will guarantee a lot of messing up). Now stop the group and ask, "Did anyone find this exercise easy? Did anyone find it difficult?" If they made a mistake, ask what they did and draw out a range of responses (e.g., "I cringed," "I cursed," "I blamed the other person," "I laughed nervously"). For the second round, instead of saying the number "one" the first person will snap their fingers, while the second and third numbers will remain the same. The partners will alternate back and forth as in the first round with a "[snap], two, three" rather than a "one, two, three" order. This time, however, instruct participants that any time someone feels that they messed up, both partners should raise their hands in the air and say "Woohoo!" Once you've completed the second round, ask the participants to note the difference in how their work was approached with this attitude and behavior shift. Identify the positive spirit, trust, good-natured failure, and excitement that filled the room. For a third and fourth round, replace "two" with a hand clap and then the "three" with a foot stomp. Make sure to keep the "Woohoo!" (I'd advise walking around and encouraging anyone who looks like they're not fully committing to do so).

Debrief questions: What happens when you make mistakes? Do you treat them as the end of the world, judge yourself constantly, blame others, or something similar? Or do you find ways to learn from them, let go, and move on with a positive attitude? How well do you adapt to change?

Applications: This exercise underscores how well each of us can adapt to change, manage failure and the unexpected, and free ourselves from the grip of mistakes and disappointments in our lives. It also establishes a positive climate and mood with a group from the outset.

Variation: For another simple variation on this exercise, get the partners to face one another and then have the first person say "ha." The second will respond with "ha ha." The first person will then say "ha ha ha." You can choose to have them return to only one "ha" or keep going numerically so the next response is "ha ha ha ha," etc.[23] Just about every group I have ever done this variation with has immediately broken out into laughter, establishing rapport between the participants.

Shared Memory

For this activity, everyone should get into groups of three or four. As Stockley notes, it's best to demonstrate in front of everyone first and underscore that the goal will be to "listen, accept, add, and adapt." The three or four participants will make up a shared memory. The first person will say the line "Remember when we went to _____" and insert a place to create a made-up shared memory for the group (e.g., "Remember when we went

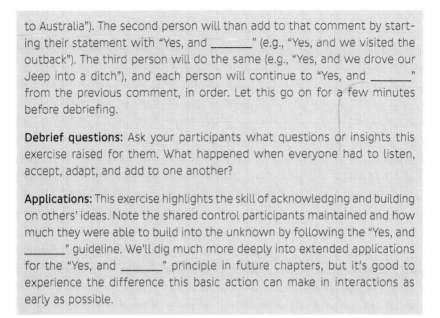

to Australia"). The second person will than add to that comment by start-ing their statement with "Yes, and _____" (e.g., "Yes, and we visited the outback"). The third person will do the same (e.g., "Yes, and we drove our Jeep into a ditch"), and each person will continue to "Yes, and _____" from the previous comment, in order. Let this go on for a few minutes before debriefing.

Debrief questions: Ask your participants what questions or insights this exercise raised for them. What happened when everyone had to listen, accept, adapt, and add to one another?

Applications: This exercise highlights the skill of acknowledging and building on others' ideas. Note the shared control participants maintained and how much they were able to build into the unknown by following the "Yes, and _____" guideline. We'll dig much more deeply into extended applications for the "Yes, and _____" principle in future chapters, but it's good to experience the difference this basic action can make in interactions as early as possible.

The Enemy of Democracy: Our Default Settings

In the exercises in box 1.1, I hope you're struck by the immediate connec-tions and positivity fostered between the participants. This kind of teaching jolts people out of routine habits that often prevent them from being effec-tive with others. Some scholars call these personal or group patterns our "default settings."[24] Default settings are typical ways of thinking and acting that prevent us from seeing the broader choices we have in any situation. They're essentially our comfort zones. If you never voice your opinion in large meetings, that's a default setting. If you're in a conversation with a friend and always thinking ahead about what you're going to say instead of actually listening to what they're saying, that's a default setting too.

While our default settings are certainly useful at times, the main prob-lem is that they can keep us from truly engaging with others, entertaining new ideas, or being adaptable. Our default settings reflect the ways we try to stay safe or avoid uncertainty when changes happen. That's why I call default settings the enemy of democracy: to learn how to get along with one another well, we have to rise above our typical habits and positions to entertain the perspectives and experiences of others.

Emphasizing how we all need to move beyond our default settings, Jamie Holmes, author of *Nonsense: The Power of Not Knowing*, says that "we're programmed to get rid of ambiguity, and yet if we engage with it we can make better decisions, we can be more creative, and we can even be a little more empathetic."[25] For example, when stressed we tend to close ourselves off from alternative perspectives—as many people did after the horrifying events of September 11, 2001, in the US—hampering critical thought and a potentially broader range of responses to the situation.[26] At such moments, people can easily forget to see how they're reverting to typical attitudes, thought processes, roles, or ways of communicating that keep us from being more creative in discovering or fashioning solutions.

In a media environment where we often find ourselves texting, surfing the web, and engaging in all kinds of other technology-related behaviors that prevent us from being present with other people, the need for this kind of work only deepens. When on the internet, we're often caught in "online filter bubbles" that reinforce what we already believe, keeping us disconnected from alternative viewpoints, flexible thought, and concern for one another.[27] Even when interactions across differences do take place online, just scrolling through the average Facebook discussion during election season more than proves the point that incivility has become a go-to habit in many of our lives. If we're to be constructive participants rather than spectators in the life of democracy, we need to supplement the algorithms of our online lives with the algorithms of real human presence and connection.

Applied improvisation provides one path for getting us there. Framing all applied improv training as a way to move beyond our default settings focuses how each of us can expand our range of communication, leadership, and civic choices. Cathy Salit highlights how "*everything* you do is a performance"; human development only takes place when we stretch beyond the usual, so a goal should be to "perform outside our normal roles" by playing different characters and taking risks that make growth possible.[28] Many people use convergent thinking, or set modes of thought and behavior, as they make their way through everyday life.[29] But research demonstrates that improvisation expands divergent thought, or the "breaking away from set patterns of thinking" to allow people to access more solutions and diverse ways of operating.[30] It promotes an "elasticity to meet momentary necessities."[31]

With different people all across the world, I've found that raising the idea of default settings as a foil for applied improv training provides an accessible concept for introducing the why behind what we'll be doing. It gives us a great place to start. Since many people still associate improv with merely winging it and other assumptions, though, it's critical to ground this type of education in solid evidence and in connection to leading ideas. What applied improvisation most needs is a cohesive conceptual framework that showcases the high-level nature of this work. Before diving into the evidence, take a look at Paul Z. Jackson's video "Applying Improvisation," where he primes us for this task by showcasing, for instance, how applied improvisation has found its way into many organizations and communities that you might not expect (again, I give full details and links for videos and multimedia in the endnotes and bibliography).[32]

Connecting Applied Improv with Leading Ideas

In years of speaking with a global network of practitioners and scholars, I have yet to meet any teacher or trainer who hasn't been impacted by using applied improvisational exercises. But the case for applied improvisation can also be made from broader evidence. It's one thing to tell your own stories about influence, but another to link these with wider projects across the world. At some point, you'll find yourself needing to make a case, since there are many assumptions that different people bring to the idea of improv (e.g., "improv is an ability that you either have or don't," "this will only be about having fun").

To highlight the value of this type of education, instructors can draw connections between applied improvisation and many leading ideas. Cutting-edge educational and pedagogical theories especially align with these methods. Scholars have long recognized that one flaw in education writ large has been a fixation on writing, reading, and math, resulting in the underdevelopment of equally valuable modes of expression such as creativity, divergent thought, and nonverbal communication[33]—forms that I'd add are instrumental to civic education and democracy building. A great deal of empirical research supports active learning as a superior approach to more passive forms of education,[34] but many educational institutions have yet to catch up to this reality.

To put it squarely, over 1000 scholarly journal articles and 120 studies on the need for learner-centered education testify to how teachers and trainers need to adapt to current students' multiple intelligences, desire for collaboration, and need for lively instruction.[35] Grounded in experiential education, Ronald Berk and Rosalind Trieber note that improvisational games and experiences work with the "active, participatory, visual, collaborative, fast moving, quick thinking, rapid responding, emotionally freeing, spontaneous, combustible vehicle they so badly desire."[36] Applied improv uses active learning theories that have participants engage in most of the work through multi-sensory, variety-filled, scaffolded classes, moving beyond a narrow focus on auditory listening or low-level factual learning and the insufficient use of individual styles or participants' expertise in lectures.[37]

Many educators have called for more democratic approaches to the classroom that counter traditional forms of "teaching as telling."[38] As my friend Drew Tarvin asks, what leaves a more lasting impression: being told not to touch the hot stove or touching it and learning to never do that again? (Please don't try this at home.) Or, if you wanted to learn to play the violin, how good would you get by simply watching slideshows about it?[39] Experiencing learning supersedes teaching as telling. Donald Finkel even advocates for "teaching with your mouth shut," which requires prioritizing learning over teaching, different activities focusing on student inquiry, instructors who can listen well and tolerate unpredictability, seminars that are open-ended and not predetermined, and knowledge development based on processes rather than authority.[40] Finkel argues that this has always been the best way to educate, since students don't naturally come to classrooms interested in abstractions like history or math. Instead, their interests first stem from their experiences, or the "obstacles, perplexities, and blind spots that emerge from their own present, lived circumstances," so instructors should be "converting products of knowledge into processes that lead to them."[41]

In this spirit, educators around the world have finally realized that games can play a critical role in learning and development. Some in secondary and higher education falsely assume that games are an impediment to academic development, rather than a pathway to it.[42] Countering these assumptions, professors like Barnard College's Mark Carnes and many others have researched and promoted immersive experiences in game-like formats as far more effective than traditional educational approaches, even for the most academic of subjects.[43] It's one thing to talk about the War of 1812, but having students actually role-play key characters from history brings the experience to life and turns what may have been a passive, detached instructional experience into an engaging event. Games have participants confront their own values and attitudes in real time, such as the classic prisoner's dilemma simulation, "which brings out competitive rather than cooperative instincts that people didn't even know run latent."[44] Many other widely used, effective activities such as the intercultural training game Bafa Bafa have also provided countless students with new experiences and perspectives leading to sustained behavior change. Albert Einstein even noted that "games are the most elevated form of investigation."[45]

According to many leading thinkers, games can therefore improve the world. Jane McGonigal writes that "gamers want to know: Where, in the real world, is that gamer sense of being fully alive, focused, and engaged in every moment? Where is the gamer feeling of power, heroic purpose, and community? Where are the bursts of exhilarating and creative game accomplishment?"[46] She finds, just as I am aiming to show in this book, that games can improve educational outcomes (as demonstrated, for example, by a charter school in New York City that uses game design for learning), reduce stress, provide structures for treating illnesses, and enhance participation.[47] Experiential and game-based education relate to sensory theories of learning, which have long supported the idea that all of participants' senses should be addressed in pedagogy.[48] In fact, some game advocates raise the stakes for games far beyond their typical purview, seeing the very future of the planet as tied to our ability to replace the incessant, historical zero-sum war games that groups and nations have waged with collaborative games in which peace and understanding are necessary to human survival.[49]

Experiential activities like role-plays make didactic approaches more effective, as "games lead to more personal awareness of attitudes and beliefs" than film viewings and similar methods, encouraging participation in ways that can foster multicultural learning.[50] With focused debriefs and time for processing, these methods make learning relevant and personal, increasing the likelihood that participants will remember and apply lessons. For those concerned about a culture of relentless testing in schools, applied improv provides an alternative, sensory-rich education where playful interaction is as much a part of students' development as other techniques.

Moreover, applied improv shares many connections with current work on "brain-based learning." There are brain-friendly ways of educating. Eric Jensen finds that many outdated models of education have been based on operant conditioning (punishment and rewards), but "a more brain-based approach would be to increase classroom engagement, greet all students with a smile, increase . . . social connectedness, and boost involvement in school activities like martial arts, theater, [and] music."[51] He urges educational policymakers to switch from a focus on testing and stress-based learning (or learning that is impaired by high levels of cortisol) to producing "happy, well-adjusted human beings who can think, care about others, and innovate."[52] The brain, after all, "is wired to pay attention to novelty, movement, intensity, contrast, and saturation."[53] This means that teachers need to facilitate energizers, stretching, breathing exercises, role-playing, movement games, and similar activities in the classroom.

In light of how much is known about what it takes to create an effective and memorable learning atmosphere, willful ignorance about the best methods of teaching should no longer be an option. Long ago Confucius asserted, "What I hear, I forget; what I see, I remember; what I do, I understand."[54] Education is a complex phenomenon, so there's much more to how learning works than this simple scheme provides,[55] but there's still some truth to its content. If there's anything we've learned about learning, it's that it's not a passive experience.[56] Repeatedly we see that games, simulations, and experiential approaches can develop affective, behavioral, and cognitive learning and student motivation over more traditional ways of teaching.[57]

Applied improv further addresses a documented decline in opportunities for play and a subsequent rise in mental disorders among children.[58] The decrease in time for recess and unstructured time in schools, especially in the US, has not escaped the notice of educational critics. Due to pressures related to federal educational dollars, testing, and time constraints, "an astonishingly low 36 percent of K-12 students in the United States participate in a daily physical education program."[59] As a parent of a child currently in a public elementary school where only twenty minutes of the school day is devoted to play and recess, I see this as a national crisis. As the Albert Einstein College of Medicine found, "children with more recess time learned more, developed better emotional and cognitive skills, were healthier, behaved better, and managed stress better."[60]

Our bodies can't be separated from our brains. The verdict has been in for some time on this: feeling and thinking go together. Without the guidance of emotions the brain will actually engage in illogical thought.[61] As a result, Larry Abraham, a kinesiologist at the University of Texas, notes how it's critical to make movement a central part of classes primarily devoted to content.[62] In essence, "Exercises that encourage limb movement across the body's lateral center can stimulate both sides of the brain and energize thinking. . . . A large group of studies has linked physical activity with cognition, and they all have solid conclusions about how physical experience affects the brain. . . . Physical activity, drama, and the arts all add to, rather than detract from, the core curriculum."[63] As was known by the ancient Greek peripatetics, a school of philosophers who would converse while traveling from place to place, even the addition of walking to a curriculum can make a difference. Leading figures from improv theater similarly share how they believe that "improvisation should be mandatory for all college students, not only to enhance studying but to increase confidence and build self-esteem."[64] Among other solutions, our schools need the play time, open spaces, and creative outlets that applied improv can provide.

Some important psychological concepts bear on this work, especially for building citizenship skills. The "broaden and build theory of positive emotions" highlights the 3:1 ratio of positive to negative emotions that should generally occur in people's lives to have flourishing relationships at home and work.[65] Gordon Bermant has noted the astonishing links between applied improv and important psychological concepts such as being able to "work without a net," becoming aware of "embodiment" (a greater awareness about one's body), "act[ing] well to be well," and having an "unconditional positive regard" toward others.[66] Applied improv aims to develop positive emotions and cultures, following research highlighting that when groups like doctors, students, and negotiators approach life in this way, they become upbeat, flexible problem-solvers.[67]

The concept of mindfulness also shares connection with applied improv. With roots in groundbreaking works from Ellen Langer,[68] this topic has had a resurgence in recent years. Langer emphasizes that mindfulness stands opposite mindlessness, or "an inactive state of mind characterized by reliance on distinctions/categories drawn in the past. Here (1) the past overdetermines the present; (2) we are trapped in a single perspective but oblivious to that entrapment; (3) we're insensitive to context; and (4) rules and routines govern rather than guide our behavior. Moreover, mindlessness typically comes about by *default* not by design."[69] If there's any definition for how default settings stand as a foil for democracy, this is it. Trapped in a narrow world of limited thoughts, a closedness to others, and inflexible strategies that fail to adapt to changes in our worlds, mindlessness, in this sense, constitutes an anti-democratic, fundamentalist orientation.

On the other hand, Ted Desmaisons says that mindfulness involves being more conscious about oneself and one's environment, while bringing greater presence, kindness, curiosity, and purpose to the world. Mindfulness can bring a depth to improv, while improv can bring joy to the usually serious nature of mindfulness practices. Ultimately, in just about any situation where we might normally have a stimulus and immediate response, Desmaisons notes how mindfulness encourages us to pause and generate multiple choices or responses to stimuli.[70] In a conflict with a co-worker, for example, both applied improv and mindfulness remind us that there's always a wider range of responses available beyond knee-jerk responses of anger or self-defense.

It's surprising that the connection has yet to be made in a systematic way, but leading ideas about culture and power share tremendous connections with applied improvisation. Caryn Musil writes that feminist perspectives, for example, bring to teaching a focus on "cultivating student voice and empowerment, endorsing students as creators and not merely receivers of knowledge, de-centering the classroom to promote more active and collaborative learning, engaging in dialogue across differences, and applying knowledge to address real world issues."[71] By each measure, this approach comports with many outcomes that applied improv targets, both in terms of content and processes (such as holding multiple perspectives, engaging in active learning, and finding joy in interactions with others). Even improv guru Charna Halpern once noted that there's a feminist angle to improvisation, since it seeks to cultivate values such as giving, nurturing, or caring.[72]

Many changes in our larger public communication environment further underscore a central role for improv in civic education and democracy building. Models of policymaking have long relied on theories of rational, ordered administration, but have failed to get a firmer grasp on the improvisational aspects of public affairs.[73] By the same token, Doris Graber argues that one of the biggest challenges facing public sector organizations is "innovation," mostly due to the sector's lack of a profit motivation and, as others have found, the sheer number of technically minded folks attracted to government jobs.[74] Up to now, applied improv has largely been used in corporate environments, yet given the nature of public administration this form of professional development stands to contribute even more to the public sector.

Indeed, as the central argument of this book, it's our social and political environments that most beg for the kind of learning that applied improv delivers. Michael Crozier finds that people have an exponentially greater number of media to choose from than in the past and now orient themselves to the world in interactive ways. Gone are the days when politicians could just hop onto a television show and broadcast their messages to the public in a one-way fashion. Nowadays, people tweet through presidential debates, write their views about public issues on internet sites, and can generally broadcast their views around the globe on any issue at a moment's notice.[75] Since "improvisation is an arts technique that is characterized by spontaneity, mutual interaction, and lack of an authorial voice," public administrators need methods for learning to develop an improvisational, collaborative mindset given the contingencies of the governing environment.[76]

More than ever, leaders will need to work across silos as a regular part of building organizational culture. They will have to maintain a "laser-like focus on employee commitment and engagement across generational, global, cultural, and demographic boundaries."[77] If anything, public figures now have to be skilled improvisers to react to all the variables continually beyond their control, being ready to listen and act in responsive and credible ways. The parallels between improv and the skills needed to engage in effective public crisis management are especially focused here. Chris MacDonald highlights how "human life is complicated in a way that far exceeds the level of detail achieved by the even the most complex and subtly nuanced set of rules we can imagine," so knowing what rules to make relevant and how to adapt them to various stakeholders requires improvisational skills that every leader now needs.[78] In this sense, given the advance of algorithms in our online and mobile lives, I like to think about applied improvisation as the building of democratic, anti-algorithmic cultures.

Above all, with so much disengagement, distrust, and cynicism about politics and public life, the most important task for applied improvisation will be to help people work with ideas that can make a difference in their roles as citizens. Games can help us get there. Joshua Lerner highlights that "what sets games apart . . . is that they are also models of and for democracy."[79] They are inherently democratic in their design, involving participation and decision-making and building forms of trust and engagement sorely lacking in traditional ways of cultivating democracy.[80] These emerging ideas show how applied improv should aim high, aspiring to address problems at the level of communities and nations. We already know a lot about how this work can influence communication and leadership skills (and, as this book will show, these remain critical parts of building democracy), but we need to go further in showing how applied improv games and exercises can promote improvements in empowering peoples' voices as active participants in society as well.

Through connections with leading ideas, the case for applied improv to reach this goal has never been greater. Spolin summarized these connections well: "theater games are a process applicable to any field, discipline, or subject matter which creates a place where full participation, communication, and transformation can take place."[81] To further build this case, we'll next turn to emerging evidence on the specific benefits of applied improvisation. Before we do so, take a look at box 1.2 for some examples of exercises that can lead to many of the outcomes already discussed.

Box 1.2
Heightening Awareness, External Focus, and Connection

Here are two foundational, widely used exercises that I run in just about every applied improv session. They're simple but have profound applications to our personal and professional lives. I recommend running them early in a session, since they're low-risk, easy to understand, and get groups bonding quickly.

Creating Connections

Have your participants stand in a circle. Explain to them that they'll be passing the words "Zip," "Zap," and "Zop," in order, around the circle (make sure to spell out the words to get everyone on the same page). Demonstrate what this looks like by pointing at someone and saying "Zip." Ask that person to then point at and say "Zap" to someone else, then that person will say "Zop" to another person, the next person will go back to "Zip," and so on. Ask everyone to try to go as fast as possible in passing the zip, zap, and zop around. When someone first makes a mistake—by saying "Zip," "Zap," or "Zop" out of order, by saying something else, by not picking up that it's their turn, or when two or more people are unclear that a zip, zap, or zop has been passed to them—tell the group that we'll always take collective responsibility for any errors. Have everyone join together by putting their arms over the shoulders of the people on their left and right, step forward and kick one leg into the circle, and say "Awooga!"[82] I usually demonstrate this myself first, and then invite everyone to do it with me. Much laughter usually follows. Once the group has this down, get back to sending the zip, zap, and zop around the circle, and encourage everyone to go fast and risk making mistakes so that they're not in their heads trying to get it right every time (you can say, "We'll just 'awooga' the mistakes out of existence, so there's nothing to worry about").[83]

Debrief questions: How committed to the message did each person seem? Was it clear that a zip, zap, or zop was sent to a particular person each time? For those on the receiving end, how ready were they to receive messages from others? Do you see any parallels between this exercise and how we communicate in the workplace or other organizations?

Applications: There are a number of lessons in this simple exercise. First, note how well participants are sending and receiving messages to one another. Every time I've run this there are always two or three people who aren't sure if the message has been passed to them or someone else, usu-ally because the sender is trying to play it cool by not fully investing in the message. This exercise makes it nearly impossible to focus on oneself. By heightening awareness and expanding their peripheral visions, participants should note that they had to push their focus outward to make this work (I go into much more detail on this "external focus" lesson in chapter 3). Second, when we approach mistakes positively, the fear in the room dissi-pates, the speed of communication picks up, and we feel more connected to others (similar to the "Working with Change" exercise in box 1.1). Third, the participants should note that those who used both verbal and nonverbal communication tended to be more successful; aligning their words with expressiveness and bodily behavior (e.g., gesturing toward others rather than standing static) greatly increases the flow and clarity of the exercise. Last, this is just a great physical and mental warm-up that gets us ready for more advanced applications.[84]

Rapid Relationships

I like to follow up with this exercise, which takes many of the lessons from the last exercise to the next level.[85] With everyone in a circle, demonstrate that one person, who has an imaginary red ball in their hand, will look at another person in the circle and say, "Red ball." The person on the receiving end will then say "Thank you, red ball." The first person holding the red ball should *then* mime passing the ball to the other person, who should also mime catching it. It's critical for everyone to note that it's *only* after you say "Red ball" and the other person says "Thank you, red ball" that you should pass the ball. There should be a connection made between the two participants before the passing takes place. Many in the group will want to say "Red ball" and pass it to other people at the same time, which itself is a lesson—many of us simply broadcast messages at other people without looking for evidence that what we're saying has been received. Commu-nication is a two-way street. Have everyone pass the ball around and get used to the format for a while. When they've got it down, turn to another participant and hand them a "Yellow ball." Tell the group to keep passing the red ball around and that a yellow ball will also now be involved. They'll need to heighten their focus on the others in the circle even more to both send and receive these messages. For those sending the ball around, they'll also need to push their volume up and act more confidently, as the other ball being passed around will create external noise that interferes with their messages. Once this is going well, add in a purple ball. You can even start to add other types. I usually throw in a basketball and, for fun, a "ball of death" (the group usually gets a kick out of this). You can also add just about anything else you want (a porcupine, a scepter, the Mona Lisa, etc.). In my experience, you won't want to go over about five balls for a group of thirty people, but you can adjust up or down depending on the number of participants. At the end, you should ask who has each ball or object and see if any are missing.

Debrief questions: What did we have to do to make this exercise work well? How did you personally deal with the increasing noise in this situation? What applications to work or our social lives can be made here? Is there a process or other activity that you currently do that could be improved with this kind of outward focus and commitment?

Applications: Building from the last exercise, I always draw participants' attention to the amplified "external focus" that this exercise required (especially when many balls were in the air) and how everyone had to shift their concentration outward to meet the compounding challenges. You can note how energetic and invested the group became in this exercise. You can't be thinking of the past or daydreaming about the future to do this well—you have to be fully present with everyone else. Over time, you'll find your own unique applications for this exercise too.

Evidence for Applied Improvisation

There is still much work to do in researching and assessing applied improv, particularly through well-designed, across-time experiments or quasi-experiments with control conditions. Yet across a variety of fields, important evidence has established how this work can affect people skills and more. With every passing year, researchers are growing our collective knowledge base in this area, so the goal of this section is less to cover every study out there than to provide a bird's-eye overview of this work to make a case for applied improv's curricular value for our organizations and our world.[86]

Let's start with a real-life scenario. Have you ever felt ignored, demeaned, or less than informed from an interaction with a doctor? Maybe the doctor seemed rushed or unclear about what was ailing you and what to do about it. You wouldn't be alone in feeling this way. A host of studies find that people experience these problems on a frequent basis with healthcare personnel. To address these issues, one promising line of research and practice is "medical improv." Medical improv is "the adaptation of improvisational theater principles and exercises to enhance such medical skills as communication, teamwork, and cognition."[87] With the healthcare field growing exponentially, the need to train doctors, nurses, and other staff to communicate and adapt well to their patients has never been greater. Scholarly work now shows that improv training creates excellent doctor-patient communication, which has been linked to better patient care, improved satisfaction, chronic disease management, and a decrease in medical malpractice lawsuits and messages that lead to costly errors.[88]

Katie Watson, a professor of medical education, bioethics, and medical humanities in the Feinberg School of Medicine at Northwestern University, tracked eight years of evaluations for a medical improv seminar at her school. Across that time, an astonishing 95 percent of students agreed with the statement that "studying improv could make me a better doctor" and 100 percent agreed with "I would recommend this class to other medical students."[89] In healthcare settings, Watson found that in-demand skills such as dealing with unpredictability, listening, empathy, respect for multiple viewpoints, reading people, confidence, group bonding, creativity, spontaneity, stress relief, and honesty were all fostered by improvisational interventions. As so many of us have found through teaching and training in this way, she notes that "students invest medical improv exercises and discussions with a degree of enthusiasm and joy I rarely see in other medical school classes."[90]

Positive responses to medical improv courses for improving patient interactions has manifest elsewhere. In the training of pediatric residents in trust-building and the "need to offer something the internet cannot fully emulate: empathetic imagination and an ability to instantaneously tailor messages to reach and teach worried and often confused audiences effectively," applied improvisation resulted in gains in communication skills and confidence.[91] In a different class, healthcare staff found two outcomes especially stood out: learning to listen and act more humanely, and providing a nuanced vocabulary for understanding their interactions.[92] In another course, healthcare teams showed enthusiasm for an applied improv program that facilitated working across silos to target improved patient safety and satisfaction.[93] Improv exercises further helped pharmacy students' performance in many aspects of standard patient examinations. Although some students found the training challenging, "course evaluations and student comments reflected their perception that the improvisational exercises significantly improved their communication skills."[94]

As mentioned, since half of the top twenty MBA programs in the world now incorporate some variation of applied improv into their curricula, many of the biggest success stories for improv training have come out of business environments. A look at just about any improv theater's website demonstrates that almost every major company in the US (Google, Apple, etc.) has testified to the value of applied improv trainings in their work. The popular press is replete with stories of educators bringing improv into corporate environments, with countless testimonies available about how it has influenced people's lives.[95]

Julie Huffaker and Ellen West differentiate this skill set from most cognitive, judgment-centered business courses, noting how in their classes with many different types of business professionals, participants demonstrated higher levels of listening, innovative thought, and diverse and constructive discussions after using improv exercises in warm-ups.[96] This work points to one low barrier to entry underscored in this book: you don't need to teach an entire class in applied improv. Embedding applied improv games and exercises in a variety of courses can be a precursor to learning technical knowledge or making regular classroom conversations more energized and inclusive.

Noting how deviations from plans are a regular part of work life that should be expected and managed well, management researchers continue to highlight the ties between improv and many of the competencies their field most values.[97] Both academic and professional organizations have used improv training in the management classroom to improve meeting skills, creativity with clients, negotiations, and idea generation.[98] For over twenty years, David Corsun and his colleagues have used improvisational exercises in workshops in a way that "allows participants to surface their perceptual shortcuts, practice alternative behaviors, overcome biases, and expand their repertoire of managerial skills."[99] Additionally, given the rise of social media and a general diffusion of message control in firms, managers increasingly need training in how to be adaptable and responsive to different audiences at a moment's notice.

Advancing decades of research with the Harvard Negotiation Project, Michael Wheeler and his colleagues have recently recognized the central role that improvisation plays in negotiations, highlighting how there has been too much emphasis on structure and sequence in the negotiation literature.[100] Following on this, improv for negotiation and mediation courses have been successfully run at many universities around the US.[101] Barbara Tint writes that in bringing together applied improvisation and work in this area, "time and again, participants express that they have never been so impacted by a conflict resolution training before. Because the learning happens on so many levels—cognitive, emotional, physical, relational—participants often report being freed up in new and empowering ways, counterbalancing the more traditional structures and expectations of law school, mediation agencies, and conflict resolution programs."[102] Practitioners can learn the improvisational skills of reading the mood in a room, making moves that can quickly change unproductive courses of action, and diversifying their repertoire of moves, and in doing so model an environment where all parties are encouraged to act more creatively.[103]

This move to a more adaptive, process-oriented view of subjects like negotiation fits well with one of the core tenets of the coordinated management of meaning (CMM) theory. Focusing attention on the process, or the pattern of communication as it unfolds, can enable interlocutors to make more adjustments than they otherwise might, leading to better outcomes for both.[104] In other words, when people learn to take joint ownership of the patterns that they create in their lives, they become better observers of how moment-to-moment communication constructs the social worlds in which they live, opening up space for a greater range of communicative choices.

Along similar lines, in a field experiment teaching sales students how to be more adaptive with clients, researchers compared a control group who had no improv training with a group who had been through such training. After a four-week sales project that involved selling tickets for sports teams, the study found "increased ticket sales performance among the improv group students."[105] Customer service firms can also benefit from improv training as a method "for delivering warm, unmechanical service without breaking the training budget."[106] And embedded within a marketing class, Finsterwalder and O'Steen found that "a preliminary analysis of the data indicates that students see this model as an effective method for learning marketing skills."[107] The advertising and marketing industries themselves have continually turned to theaters such as the Upright Citizens Brigade and Second City for development of new content and ads.[108]

From a larger level, applied improvisation can impact organizations. Improv connects with organizational study and development, especially in dealing with unpredictability, a focus on process (and not just outcomes), and its ability to hone awareness, forge agreement, and promote collaborative skills.[109] Key historical examples such as the Apollo XIII astronaut crisis, in which NASA scientists and astronauts had to adjust their organizational approaches quickly, show that improvisational processes grounded in shared leadership, a wide knowledge base, and drawing on what's available remain central to effective institutional decisions.[110]

Many people think improv is only about individual performance, so it's critical to highlight these links to organizational goals. Jordana Cole found that improv can improve "organizational well-being" through its "ability to generate positive social connections and strengthen workplace relationships by improving communication, collaboration, and interpersonal understanding."[111] The improv principles of co-creation, presence, and building on others' offers especially link with a number of goals in positive and industrial psychology, so she recommends embedding improv within the organizational culture and typical work activities. Renowned scholar Karl Weick has written extensively on these connections, stressing how organizational studies needs to under-stand improvisation relative to growing societal concerns about "how to cope with discontinuity, multiple commitments, interruptions, and transient purposes that dissolve without warning."[112] For organizational development consultants, theatrical techniques can also move clients beyond positivistic, diagnostic forms of behavior change to "develop more advanced skills such as reciprocity and collaborating . . . shared meaning making, multiple realities, and collaborative solutions."[113]

Alongside skills in math, language, critical thinking, scientific literacy, and others, applied improv targets many benchmarks in education. Com-munity college students introduced to improvisation practiced the craft and continued to use improv in both their personal and school lives.[114] This evidence is significant, since a gap has emerged between the preparation employers expect and what students bring to professional life, most notably in the areas of oral communication, an ability to work well in teams, inno-vation, and dealing with diversity.[115] Consistent with themes I raised earlier in this chapter, the AACU's National Leadership Council has called for "a far-reaching shift in the focus of school from accumulating course credits to building real-world capabilities."[116] In addition to embedding applied improv exercises in a variety of courses, these findings and calls advance the idea that applied improv should be a class in every college curriculum.

Some research demonstrates improv's effectiveness in the classroom and its capacity to improve teaching itself.[117] Theresa Becker's work on improvisation training for pre-service teachers demonstrated "a significant difference in participants' self-efficacy for teaching measured before and after the improvisation training," with the teachers reporting personal benefits and having used the training in their post-intervention interactions with students.[118] Through improvisation, the teachers implemented new strategies for using "body language, emotional mirroring, vocal prosody, and acceptance to foster interaction and communication with the student."[119] The training was especially valuable for participants working with students who had communication difficulties. In another study, research by Cassandra Kisiel and her colleagues showed that, after six three-hour workshops in applied improvisation, on three key behavioral and psychological outcomes elementary-school-age children exhibited less aggressive and more prosocial behaviors, including decreased hyperactivity and greater scholastic engagement when compared to their control condition.[120] They also argue that these educational methods are more in line with current educational theories than many traditional strategies.

Improv training for social workers who conduct interviews manifests similar results. Researchers discovered three factors with real-world applications: "unconscious and emotional knowledge, the relational nature of practice, and the variability and unpredictability of the interview."[121] The value of applied improvisation for diverse, interdisciplinary research collaborations, constructing classroom communities in non-hierarchical ways, and engaging in organizational development in higher education is also beginning to be recognized.[122] Improv has even been used as a "tool for enhancing cooperation in academic libraries."[123]

Doctoral students, especially in more technical fields like the sciences, often have a difficult time communicating and translating their research. With clear results, applied improv training has been used to help graduate students loosen up and communicate in more expressive and impactful ways.[124] Former television star Alan Alda now runs the Center for Communicating Science at the State University of New York at Albany, which uses improvisational exercises to reach these goals. The center has collected all kinds of data from participants completing these sessions. One trainee's comment is illustrative: "It was as if the three-hour improv session finally, after many years, broke something in my brain loose. I gave the best presentation I have ever given and felt very 'present' and in control as I gave it."[125] To see the difference that this type of education has made for science students both "before" and "after" applied improv interventions, I highly recommend watching Alda's "Improv for Scientists" video, available on YouTube (see the endnote).[126]

A recognition of improv's contributions to technical disciplines has further begun to form, such as "engineering improv." Engineers are gradually recognizing that their work should bring together technical concepts with embodied education. Joseph Holtgrieve offers a college course in the subject and tells his students that

> all successful improvisation—and effective engineering—begins and ends with paying attention. I tell students to think of their attention as a flashlight. It creates a beam of light, and whatever that light illuminates represents their awareness. In addition, wherever they shine that light represents their intention. For many students, the flashlight is constantly being jerked back and forth by deadlines, crises or failed expectations, leaving them feeling ungrounded and exhausted much of the time. Early in the course, we introduce the idea of the flashlight, telling the students that when they realize they are the one holding it, they will come to understand that they also hold the power to be intentional. By deciding where to direct the light, they can choose to illuminate things that feed their energy rather than consume it with thoughts that haunt or distract.[127]

There's good reason to place so much value on attention in training. In the field of psychology, it's well established that "we create ourselves by how we invest this [attentional] energy. . . . attention is our most important tool in the task of improving the quality of experience."[128] What we pay attention to becomes the patterns of our very identities. In a response that those of us who teach applied improv often find, a student in this course shared with Holtgrieve "that Engineering Improv is the only course he has taken that has changed how he lives his life."[129]

In one of its most stunning applications, applied improv has become a tool for working with issues like mental health and autism. One study had participants engage in improvisational exercises designed to show what it's like to deal with psychiatric conditions, promoting understanding and empathy for others dealing with these issues. Participants universally rated the experience as positive.[130] Researchers find that improvisation has tremendous potential for helping "people with autism, dementia, anxiety, and trauma. Therapists, social workers, and psychiatrists are beginning to see that using the rules of improvisation in their practices leads to sessions in which patients and counselors build realities collaboratively without being inhibited by fear of judgment or failure."[131] In therapeutic applications, practitioners have adapted improv exercises to increase trust, personal awareness, and attentiveness to others.[132] It has also been used as an effective intervention for treating social anxiety disorder, as distinguished from similar forms of treatment like psychodrama and drama therapy.[133]

Increasingly, the applications of this work for autism are coming into focus. I have heard countless stories about professionals forwarding this new line of practice in their work, especially for young children such as

> 8-year-old Shaw. . . . From the moment he walks in, he can't wait. The blonde boy, in his gray and black zip up sweatshirt, is eager to shake his limbs. Scream a countdown. And then, he's ready. Like the other children gathered beneath the bright fluorescent lights at Indiana State University's psychology clinic, Shaw's here for a class specifically designed for 6- to 9-year-olds with high functioning autism. He's here to practice a skill that, until recently, seemed reserved for comedians and actors. Improv theater. But, instead of entertainment, tonight it's being used by one of a growing number of groups that use improv to teach social skills to children with autism. . . . "[Improv] is being recognized as kind of a technology for human connection and communication," says Jim Ansaldo, a research scholar at Indiana University.[134]

Since many "neurodivergent youth have a limited range of specialized interests, are dependent on routines, and struggle responding to unfamiliar situations," improv provides an "opportunity to Yes And youth interests and rewards flexibility and spontaneity"—even exercises based on having participants make a "new choice" can inform moments in life when redirection is helpful.[135]

Others are also forwarding these fascinating applications with neurodiverse individuals. Nancy Krusen suggests using "improvisational techniques as an adaptive skill to effectively blend art and science for occupational therapy practice" in unpredictable and fast-paced environments.[136] Moreover, patients with Parkinson's disease going through a twelve-week improv session led to a significant improvement in daily living activities, with the vast majority enjoying the class and believing it helped with their symptoms.[137]

In a cutting-edge application mentioned earlier, researchers and practitioners have begun using applied improv to train humanitarian and disaster workers to better prepare for the unexpected. Humanitarian workers operate in what's been called a volatile, uncertain, complex, and ambiguous (VUCA) world, and interviews with individuals who have completed applied improv training overwhelmingly maintain that they feel better prepped to engage that world with agility, speed, focus, and confidence.[138] Too many training programs focus on technical content to the exclusion of skills in communication, thinking on your feet, and "acquiring and building a capacity for peripheral vision."[139] With its focus on non-routine situations and unplanned contingencies, improv training is now seen as critical for emergency management personnel as well.[140]

Emerging work on leadership development, which I'll cover more fully in chapter 4, may provide one of the best justifications for embedding and scaling applied improv across organizations. In a study of sixty-seven leaders from different industries, regions, and organizations, qualitative and quantitative data from an applied improvisational training improved participants' abilities to lead, work with others, and more. Every single leader said that their listening skills had improved, with competent risk-taking, reduced stress, and enhanced mindfulness resulting from the project.

Overall, across many fields emerging studies provide a case for the value of applied improvisation. Armed with these arguments, teachers, trainers, and readers of all kinds now have a background for this curriculum and information that supports putting an applied improvisational philosophy, methods, and program into practice. While it's critical to know why we need to implement this vision for education more broadly across our educational systems and public life, I want you to hew closely to *how* this can be carried out on the ground, so here are two more exercises in box 1.3 before we turn to the next chapter.

Box 1.3
Teamwork and Commitment

These two exercises get participants into a playful mode, providing a burst of energy that has them commit more confidently to their messages and interactions with one another. They also open up participants' physicality, voices, and emotional range.

What's Needed Here?

Have everyone get into groups of three. If there is an even number, a group of four will also work. Ask the groups to stand back to back in a triangle shape without touching. This is like the game "Rock, Paper, Scissors." Tell everyone that you will say "One, two, three, go," and on the "go" they'll turn around and commit to one of three characters. The first character is a tiger, which you should demonstrate by putting your hands up in the air and giving a roar. Everyone should then practice this. The second character is a Martian. Put your index fingers at the side of your head and make an alien sound (whatever comes to mind is fine), and have everyone do the same motion. The last is a salesperson. Put your hand out for a handshake and say "Hi, how are ya?" Emphasize that everyone should turn back-to-back and decide beforehand what character they will fully commit to; there should not be any hesitation when they turn around. Play a number of rounds and allow laughter and talking after each. In a subsequent round—and this is critical—ask everyone to think about what their teammates *need* them to do, instead of thinking in advance of what they individually *want* to do. There will usually be more matches as a result of this mental switch.

Debrief questions: As with all applied improv exercises, it's best if participants talk about what they learned first. What does this exercise illustrate for each of us? Were there any surprises when each person decided to think about what the others *needed* rather than what each participant individually wanted to do? What would be a first step for bringing that attitude or approach into their personal or work lives?

Applications: This exercise teaches us to be fully committed and to worry less about mistakes, and it highlights the importance of celebrating small wins and disposing of our own ideas to try to focus on what our collaborators need. That last takeaway is usually the one to zero in on the most. Exercises like these help us make a mental switch from "How am I being perceived?" to "What is needed by my partner?"[141] This game is a winner with small or large groups.[142]

Pass the Expression

Everyone should stand in a circle. Tell the group that you will make a sound and a movement (you must do both!) that the person to your left will copy and pass to the person on their left. Each receiving person should mimic the sound and movement exactly, turning to the person to their left as quickly as possible. Once the sound and movement has gone fully around the circle, have the person to your left start a new sound and movement that everyone in the group will copy. Go around the circle again and then have the person to their left start a new sound and movement once it reaches them, and so on. You can increase or decrease the speed at which the exercise takes place.[143]

Debrief question: This is a warm-up exercise, so you can simply ask the group if everyone is feeling more energized and connected after.

Applications: This exercise gets everyone laughing and connected, and it frees up the body, voice, and emotions quickly. You can underscore how we're seeking to peel off the layers of self- and other-judgment and open up space for affective and behavioral learning.

Variation: One variation is to simply pass a clap around the circle. Turn to the person on your left and say "We're going to clap at the same time." Once you do so, they'll turn to the person on their left and try to clap at the same time, and so on. Pick up the speed as they get the format, but slow it down if they're going too quickly and not making connections with one another. Some improv teachers note that "if students are having trouble clapping simultaneously, try this demonstration: ask several pairs of students to face each other. Instruct them to look at each other's hands and clap. Almost always, looking into a partner's eyes is more effective."[144] They mention that you can also reverse the direction of the clap by clapping again with the person who just passed a clap to you, by adding more claps into the circle, or allowing the participants to pass a clap to anyone in the circle. These introduce more unpredictability into the exercise, so debriefs should focus on what each person needs to *do* to deal with the sudden changes.

By now you should see some of the directions this work has taken. In the next chapter, we'll turn to how you can best prepare to implement this work, including a mini-curriculum of field-tested exercises that I and others have run all over the world to help you get started before we turn to more advanced themes. By the end, my greatest hope is that you'll find that improv for democracy can play a major role in helping us graduate from old practices in a new world.[145]

Chapter 2

How to Prepare for and Practice Improv for Democracy

In developing skills for citizenship, we want our participants to become more engaged, innovative, and flexible human beings through applied improvisational methods. But there's one part that we don't want to improvise: our preparation for running courses, conducting workshops, or integrating improv's lessons and practices into existing initiatives in any format. This chapter gets straight to the point on what you'll need to bring to this curriculum, some foundational principles that should guide your thinking throughout this work (especially before moving to more advanced applications in the next chapters), and a mini-curriculum of ten exercises that shows how this kind of teaching and training can be structured for best effect.

What to Bring to This Curriculum

Before jumping into the three main democracy-building skills and the many exercises in this book that support them, instructors of all kinds should prepare to bring certain practices to this curriculum. The following guidelines can help frame and provide the best chance for applied improv to inspire and transform participants' behaviors.

First, you should bring a fun spirit to this mode of teaching and training. For many people not used to working in this way, there's good news. This isn't about being funny, putting on a show, constantly having participants tell jokes, or drinking three Red Bulls before a workshop. The key to cultivating a fun spirit lies in one factor: bring a "playful attitude" to the session.[1] Any of us can access a playful attitude. Although it may be rare to hear teachers speak of having fun in a classroom, teaching in which "controlled unpredictability" purposefully plays a part will tend to generate the atmosphere this kind of training thrives in.[2] James Carse clarifies: "To be playful is not to be trivial or frivolous, or to act as if nothing of consequence will happen. On the contrary, when we are playful with one another, we relate as free persons, and the relationship is open to surprise; everything that happens is of consequence, for seriousness is a dread of the unpredictable outcomes of open possibility. To be serious is to press for a specified conclusion. To be playful is to allow for unlimited possibility."[3] A great deal of research supports the relationship between mood and creativity.[4] Most of the positive energy in the room will emerge naturally from what the applied improv exercises have participants *do*, but it's critical that those leading these lessons and practices model a playful approach from the outset.

Second, educators should make sure to repeat many of the fundamental improv exercises from session to session. Unlike classes or workshops in which a subject is covered once before moving on, the value of applied improv lies in continual application and feedback on core practices. Communication research has shown that opportunities for repeating exercises or performances in classrooms helps participants master skills,[5] and improv training is no different in this regard. From experience, I'd suggest repeating at least four to five exercises in each course or workshop series. The participants will enjoy having a chance to return to previous activities and getting to see the improvements they're making in successive rounds.

Third, everyone should be included and engaged. In applied improv, there's no hiding. The nature of most applied improv exercises makes it nearly impossible for participants to have their heads buried in their cell phones or decide not to make a contribution to the session. While it may take you and your participants time to get used to this way of learning, once you've experienced it, you'll find these approaches superior to others that require less than full participation. As you'll see when you carry out some of the exercises already described in this book (e.g., "What's Needed Here" in chapter 1), anyone who comes to these sessions with a negative attitude will quickly find themselves isolated amid the camaraderie, laughter, and positivity that quickly develops among their colleagues. Many of these exercises make it difficult to pout or judge, flipping the switch on typical negative behaviors. But I've also found it useful to provide participants with one exception to joining in. For any of the more physical exercises, you should always let them know that if they have any physical issues, they should sit out and play the role of observer for the debrief. Make it a rule that they are not allowed to comment on the exercise while it's underway; they should save their constructive observations only for when it's completed.

Compared to many traditional ways of organizing education (such as lectures or open discussions), the standard that almost all activities should be both inclusive and engaging also fits with a growing movement to implement more "liberating structures" in organizations.[6] For instance, to vary the way you conduct debriefs or to have participants engage in a discussion about exercises that they have participated in, you can use a liberating structures method like "One-Two-Four-All" (pose a question; have each person write down their individual response to it and share that response with one other person, then with a group of four, and then with the whole group).

Using variety is also important. Mick Napier highlights that "constant change-up is what keeps an audience on their toes. It keeps them guessing, jolts them into new feelings and realities, and catches them off guard in a great way."[7] Some exercises should have everyone working in pairs, some in a circle in a big group, while for others everyone can be seated watching a few people up front. The general principle here is to create change in ways that feel qualitatively different than the passive setup in so much formal education.

Fourth, solid preparation and debriefing remain critical to the success of applied improv. Once again, applied improv isn't simply "winging it." This book will help you with that preparation by spotlighting many of the key lessons for your lessons or trainings. But as a matter of course, I've always found it best to let those in the class or workshop express what they're learning first, before providing at least one insight or theme that each exercise underscores. Much of the time, I'd also recommend explaining up front what participants will be doing and how it connects with their lives, since one active learning mistake is to "plunge into active learning with no explanation."[8] You don't need to give away all your insights up front, but providing some orientation to what you'll be doing and why you're doing it can put your participants at ease.

Many of this book's exercises can be run with the goal of merely promoting fun or a series of icebreakers with a group. However, having run thousands of these sessions, what I can tell you is that without any debriefs or mini-lessons, "we had a lot of fun" is what many people not used to applied improv will take away. Since there's much more than meets the eye and multiple lessons for just about every applied improv exercise, instructors should focus debriefs on the ideas and applications that go with each. This also models for participants the level of thought we want them putting into their own insights and connections.

Most important, you'll want to make debriefings as relevant to your audience as possible by investigating their learning needs. In advance or at the start of a course or workshop, find out what their pain points are, what they would like to do better, and the kinds of outcomes that matter most to them. Educational experts share that "if the energy that drives the course flows from the students' real *need* to investigate the question they hold in common, then the learning that results can touch students deeply."[9] With the idea that we're trying to lead participants through processes that lead to knowledge, if you know a fair amount about what the group needs to address, you can even create class or workshop titles that imply a question to be addressed rather than ground to be covered.[10] Ken Bain shares that "people are most likely to take a deep approach to learning when they are trying to answer questions or solve problems that they regard as important, intriguing, or just beautiful. . . . In most classes, however, students usually aren't in charge of the questions, leaving an enormous gap between the realities of schooling and the conditions that promote deep approaches."[11] Instructors can facilitate deeper approaches to learning by having participants identify what's important to them and, especially during debriefs, by providing opportunities for them to create the meanings for the exercises on their own terms first.

Relate what has occurred to real-world contexts, with questions such as "How does this apply to [X situation]?" "How might you use this?" "What might you do differently than you have done before?" and "What has become clear to you?"[12] Some other general questions can include "What did you learn about yourself in these activities?" "What did you learn about collaborative learning climates?" and other questions that center on motivation, trust, assertiveness, listening, feedback, and a variety of other democracy-building skills.[13]

Fifth, when running improvisational games or exercises, you don't want to wait until the end of each before you intervene. One of improv's novel contributions to teaching involves "side-coaching," or intervening with quick commentary and feedback *during* a game or exercise.[14] You don't want to do this so much that it interferes with the flow of the participants' training, but using side-coaching at key moments provides a way for the lessons and takeaways that we're after to sink more deeply into practice. If you notice during the "Working with Change" exercise described in box 1.1 that a participant is hemming and hawing their way through, a quick note to "speed it up" or "commit" can nudge the trainee toward the learning outcome *in the actual moment when it's needed*. Spolin underscored how it's essential to side-coach (or "the calling out of just that word, that phrase, or that sentence that keeps the players in focus . . . given at the time players are in movement") to help participants unlock their creativity and experience intellectual, emotional, and behavioral changes.[15]

Sixth, applied improv training works best when the instructor moves from lower- to higher-risk exercises.[16] Starting with an exercise that's too challenging can set the wrong tone from the start. Beginning with a few simple but insightful activities can build intrigue and help participants quickly understand how the sessions(s) will proceed. The exercises described in this book to this point have been fairly simple for this very reason. As you'll see in the more advanced exercises in the example mini-curriculum below, the order matters. Following active learning pedagogy, for any exercises that don't involve everyone it's best to call on people rather than ask for volunteers every time, and to vary the length of activities while staying attentive to any downtime participants experience between them.[17] I like to think of running trainings as having peaks and valleys. You don't want to be in one or the other for too long. If you start with some high-energy exercises, switch to a series of nonverbal or more reflective activities afterward. Steve Roe stresses that it's truly best to have a primary point of focus per exercise.[18] I'll be the first to admit that in the past I've overwhelmed participants with a number of lessons for each exercise. This isn't to say that you shouldn't highlight a number of concepts at play, but I have found that participants' skills tend to advance more when one primary point is prioritized and reinforced among others for each activity.

You'll want to approach this curriculum with a realistic sense for some of the challenges you may face. I like to keep a running list of objections I come across to build a case for this work and to manage expectations before and during trainings. Knowing that some decision makers may worry that a workshop will be "fun only," for example, can help you pitch this as deep, serious work that focuses on "behavioral change" rather than simply "informing" participants about what they need to know. With some discussion, you can usually get a decision maker to admit this approach is preferable, since the assumption that "experience is what counts most" runs deep in most organizations. In applied improv trainings, others have also noted that "most of the challenges facilitators encounter have to do with fluctuations in group energy levels, group self-consciousness, and preoccupation with the 'rules' and 'doing it right.' "[19] Over time, with this book's guidelines in hand, you'll be ready to address the kinds of assumptions or questions that participants typically bring to this work.

Seventh, try to accept yourself, others, and what is happening right now. An improvisational virtue involves "letting go" and accepting the choices you and others have made. Improvisers take what's in front of them at face value and work with it. They don't keep rehashing mistakes in the hope that they or someone else could have made different choices. We work with the reality we're given to improve it, but we don't get ensnared by what we can't change. In a classroom, for example, if you notice that a student keeps getting hung up on making a mistake or finding an exercise difficult, have them "woohoo" it out of existence to move on (see box 1.1 again). One of the most valuable improv lessons is that at times we've got to get out of our own way.

Eighth and last, the basics of excellent teaching don't go away with these practices. Facilitators should read the room and be attentive to students' needs, and work on making each session a safe space in which to engage in these practices. Over 10,000 studies of teaching effectiveness show that great instructors of all kinds know their subject, are clear about ideas and their relationships, motivate participants, structure their information, and work on being open, reasonable, caring, and creative in their teaching.[20] From a communication viewpoint, educators who work on being "assertive, responsive, clear, relevant, competent, trustworthy, caring, immediate, humorous, [and provide self-]disclosure" are engaging in research-supported behaviors, with "clarity, competence, and relevance" as the most important.[21] We all can and should aspire to these qualities.

The Background Basics

Whether you're new to improvisation or a veteran, there are some fundamental actions from theatrical improvisation to keep in mind. I use the word "actions" purposely here. I believe that applied improv instruction should focus on behaviors rather than just awareness of concepts.[22] Simply having knowledge doesn't necessarily translate into practice, so I have positioned all of this book's lessons and concepts in actionable terms. Characterizing every applied improv lesson as a behavior has the additional benefit of being observable and measurable, which can be important for demonstrating the results of this work to your boss, administrators, clients, funders, or other decision makers.

If you take a class at just about any improv theater in the world, you'll run into at least some of these fundamental actions at one point or another.

This list isn't meant to be exhaustive, but it should help readers note some basic themes that run across learning objectives, outcomes, and overall curricular development with applied improv. It will also act as springboard for many of the lessons and debriefs that we'll cover in the following chapters on using improv for communication, leadership, and civic skills. We want to use and be inspired by these principles, but also to move beyond them to focus on new ways of doing this work.

SAY "YES, AND . . ."

This is the most basic and famous guideline in all of improv: affirm and build upon others' ideas and actions. In the world of improv theater, this means accepting the reality your partner offers you and then adding information to it (for instance, in a theatrical scene, person 1 might say, "Captain, the ship can't handle this kind of weather," to which person 2 could respond, "Yes, and we just lost our sail!"). With this orientation, improvisers can support and collaborate with each other. On the other hand, if an individual is too quick to negate others' ideas, the scene will stop dead in its tracks as the improvisers fail to co-create a reality together (person 1: "Captain, the ship can't handle this kind of weather"; person 2: "No, this isn't a ship, it's a car"). As you'd hear from any improviser, some of the themes that run parallel to this basic principle include seeing everything that the other person offers you as a gift, always trying to make others look good, or treating everyone as "a genius or a poet."[23] To do so, we have to be present with others.

For our personal and professional lives, this guideline teaches us to truly listen to people and build on their ideas before negating or critiquing too quickly. For those of us whose first impulse is to argue, saying "Yes, and" retrains us to synchronize before moving to areas of difference. In fact, once one has been trained to see life in terms of others' "offers," everyday interactions become more productive and enjoyable. It gets us to practice affirmations consciously and strategically.

It's important to note that saying "Yes, and," like other guidelines, goes beyond face-to-face communication. When responding to an email, this fundamental would have us consider questions such as "What would it be like to affirm and build on others' email messages rather than ignore or critique them automatically?" There are many other lessons in this simple precept for communication, leadership, and civic skills that we'll cover, but for now it's important to make sure this most basic of ideas is understood before moving forward. The "Shared Memory" exercise in box 1.1 teaches the "Yes, and" principle. Given the culture of single-minded debate and advocacy in much of contemporary politics, there's likely no other skill so underdeveloped in civic education as learning to build on rather than continually negate others' offers.

Give and Take

Applied improv teaches people to become more comfortable with both giving and receiving. Many exercises are designed to show us how deeply the impulses for controlling a situation or other people may be. If someone likes to monologue extensively in meetings, this training brings that out. Alternately, these exercises can show us if we cede control too easily and seldom step forward to make contributions of our own. In a conversation with a friend, for example, applied improv can provide insights into how one person barely ever contributes to discussions. With improv's emphases on co-creation, we become better leaders and followers as a result of this work. As some improv instructors put it, "the ideal improviser is wonderfully fecund when ideas are required, but perfectly happy to let their partner run the scene for a while if they look inspired."[24] We aspire to be good colleagues, letting others know that we're with them. At the level of democracy building, can you imagine what could happen if more of our representatives and leaders made give and take a foundational part of their work?

Welcome the Unexpected

Those who have gone through applied improv trainings see changes as opportunities, embrace or move beyond slip-ups, and generally view the unpredictable aspects of life as welcome occasions for expanding our range of thought and behavior. In a theatrical scene, you'll often see the most unexpected moments become the highlights of a show. The applications to life are ample. Public speakers who can handle an unexpected question from an audience member are in a different league than those who come to such encounters afraid of what can happen, or freak out at the slightest deviation from their plans. We learn to work with what's actually happening and the many variables that are always at play and that we can never fully control for in any situation. For our civic lives, welcoming the unexpected means practicing curiosity, being open to surprises, and cultivating an ability to change when needed.

Use Inner and Outer Awareness

Applied improv teaches you to become more aware of your inner thoughts and rhythms and external behaviors such as verbal tics, nonverbal habits, and more. We learn to recognize that there's far more going on in communication than words. Participants learn to think more about the tempo at which they and others operate (i.e., in speech and other behavior does a person orient themselves to the world in slow, medium, or fast ways in different situations?). They learn to think about their emotions and the emotional climates they're in, the character and role choices people make in different settings, dialogue tendencies, and so forth. They focus on who they're being, where they are, and what's going on at a much more mindful level.

In effect, applied improvisers become skillful in working with multiple viewpoints and learning to play with different opinions, attitudes, and behaviors. They also know that every behavior implies a certain status or power level (more on this in chapter 4). Both applied improv and improv for theater also teach you to think about external elements in the environment, such as how the shape of a chair affects how people feel, what kind of relationship is broadcast to others by observing the interactions between people, and the nuances of how people stand or behave nonverbally relative to one another.[25] Citizens who become skilled in these matters can cross situations, cultures, and differences with ease.

Interrupt Routines

Applied improvisers are trained to become quick storytellers. They know that humans are story-making machines. As soon as one person stands in front of another, the mind automatically generates stories about who they are, where they come from, their mood, and more.[26] Good stories start from a place of authenticity, establishing a platform or status quo to which an audience can connect. They then "tilt" that base reality to show aberrations, anything abnormal, or a disruption in the lives of characters' routines.[27] Think about the beginning of just about any movie you've seen. There's usually a central character whose life is changed in some way by external events, characters, or other elements. Keith Johnstone advised against trying to think up stories, proposing that actors instead think of "*interrupting routines*" to free up their creative processes.[28] As an example, it's easier to create a story by filling in the blank in "you're practicing the piano when _____" than to think up six incidents that happened to a piano student.[29] What's the application to the outside world? In applied improv, we look for constructive opportunities to interrupt routines. We become more observant of ways to move beyond habitual practices to improve the stories we and others are living within.

When I was new to a job many years ago, I remember colleagues telling me to watch out for another employee, Tracy (name changed), because of her generally bad attitude and rude behavior with everyone. Without dismissing Tracy's role in this problem, I wondered if her attitude and behavior were also a result of everyone expecting this from her—in other words, a typical office routine had become "let's treat Tracy as if we always expect the worst from her." I decided to interrupt that routine by treating Tracy as amicably as possible every time we met, and I was surprised to see that she responded in kind, becoming a great colleague. A new reality was created. All she needed was for someone to interrupt the routine and treat her more graciously. To build democracies, we have to learn to interrupt routines well.

Let Go

You've seen this fundamental in this book already, and for good reason. It's vital on stage and in life. Similar to the last guideline, improvisers don't get fixed on the one right way of doing things, and try not to dwell on what could and should have been. Instead, they "let go" to deal with what's actually happening and possible in the present. I've heard many improvisers call this "disposability." If we can easily dispose of judgments, grudges, and the like, we broaden our worldview and make it easier to say "yes, and" and give and take with others. In essence, "your ultimate goal as an improviser should be to *let go*, which means going somewhere you had no intention of going."[30] In improv theater, we let go to stay open to different choices and the ensemble's needs.

Translated to the rest of life, the bigger point is to keep ourselves from getting fanatical about the thoughts that run through our heads and, as a result, to remain more open to all of the potential around us. The more we hold on to fixed viewpoints in our personal and professional lives, the less we are able to learn as well. This doesn't mean an individual needs to abandon their most cherished beliefs and viewpoints, but it does mean that they should remain open to new information and actions that foster flexibility and prudence. How many people do we all know (let's admit it, ourselves too) who simply cannot let go of some perceived slight in the past? It's not only individuals, of course, but entire nations that make it their platform to not let go of past slights from other leaders and countries. The implications for the building of more democratic forms of public engagement should be obvious. For everyone's sake, it's far better to let it go and find solutions with others *now* than to continually carry that rain cloud over our heads.

CARE AND COMMIT

While being open to pivot and adapt to others at any point, improvisers learn to care and commit fully to their own and others' actions. When I took classes and performed at the Groundlings improv theater in Los Angeles, the coaches would often say "play it to a ten"—meaning bring your *full* self and commitment to what's happening. Pulling back, not caring, and not being fully involved in a theatrical scene are at odds with an improvisational mindset. Among actors it's common to hear that acting is really "reacting," or being ready to be changed. Seeing people affected and altered by one another moves actions forward; if someone is unaltered by what others say and do, the scenes flatline, an agonizing reluctance fills the air, an ironic detachment can take over, and we ultimately get the feeling that there's nothing going on.[31]

The applications for our lives should be clear. We all know what it's like to be in a meeting where few people care about what's being talked about. Whether consciously or not, a decision not to care and commit to what's going on can distance coworkers from one another and suck the energy right out of a room. As another example, no one wants to listen to a speaker who doesn't seem to care and has little commitment to what they're saying. Much of the political realm is filled with such actors, who drone on and on at speeches and town-hall meetings in monotone voices that register little connection with those they wish to engage. Nothing of value ever gets accomplished without someone caring and committing.

Another way to look at all of these basic actions is to consider what happens when we're engaged in their opposites. In general, there's much consensus about the types of behaviors that run counter to applied improv: we have a tendency to block others' ideas or actions quickly, deny what they have created, provide no energy, care, or input of our own, grandstand and say a lot without much meaning, continually script our responses in an effort to control everything, judge incessantly, choose fear or egotism where we could have easily chosen joy or care, and go for cheap or demeaning humor at the expense of making real connections with others (improvisers often suggest "playing to the top of your intelligence"[32] in this regard), among other considerations.[33] These all tend to constitute anti-democratic behaviors. Keep these ideas in mind as you side-coach during teaching or training sessions.

Sequencing a Course or Workshop

By now you can hopefully see both the value of and ways to implement this kind of curriculum. Using the foil of "default settings," you should be ready to make a solid case for, and actually conduct, applied improv teaching and training. Before we move to the communication, leadership, and civics lessons and exercises covered in the rest of this book, in addition to the exercises already covered, here are ten applied improv exercises to get more acquainted with what this approach has to offer. The exercises in this book are themselves a "yes, and" to the incredible activities that so many improvisers across the world have developed in the last several decades. I have drawn many from a wide variety of sources and added my own lessons and variations from experimenting with them. Employing the following sequence will also give you more practice in the ebbs and flows of stringing together these exercises over an entire class or workshop.

Box 2.1
Ten Exercises to Get Started

Synergizer

This one's meant to be simple. It's a warm-up that immediately gets people connected, more energized and expressive, and ready to engage in further exercises. Everyone should stand in a circle and, following the instructor's cues, shake out their right arm while counting down from eight to one with each shake, "Eight, seven, six, five, four, three, two, one"; then their left arm, counting down from eight to one; then their right leg by the same count; and then their left leg. Try to pick up the pace as the exercise goes on. Once everyone has shaken each limb out from eight down to one, you'll repeat the same shake out from seven to one. After that, everyone will shake each limb from six down to one, and so forth. After everyone has gone through the final round ("one, one, one, one"), encourage them to applaud.[34] You don't need to do any debrief questions or applications for this opener, but if you would prefer to do so, highlighting the concepts described earlier of "letting go," building "inner and outer awareness," or "caring and committing" should suffice.

Pivoting on the Fly

This is a great exercise for getting the group working together quickly, adapting to changes, and being more present and "in the moment." With everyone standing in a circle, one person should swing their right arm across their body and say the word "Whoosh" to the person on their left. That next person should then "Whoosh" to the person on their left, and so on. Once the "Whoosh" has gone around the circle a couple of times, introduce a new cue, in which a person receiving the "Whoosh" from the person on their right clenches their fist, makes a hammering motion with that arm, and says the word "Bong." This reverses the direction of play. The person being "Bonged" can now "Whoosh" the person to their right or send the "Bong" back to the other person (this'll get a laugh, but encourage them to keep the motions going around the circle as much as possible). Once the group gets used to this, introduce a third cue, "Tunnel," in which the person whose turn it is can point at another player in the circle and say this word. This passes the play to the person being pointed at. You can add a fourth cue, "Ramp," by putting your hands up over the person's head to your left or right (depending in which direction the play is going). This cue skips the person who is having a ramp built over them, and play should continue with the person who made the other half of the bridge. You can also add in "Suspension bridge," which has the same dynamics as a "Ramp," but skips over two people instead. Finally, using the cue "Earthquake," everyone should shake their hands in the air, yell "Agh!" and find another spot in the circle. Play will resume with the person who yelled "Earthquake."[35] One addition for the "Ramp" cue that tends to create laughter is to tell the group that anyone being skipped over should look truly devastated.[36]

Debrief questions: How did you feel conducting this exercise? Was there anything you observed about yourself or others? How did you react when change happened unexpectedly?

Applications: This is a good exercise to zero in on the basic of "welcoming the unexpected" described earlier.

What Are You Doing?

Now we're getting to the heart of improv. Where the previous exercises mostly focused on activating participants' affective and behavioral energies, this one now adds in an intellectual component too. With everyone still standing in a circle, have one participant stand in the middle. Ask the group for a suggestion of a general activity or sport that this person can do, such as skiing. The person should immediately imagine that they're in a scene related to skiing, and both *do* and *say* something relative to that activity. Above all else, side-coach the person in the middle to immediately jump into some kind of action (this will prevent participants from freezing up and judging what they're doing). For example, the participant could start doing skiing motions and say "Lovely day for skiing down a triple black diamond." Or they might start digging with a shovel and say "Ah, looks like there's an avalanche coming, time to start digging an escape tunnel." They should keep doing the action and talking until someone from the outer circle taps them on the shoulder and says "What are you doing?" As quickly as possible, the person in the middle should then give them *any other activity* that has to do with the category (in this case, skiing) that is not the one they're currently engaged in and does not repeat what someone else has done before. So, if the person in the middle has been doing skiing motions, they could say "Building a ski cabin" or "Checking the snowmobile," but not "I'm skiing down a mountain." The person in the middle also shouldn't do the activity they're saying (make sure they continue the one they're currently engaged in while giving the new directive)—that's the next participant's job. As quickly as possible the next person should then jump into the middle and start doing the new activity and say a line—for example, they start building a ski cabin and assert "I wish there were a Home Depot close by." They should continue the scene until the next person taps them on the shoulder, and the same process takes place, with each person in the middle returning to the circle as each new participant steps in. Make sure the person asking "What are you doing?" does so with confidence; don't let participants off the hook if they enter the middle without energy and focus. When giving the next action to the person tapping in, you can also tell participants to take the "I'm" out of their instructions (e.g., "I'm . . . building a ski cabin"): that's another device for judging ideas and stalling action. After running this round for a bit, get another activity (e.g., "Washing dishes") and continue the exercise.

Debrief questions: How did it feel to name the new activity while performing the old one? Were you able to play and not plan too much?[37] Were you able to fully commit to the action or did you find that you held yourself back?

Applications: This exercise is about teaching participants to commit, engage in movement to spur thoughts, and deal with and adapt to sudden changes with greater ease.

Variations: After running the initial round with an activity or sport, I highly recommend adding the following variation. For a suggestion, ask individuals in the group for two different letters, e.g., "A" and "M." Participants in the middle will now need to provide the person tapping them on the shoulder with a first word that starts with an "A" and a second word that starts with a "M" to inspire the actions of the next round; for example, they could say "allowing mischief," "attacking mongooses," or even "artful monitoring." It's critical to emphasize that those receiving the action should immediately jump into the middle and interpret the cue however they wish—the results are almost always hilarious. To one person, "allowing mischief" could mean letting a toddler do whatever they want at a restaurant, to another it could be letting animals loose from a zoo. Getting participants to *commit to their own interpretations* is where you'll really get to see some individual creativity shine. Once the group gets used to this, change to new initials, and for a more advanced, even funnier round, get three initials instead of two. You can also do a rhyming round, where the last word in each directive must rhyme with the last word of the previous; for example, if the rhyming word is "run," directives from the person in the middle could include "lifting a ton," "basking in the sun," or "eating a hot cross bun." Like all applied improv exercises where everyone first stands in a circle, you can also split into smaller groups so participants get more practice once they get the format down.

Following Through

Since your participants have been standing in a circle for the first three exercises, for variation it's now time to switch it up. Have your participants get into pairs; one person should be A and the other B. Instruct the A's to begin a conversation about anything at all. If you think it would help, you can also ask the group to come up with a topic that would be easy to have a conversation about (where to go on vacation this year, what's happening at work, etc.). When A finishes their sentence, B must begin their sentence/response in the conversation with a word that begins with the same letter as the last letter in A's last word. So, for example, if A said "I want to go to South America for my vacation this year," B would zero in on the letter "r" (since "year" was the last word and "r" the last letter of the sentence).

B would then need to begin their sentence with an "r" word, e.g., "Right now I was thinking just the same thing," and so on back and forth between A and B.[38] Let this go on for a minute or two.

Debrief questions: Have your participants debrief on what the conversations were like, what they found difficult, and what having practiced this rule taught them. In our everyday lives, how much focus do we put on other people and what they're saying?

Applications: This exercise is primarily about listening. Many of us get into the bad habit of formulating what we are going to say while other people are talking, preventing us from truly listening. Sometimes we also fail to show that we're trying to hear what others are saying, with our heads down or minds elsewhere, signaling that we're uninterested. Or, we grab on to one thing the other person says that relates to something in our own lives, instead of trying to build on or explore what they offered. It's not always bad to talk about ourselves in response to someone else's comments in a conversation, but this exercise demonstrates how we may get stuck in that default setting, perhaps failing to ever ask follow-up questions or stick with what the other person wants to talk about. One improv coach notes how "there is no way that you can be thinking ahead while playing this game"; it "gets you out of your head and paying attention to your partner."[39] The goal of last letter, first letter isn't to have participants focus on letters in everyday conversations, of course: the main takeaway is to focus and build on others' communication more intently. Early in my career I worked in radio and once asked some talk-show hosts what they did to prepare for interviews with guests who would come on their programs. I'll never forget learning from one talk-show host how his key to effective on-air conversations involved simply listening closely to what his guests would say, but especially the last thing they mentioned. By approaching others in this way, he said that whatever he needed to say next would always suggest itself. Most people are not used to listening to others in this way, but it can transform interactions.

Variation: Another common and easier way to run this exercise is to have participants simply start their sentences with the last word (rather than letter) the other person said. You can also build in a challenge outside the class or workshop by having participants do this with people they encounter throughout their week. Advise them not to do it too much or obviously, but it can be a fun assignment that participants can reflect on for a next session.

Line Up

At this point, we turn to a quick, nonverbal exercise that works on a different skillset. As mentioned, sequencing a group of applied improv exercises is best done in ebb and flow fashion. There should be peaks and valleys to the teaching and training, since continuous, energetic exercises can become exhausting, just as too many slower, reflective ones can fail to build momentum and cohesion. For its simplicity, I consider this a good transition between the last and next exercises. Tell everyone that there should be absolutely no talking: this is a nonverbal exercise where they will have to communicate without speech or words. Tell them that when you say "Go," everyone must line up in order of their birthdate, with January 1st at one end of the room (show them all exactly where that spot will be), all the way to December 31st at the other end of the room. Say "Go" and observe what happens, making sure to enforce the no-talking rule. I like to place a time limit on this activity; when it looks like they may all be close (but not finished), give them a ten-second countdown. Then go through the line and have each person say the day and month of their birthdate, starting from the person on or closest to January 1st.

Debrief questions: How did you communicate effectively with others without the use of words? This exercise is mostly a setup for the next, so you can debrief quickly.

Applications: The idea of developing greater inner and outer awareness can be focused. The next two exercises further advance this lesson in different ways.

Variations: You can also do more rounds (I find that two is about the most you'll want to cover), including nonverbal line-ups in terms of shoe sizes or any other category that can translate to consecutive numbers.[40] The prompts "Line up in order of where you were born" and "Line up in order of where you now live" can be particularly challenging, with the start of the line as the place where those who were born or live closest to the room you're in will stand, and the end of the line as the place where those who were born or live the furthest away from the room should stand. You can further alternate the verbal and nonverbal rule, with some prompts allowing the participants to speak and in others to remain silent.

Three-Word Conversations

Have participants pair up. If there's an odd number, there can be one group of three. Ask them to start a conversation. The only rule for this conversation will be that each person must say three words and only three words (not one, two, or four; they must get to three only). I like to demonstrate this with another person so everyone can see what this might look like: for example, "How are you?" "I'm good, you?" "Fantastic, great weather," and so forth. Say "Go" and let them proceed with their conversations for about two minutes. Tell them to keep the conversation going no matter what.

Debrief questions: What did you observe during this exercise? (Okay, aside from maybe speaking like cave people.) How did only having three words impact your communication? Did you find yourself slowing down for emphasis, gesturing more, or becoming more animated?

Applications: Let's face it, many of us communicate with a great deal of verbosity. We over talk or even monologue in desperate attempts to create meaning, only to realize that, at times, there are actually diminishing returns from the amount of verbal communication we use with others. Sometimes more meaning is created when we take greater pause, use silence strategically, or think about what kind of impact we want our words to have. This exercise builds from the previous one to have participants experience what it's like to slow down a bit and bring more of our nonverbal life to communication. Among other lessons, participants typically respond that they found themselves selecting their words much more carefully than usual, used more gestures, and became animated to bring more meaning to their communication. Being restricted to only three words demonstrates that there's sometimes as much meaning in what's not said as what is. It's quite an enlightening exercise with a variety of applications; it "imposes a slowness that ups emotional involvement," surfacing physical rather than purely verbal solutions in our interactions with others.[41] The exercise highlights how we're often desperate to fill the silence (hence the use of filler words like "um," "uh," etc.), and that we can communicate more purposefully as individuals, leaders, and citizens by making our words matter.

Variation: You can also vary the number of words that participants are allowed to use, although I've found that using three words tends to awaken participants' nonverbals and gets them to be more precise in a way that's more difficult with other numbers.

That Is . . .

Building on the previous exercise, this activity has everyone working on their own rather than in a group or pairs. I've never seen this exercise fail to be anything but a major revelation for participants. It leads to a lesson that's hard to ignore in everyday practice.[42] First, ask everyone to walk around the room. They shouldn't follow any pattern (e.g., a circle), but just walk around randomly by themselves. In this initial round, ask everyone to point at things in the room (or wherever you are) and say exactly what they *are*. Demonstrate this for everyone by pointing at a chair and saying "chair," pointing at the ceiling and saying "ceiling," and so forth. Say "Go" and let participants engage in this activity for about a minute, telling everyone to go as quickly as possible. They'll be feeling pretty good about themselves at this point. In the second round, ask the participants to now point at things and only say the last thing they pointed to. Demonstrate this by pointing, for instance, at the wall first and then pointing at the floor (at which point you'll say "wall"), and then a table (at which point you'll say "floor"), and so on. You'll notice the energy in the room change as the participants struggle with this new rule. Let this go for another minute. For the third and final round, without any other instructions or a demonstration, tell everyone to point at things in the room and say anything other but what they actually are. Say "Go" quickly so that they don't have too much time to think about this. Observe what happens in the room and let this go on for another minute or so.

Debrief questions: For the debrief, first ask your participants which of the three rounds they found the hardest and why. You'll often get a mix of the second and third conditions, depending on the group. For those who found the second condition hardest, ask them why they found it challenging. Ask the same question to those who found the third condition the most difficult.

Applications: In both my and other trainers' experiences, the third round is often played the slowest. You hear more silence and struggles among the participants the longer it runs. So here's the rub. The second round has a *real* rule built into it, so it's clear when the participants are either doing it "right" or "wrong." As an observer, empathize and share that you felt their pain, it was a genuinely hard rule that made almost everyone struggle with their short-term memories. But in the third round, note that it was difficult to be wrong. You essentially just gave the instruction to point and call out anything they wanted. To repeat, that's anything at all; what an incredible universe of options to choose from! So why did this version of the exercise cause so much consternation, anxiety, and hesitation, especially as time went on? Tom Salinsky and Deborah Frances-White share that one explanation could be that there are lots of options but no criteria. All of us went to school and learned that there are right and wrong answers to many of life's questions, but this circumstance provided no criteria. As they mention, "you don't know if calling the chair a beehive earns you a tick or not."[43] In this sense, the second round should feel like the kind of challenge we're used to. In the third, however, we end up inventing rules out of thin air to fill the criteria void; you'll point at a window and want to say "dog," but thinking that's not imaginative enough, censor yourself and instead stretch for "viaduct."[44] Participants often end up inventing rules that don't exist and start applying them unconsciously, such as "Everything I say must be different and original," when the original instruction would have equally allowed pointing at every object and saying the word "apple" over and over again. We become less fluent from the first to the third condition because in the second there's a real rule to struggle against, and in the third we end up inventing our own obstacles. It's a lesson that countless improvisers and improv teachers around the world will highlight about this work: one of the greatest goals of this teaching and training is to help each of us *get out of our own way*. Stephen Nachmanovitch relates that "the work of creativity is not a matter of making the material come, but of unblocking the obstacles to its natural flow."[45] It's also a way of taking care of ourselves so that we're taking care of our partners—clear choices and commitments are offers for others to build on.[46] The exercise shows that we generate a lot of learning anxiety ourselves, teaching participants about the attitudes we bring to challenges without even thinking about them. Pose a final question: where else in life are we each applying these kinds of unnecessary constraints or complications where none are needed?[47] You may also wish to discuss the following quote in this context: "What will undo any boundary is the awareness that it is our vision, and not what we are viewing, that is limited."[48] If the participants are fortunate to continue beyond a first class or workshop, keep returning to this theme.

Variations: You can do a follow-up to this debrief by asking everyone to repeat the third round by pointing at things and saying the first words that come to their mind without self-censoring. Emphasize that speed and walking around are still critical to this final attempt. Everyone should find it easier. This exercise teaches people that trying to look dull or like they're not good at certain activities are themselves strategies in need of replacement. For imagination and creativity to flow, we have to start with ourselves and all the ways we impede our own progress unwittingly. Another variation of this exercise involves having some middle rounds where other rules or self-limitations play out, such as that everything pointed to must begin with the letter C.[49]

Campaign

Put your participants in teams of four or five people. Have each group sit in chairs in a circle. Ask one person in the group to be a note taker. To get started, ask all the participants for a great product that doesn't yet exist but should (e.g., a time travel machine). Get a few suggestions and then pick one that seems interesting.[50] For the first round, ask everyone to go clockwise around the circle and each provide a suggestion of a "name" for this product. Here's the really critical part: as each person provides a suggestion, everyone in the group must throw their hands in the air and yell "Yay!" each time a group member does so. Enforce enthusiasm here and make sure the note taker writes down each suggestion. Once everyone has had a chance to provide one name, keep going around the circle for more name suggestions. Have this go for a minute or two.

Debrief questions: I like to do a quick debrief after this first round. How did it feel to support one another's suggestions so enthusiastically? Did you see the "yes, and" principle at work here? What would have happened in your group if you hadn't done the "Yay!" each time?

Applications: This is one of my favorite exercises for showing how the "yes, and" principle can supercharge our creativity. I have used it in many classes and workshops that have nothing to do with improv, to demonstrate what can happen when we commit to simple changes in our interactions with others. We often think of creativity as an individual accomplishment, but this exercise shows how it can equally be about the unconscious or conscious communication norms we put in place with one another, which either challenge or foster our capacity to be creative. I highly recommend building on the initial round with the following variations below, and then conducting a final debrief that focuses on how the improv principles of give and take, letting go, and caring and committing informed this experience too.

Variations: Have the participants generate other aspects of this product campaign. Using the exact same process, have them come up with a "priority audience" for this product for one to two minutes, then a "slogan" for the product, a "celebrity endorser," and even a "short advertising jingle" that might go with a commercial for it. I've found that four to five rounds of idea generation is usually enough to make the point and keep everyone interested. At the end, every group should pick a final name, priority audience, slogan, celebrity endorser, and jingle from the lists they've generated. Go around each group and have them share out what they came up with. The results are usually entertaining.

Adaptor

This one's a classic.[51] There's probably no better applied improv exercise for building participants' ability to adapt to change than this, since it has a step-by-step progression toward increasingly difficult adaptations built into its structure. I call it "Adaptor" because it requires rapid adaptations that keep everyone on their toes. Everyone should stand in a circle. One volunteer will start in the middle and have one of two choices that they can make. They should walk around and say either the words "Bippity bippity bopp" (have everyone practice saying this a few times, and make sure those in the circle are saying all three words each time) or "Bopp" to individuals in the circle at random. If they say "Bippity bippity bopp" to someone, that person must respond with the word "Bopp" before the person in the middle completes the phrase. If the person on the receiving end fails to do so (or if they say anything else than "Bopp"), they should now trade places and continue the task of saying one of the two phrases to others in the circle. Alternatively, if the participant in the middle of the circle says "Bopp" to anyone, that person must stay silent. If the person receiving the "Bopp" says anything at all, that person should now switch places with the person in the middle. You'll see everyone suddenly listening at a deeper level and becoming more focused once they get the hang of this. Tell the person in the middle not to necessarily go around the circle in order; instead, they should strategically try to throw people off balance by trying a mix of strategies that might work (for example, darting from one person to someone four people away quickly). Once the group gets used to the format, this is where the exercise really gets fun. Give the person in the middle a third tool: they can say the word "Elephant" to anyone and then count from one to ten. In response to "Elephant" and the subsequent ten count, the receiving person should put their right arm out (this will be the trunk), cross their left arm under their right arm and bring that hand up to their face (i.e., so that the left arm will act as the elephant's face).

Have everyone practice this. The two people on each side of this person should, in turn, create the elephant's ears by putting one arm up in the air and another down below (i.e., the individual on the left of the person creating the elephant will basically create a "C" shape with their arms, and the person on the other side will do a reverse "C"). If *any* of the three people have their part of the elephant picture out of place by the time the person in the middle counts to ten, then they should trade places and be the new person in the middle. If two or all three mess up, just pick the person who seemed to mess up the most. Remind everyone that the tools of "Bippity bippity bopp" and "Bopp" are still in play, however, so the person in the middle now has three choices. After the participants have gotten used to this new tool, throw in a final one that can be used. The person in the middle can now also call "Airplane" and count to ten. Anyone receiving this cue must put their thumb and index fingers in an "O" shape on both hands and place them over their eyes (i.e. these should look like a pilot's goggles). The person to their right must put their right arm straight out to their side (the plane's right wing), and the person to the left must do the same with their left arm (the plane's left wing). As with "Elephant," anyone who messes up by the ten count must trade places with the person in the middle.[52] After a few rounds of this, turn to what I call the "chaos" round, which requires a heightened level of action and attentiveness among everyone in the room. Add another person into the middle so there are now two people inside the circle calling out one of the four tools at a time to individuals on the perimeter. Then add another volunteer, and another, and another. With a group of about thirty people, I've found that five people in the middle marks the limit of what can be handled.

Debrief questions: How did you feel during this exercise? Did you notice that as the rounds progressed you became more attentive and adaptable to what was happening? What other lessons do you think this exercise teaches us?

Applications: External focus, being fully present, managing and adapting to change, and welcoming the unexpected.

Countdown

I love using this exercise at the end of a workshop. It's impressive and under-scores many of the lessons that we're seeking to translate into practice. Have everyone in the group circle up, put their hands over one another's shoulders, lean forward, and close their eyes. Start by saying the number "twenty." From there, another person in the circle should say "nineteen," then another "eighteen," and so on down to "one." Each number must be given by a different person in the group, and the participants shouldn't simply go around from left to right or right to left with each person in turn providing a descending number. If anyone speaks at the same time at any point, the group has to start back at twenty again. Typically, groups will try to rush through the first few times, so tell them to slow down a bit and connect with one another. After a workshop filled with collaborative exercises, what many improvisers call a "group mind" often develops where participants become much more sensitive to each other's energies and what's happening in the room. Most times when I run this at the end of a full class or workshop, the participants eventually do get all the way from twenty to one and express great joy at doing so. Even if they don't, emphasize how well they did and that (if you hopefully have a series of workshops or classes) this is one we'll return to in the next session(s).

Debrief questions: How did (or could) the group manage to do this exercise successfully? Was there a leader who emerged? And if so, would there be a way of doing this without a leader?[53]

Applications: This final exercise brings participants' energies down to a reflective, focused level, especially after the more physical and boisterous exercises. The value of silence for good communication becomes more palpable (more on this in the next chapter). This exercise is also a great way to end a session focused on democratic forms of leadership (see chapter 4).

Now it's time to "raise the stakes." That's also an improv concept. In the next several chapters, I'll show you the many exciting ways applied improv connects to communication, leadership, and civic skills, all in the service of building democratic people, organizations, and societies. Although applied improv had its origins in theater and similar areas, I believe that it's now important to pull away from those contexts to create higher-level applications for this work that move us beyond the background basics. Each step of the way, I'll ground actionable concepts with exercises that show you how to put this work directly into practice.

Chapter 3

Using Improv to
Develop Communication Excellence

In my travels and teaching, I've met countless people who say that taking an improv class was one of the best experiences they've had for improving their communication skills. Some renowned speakers even share that improv dramatically improved their presentations, heightened their ability to see and listen to others, and generally changed their attitudes toward life.[1] Year after year, studies continue to confirm that communication is the top professional skill to master. Through rigorous research, Sherwyn Morrealle, Joseph Valenzano, and Janessa Bauer find that "communication, and specifically oral communication education, is critical to . . . future personal and professional success."[2] The building of vibrant democracies is also founded on the quality of our communication practices. Crafting better social worlds starts with how we relate to and what we say with one another.

In essence, communication is one of society's most important assets. Repeatedly, communication education has been found critical to "enhancing organizational processes and organizational life; promoting health communication; enriching the educational enterprise; understanding crisis, safety, risk, and security; improving interpersonal communication and relationships; influencing diplomacy and government relations; being a responsible participant in the world, socially and culturally; developing as a whole person; and succeeding as an individual in one's career and in business."[3] In this chapter, I'll provide readers with high-level ideas about communication and their connections with improvisation. You can think of these as a series of concrete lessons and learning outcomes. I present each as a directive that participants should *practice*. For years, improvisers have had a go-to list of ideas that improv supports (e.g., "yes, and"; see the last chapter). At the same time, it's useful to move beyond these to develop an advanced vocabulary and exercises for this work that connect with the communication field.

One of the central claims of this chapter is that applied improvisation dovetails perfectly with state-of-the-art communication research and pedagogy. Whether you're putting together a communication class, seeking to embed applied improv lessons or teaching into your existing courses, workshops, or thinking, or looking to create an entire applied improv curriculum, this chapter will provide the substance and some practical exercises that will help you demonstrate the value of this kind of teaching and training for communication-related goals.

As a reminder, we're doing this work to counter the "default settings" that we all have—in this case, the default settings that prevent us from communicating in more productive, engaging, positive, and democratic ways. And we're going for that type of elevated learning that seeks to get the best ideas into the body, not just the head. This isn't simply about having a great class or workshop experience. We're aiming for experiential learning and hard-hitting takeaways that translate into new practices in people's everyday lives. We know that participants' retention of content is markedly better in experiential over lecture-based learning.[4] Yet we're combining these approaches to implement what researchers have found is at the very heart of educational motivation: "intellectually stimulating behaviors."[5] As such, every idea in this and subsequent chapters is framed in terms of what people should *do*. I've packaged every concept as a behavior-focused phrase that you can use in teaching or, better yet, in the moment of side-coaching participants (e.g., just like the basics of care and commit, give and take, etc.).

While this chapter explores new connections and practices for applied improvisation, it's also an effort to recover important ideas and methods from communication history. In his studies, William Keith notes that most communication instruction nowadays involves teaching "*about* communication" rather than "improving the [communication] ability, skills, and coping of students and others."[6] Earlier in the last century, pioneering communication educators valued both communication performance and the interventionist, political dimensions of such teaching to a much greater degree, especially in addressing the question "How should people in a democracy communicate?"[7]

It's important to make this connection at the outset, as applied improvisation helps us advance both historical and contemporary concerns in communication and the underlying concern of this book: that improv can support the development of democratic skills. We're after what some forecast is the future of communication education itself: a "broader vision of academic practices" that involves "generating both observations of what is constructive for people and communities and also general theories of what [communication] practices tend to improve the world."[8]

Applied Improv and Core Communication Competencies

Before reading further, I'd like to cover some credible, supported ideas about what we're going for in communication education and training writ large. If you're pressed for time, these are ideas that you can adapt and return to repeatedly. Based on a multi-year study of what core skills students and trainees should take away from communication courses, a research team identified seven core competencies: "Monitoring and Presenting Your Self, Practicing Communication Ethics, Adapting to Others, Practicing Effective Listening, Expressing Messages, Identifying and Explaining Fundamental Communication Processes, and Creating and Analyzing Message Strategies."[9] Although we could go into great detail on each of these, for practical purposes let me quickly make some connections with applied improv that you can use.

MONITORING AND PRESENTING YOUR SELF

Improv teaches us to become more aware of ourselves and others, monitoring behaviors such as how much we're listening, building on other's ideas, and more. By tapping into our default settings and getting to practice a larger repertoire of communication tools, you become more attuned to how you're presenting yourself and more adept at recognizing how people present themselves.

PRACTICING COMMUNICATION ETHICS

Every applied improv exercise promotes ethical values. It's critical to have participants recognize that we're seeking to discuss and apply ethical communication practices in each. Take the give and take concept, for example. That's not only an effective practice, but a communication ethic about the way that we should generally try to open rather than close space for other people in our communication. One idea relevant to practicing communication ethics is John Shotter's notion that moral knowledge is social, which is to say that the feeling of obligation that arises when we engage with others "is the kind of knowledge one has only from within a social situation . . . and which thus takes into account (and is accountable to) the others in the social situation."[10] Improv focuses on an obligation to build on rather than just ignore others' offers. Terms such as "mansplaining" (when someone monologues at another person about a topic that person already has expertise in, often with irrelevant details, little self- and other-awareness, and as a gendered practice)[11] have been invented to show how deeply problems like this are felt in people's everyday lives. The forwarding of communication processes that are attentive to and respectful of others' turns is at the core of what improv affords our social worlds and civic life.

Adapting to Others

There are many ways that improv helps us adapt to other people, from reading a room well to advocating for all voices to be heard in a discussion. Ultimately, the goal of all communication is less persuasion than what Kenneth Burke calls "identification,"[12] or the building of connections between two or more people. In politics, for example, leaders who win are usually those who can create words and other symbols that most people can "identify" with. In applied improvisation, we're building methods for identification and adapting well to others.

Practicing Effective Listening

Nearly every time I raise the subject of listening with a group, a participant will mention that everyone should have an entire course on getting better at this practice. I couldn't agree more. There's probably no other communication skill as critical to our lives that receives so little attention in formal education. Improv gets us to push our focus off ourselves, promoting dialogue. If you ever watch an improv comedy show by a highly skilled troupe, "you will see how not one detail slips by these players. . . . Everything is heard" and treated as "the most important idea in the world."[13] Note that this doesn't mean agreeing with others' ideas, but at least making sure that they are heard and absorbed.

Expressing Messages

Improv helps participants summon the courage to communicate in expressive and flexible ways, inviting them to become more fluid in their interactions with others and helping the brain and tongue connect more seamlessly. Many applied improv exercises empower individuals to practice confident delivery and feel more comfortable expressing themselves in a variety of situations.

They're of particular help for situations involving impromptu speaking and similar types of communication where the unexpected is at play.

IDENTIFYING AND EXPLAINING FUNDAMENTAL COMMUNICATION PROCESSES

I've discovered that almost any communication concept I might want to teach can be demonstrated through applied improvisation. A host of communication theories cover ideas about proximity, or the distance between human beings, for example. Take "expectancy violations theory," which teaches participants how the distance we stand from one another affects how persuasive we can be in particular situations.[14] In applied improvisation exercises where two or more participants converse with one another, debriefs can draw everyone's attention toward this and many other important lessons.

CREATING AND ANALYZING MESSAGE STRATEGIES

Although the weight of applied improvisational teaching and training is put on what happens in the moment of communicating, educators of all kinds can still focus on the creation and analysis of participants' message strategies. For instance, in the "Rapid Relationships" exercise discussed in the first chapter (see box 1.2), part of the debrief can ask participants what kind of messages they created to connect with others. What messages worked? What didn't work and why? As this chapter will cover, applied improv also focuses on the link between creative communication and message strategies.

Box 3.1
Getting Past the Curse of Knowledge

Friend from the Past

This is one of the best exercises I have come across for teaching about what most challenges our communication skills.[15] Ask everyone to pair up: one person will be A and the other B. Tell the A's that they are to describe to the B's what an iPhone is. Reiterate that it's really that simple, all they have to do is get across to B what an iPhone is. You could select any number of other objects, but in my field-testing of this exercise with many people in different countries, I've found this object both universal and sufficiently technical for its purposes. Now tell the B's that they are going to play a role—they are from the sixteenth century. They won't know what electricity is and will certainly never have heard of phones or even computers. Be sure to emphasize that you need them to play this role with commitment—they shouldn't make it easy for the A's to explain what an iPhone is. For example, if A says a word like "internet," push back and ask, "What's the internet?" Say "Go" and let the participants struggle through this for several minutes.

Debrief questions: After, ask the A's how it went. Typical responses will include that it was incredibly hard, that they had to adapt and hone their communication for the B's, and more. Ask the B's what worked well and what didn't in terms of A's communication strategies. (Inevitably, you'll find that "magic" gets introduced by at least one group.) Debrief questions can also be related to each of the seven core communication competencies identified above (e.g., "What principles or communication ethics does this exercise promote?").

Applications: Scholars from Stanford and Harvard Universities highlight that one of the greatest obstacles human beings face in their communication is "the curse of knowledge."[16] The curse of knowledge gets at how, ironically, the more we know the harder it can be to communicate with others. If you've ever been confused by someone's directions for how to get to a place you've never been, it's probably because they know the area so well that they have difficulty imagining what it's like not to know what they know. In essence, we're each "cursed" by the knowledge that we have when it comes to communication. Our default setting is that we forget to step into others' frames of reference first. The beauty of this exercise is that it gets participants to *experience* the curse of knowledge in a playful way. Stevie Ray notes that this activity can "develop skills of explanation, but it is more about dealing with people who have a different worldview than you. This is a fun wake-up call to how much we take for granted and how easy it is to confuse rather than clarify. . . . You will focus on satisfying their needs, rather than just talking about what you know. People like to talk about what they know, even if the other person doesn't need to hear it. The trouble is, me learning how much you know doesn't solve my problem. It actually creates more distance."[17]

Getting to the Core

Advancing the same lessons from the last exercise, this game provides a great way to break through the curse of knowledge, this time in a co-created manner.[18] Have your participants get into groups of four and have one person in each explain a real-life example of a work-related task focusing on what they must accomplish (e.g., what they do at work and why). Alternately, any complicated professional message (e.g., a nonprofit's mission statement) that one person in each group has to try to communicate to others in their line of work will suffice for this exercise. This person will turn to the participant on their left and have ninety seconds to explain the details of this message. The second person will then turn to the third person and restate this message in thirty seconds. The third person will turn to the last person and restate this message in only fifteen seconds. Finally, the last person will turn back to the first person and state the message in only four words.

Debrief questions: What did this process do to the message that the first person constructed? Did you find yourselves getting to the message's essentials as the process played out? What adaptations did each speaker make for their audience?

Applications: You can use this procedure to highlight how each person attempted to distill down to the message's essentials in an effort to overcome the curse of knowledge. Stress any observations you made about both the message and its reception between the participants. You can also highlight moments when judgment, self- or other-criticism, or the need to control the message may have prevented each participant from fully expressing themselves and advancing the group's task.

Push Your Focus Outward

Aside from the need to overcome the curse of knowledge, if you take nothing else away from this chapter, let this be it. The advice to push your focus outward illustrates perfectly what years of experimentation in improv theater has to offer other contexts. Having been in the communication field for close to two decades, I've never seen it come up in any communication textbook, but it should be fundamental to a lot of communication instruction, especially when teaching public speaking classes or workshops.

The idea is simple: to communicate effectively we have to push our focus outside ourselves as much as possible. In improv theaters you'll often hear the concept referred to as "external focus." If you're giving a speech, the more you focus on yourself, the harder it'll be to connect with your audience or make much of an impact. This sounds almost too simple, but when you realize how many public speaking problems begin and end with speakers who are *self*-focused (stuck in their heads or too attached to their scripts to connect with the audience), you'll see how deeply this issue affects us all. The exercise in box 3.2 demonstrates how to immediately show what a lack of external focus looks like in our communication, and what we should do to address this problem.

Additionally, if there's one thing that people can *do* to immediately reduce nervousness, this is it. Having an external focus gets us "to take the focus off ourselves and allow[s] us to dial down our personal judgment. When we're concentrating hard and fully present in the moment, there's no room for self-consciousness or shaky nerves. All your energy goes into the task at hand."[19] Pushing one's focus outward isn't just for public speaking. It also brings to light how much external focus takes place in conversations, in groups, and in work-related settings. There's a vast difference between an interviewee who stares off into the ether, rambling on without any sense of what's happening externally to them, and one who pushes their focus outward in an effort to connect with interviewers.

In the acting world, it's been recognized that having an "outward-directedness" gives actors "a state of magnificent responsiveness and makes [their] progress thrilling to watch," so much that "the more you are concerned with yourself, the less you are worthy of note. . . . The person with attention directed outward becomes various and provocative."[20] In its professional applications, Mike Bonifer further notes that "what separates successful improviser/entrepreneurs from the pack is the intensity of the focus they bring" to what they do.[21] This is a lesson best seen firsthand, though, so read and try the following exercises to grasp this critical concept.

Box 3.2
How to Focus Outward

From Aimlessness to Action

Like "Friend from the Past," this tends to be a hard-hitting experience in classes and workshops. Its applications to communication can be observed and remembered quickly. Have four volunteers come stand up in front of everyone. Tell them that they are to do absolutely nothing, they're to simply stand in front of the audience. Tell the class that we'll only observe the four up front and there should no commentary during the exercise. Let about a minute go by before stopping. In this first round, you'll notice that all or most of the people up front will start to look self-conscious, slightly anxious, and fidget. Now tell the four participants up front that in the next round, they should count the number of chairs in the room or the number of ceiling tiles above them (anything in the room that would take them more than a minute to count will work). Let them know that when you say "Go," they should each start the counting. Once you do so, let this go on for another minute before stopping them.

Debrief questions: Ask the volunteers how they felt in the first round compared to the second. What made a difference in how they felt? You can ask the audience the same questions.

Applications: Between the two rounds you'll notice a visible shift in the participants from a state of aimlessness to action. As they each start to count in the second round, the volunteers will look more relaxed, focused, and confident. In essence, they'll have pushed their focus outward, so now no longer have the time to judge themselves, get nervous, or get stuck in their heads, because they have a task or action to accomplish. You can quickly draw everyone's attention to the idea of pushing their focus outward, and how what just happened in the room demonstrates how we all have this need.[22]

Exercise Expressive Flexibility

I've heard that improv training is like going to the gym for your social skills. I think a better analogy is that it's like playing a sport. Going to the gym can be boring, filled with repetitive motions like climbing an elliptical. The benefit of most sports is that you get to exercise and have fun at the same time. Similarly, in improv you often have such a great time that you forget how much you're engaged in a workout for your communication skills.

Improv training highlights our needs for expressive flexibility, unleashing latent abilities in presenting, listening, emotional and physical range, and a host of other communication-related habits. In educational systems mostly set up to foster cognitive, thinking-heavy practices, many of these skills can get easily lost. As with any muscle, when we don't prioritize communication instruction, our facial muscles begin to atrophy, our voices grow weaker, and we become less able to adapt to other people.

That last part is key. Nearly two millennia of communication studies highlight that the ability to "adapt to your audience" remains critical to communicating ethically and effectively. If you share with a friend that you had a difficult day at work, and they reply by talking about another subject, you'll feel like that person is showing you little regard. We all have to adapt our communication to others to have any kind of relationship in the first place.

I use the verb "exercise" here deliberately. It's not enough to take one applied improv workshop to see a difference in these skills. This is where the gym analogy fits: it takes a long-term commitment to build these competencies and improve stamina. As Martin McDermott candidly shares, six months of improvisational training "bolstered my presentation skills far more than any professional development course I've taken. This lightning-paced, think-on-your-feet, trust-your-gut, remember-there's-an-audience, fly-by-the-seat-of-your-pants, yet-it-all-works-out-in-the-end process is like classroom teaching on an intravenous espresso drip."[23] It can take time to develop greater fluidity and range with our expressive capacities. Exercising a long-term approach also highlights why applied improvisation needs embedded and scaled across organizations in the service of democratic goals. As a result of practiced, sustained attention to these lessons, we need to build structures than can help citizens exercise this ability over the course of their lives (I expand on this point in the concluding chapter).

One of my favorite ideas that captures the stakes for this concept is "rhetorical sensitivity."[24] A key component of rhetorical sensitivity is that we have to be willing to undergo the *strain* of adapting to one another to make communication work well. That takes expressive flexibility. If we're in the mood for laughing, but have a friend who has just received news that a grandparent passed away, we had better be ready to adapt to their emotional state to communicate well with them. Signaling care would probably be the best response, and that takes some physical and emotional flexibility. I've observed introverted students who remain stoic across situations that demand more expressive flexibility. On the other hand, I've noticed raging extroverts who have a hard time pulling back from dominating conversations (i.e., being too expressive all the time). If we play our communication in a single note that never undergoes the strain of adaptation, we limit our potential to connect with people.

I've already highlighted listening skills, but what we're after here is something far more robust and whole-bodied than what we simply do with our ears. I recently learned that the traditional Chinese character for "listen"

(聽, "tīng") incorporates these multiple dimensions: using one's ears (耳), eyes (目), mind and heart (心), and overall focus captures the best listening practices. Movement can especially help us connect with others. The mind and body affect one another constantly, so why shouldn't some attention to this matter be part of every organization?

In my lessons, I always take participants through a range of movement exercises that open up or stretch their expressive capacities (see box 3.3). One of the most brilliant methods to get participants to practice expressive flexibility involves the use of "gibberish" exercises, a staple training technique from improv theater. Gibberish is made-up language. Getting participants to speak in gibberish, without using any real words (and not cheating by speaking a foreign language), can push them to try communicating in ways that don't overly rely on the verbal, activating their physical, emotional, and vocal abilities. These exercises ultimately seek to teach communication lessons that, in Annette Holba's terms, constitute an "embodied philosophical act that places our focus of attention on the intellectual play and bodily experience of the act."[25]

Box 3.3
Expanding Physical and Vocal Range

Walk About

I always use this exercise in at least one early class or workshop. I've seen it run in many ways at different improv theaters and in acting classes, but I have developed this version for application to professional contexts. Ask all of your participants to start walking around the room. As with earlier exercises, this should not be in any pattern (e.g., a circle), but a neutral walk around the space. Tell the participants that you're going to ask them to make simple physical changes such as "walk slowly," one cue at a time only (i.e., they should deal with only one change at a time; they should abandon walking slowly when the next cue is given). All they need to do is follow your cues. This technique is grounded in the idea that simple physical changes can make us feel profoundly different, and sometimes even affect our emotional life. It's working on our communication "from the outside in." When we smile, for example, it can be hard to feel anything but positive toward what's happening. Oppositely, forcing a frown can visibly dampen our mood. Once everyone is walking around, first tell them that we're going to play with being more confident.[26] Have them imagine that they're at a work party or walking into a professional networking event. On a scale from one to ten, with one being not at all confident, and ten being supremely confident, shout out new confidence levels every thirty seconds or so. After having them walk around with each confidence level for a bit, they should stop and interact with one other person in the room. Ask them to make these changes as naturally as possible, exhibiting the confidence level in their voices and postures. Note the high level of communication at ten. This doesn't necessarily mean being loud; there can be a focused, quiet energy exhibited at that level too. Ask them to think about times and places where they have demonstrated these particular confidence levels. Next, ask everyone to return to neutral while still walking around. Ask the participants to embody various emotions for twenty seconds at a time, such as "excitement," "anger," "fear," and more. You can also have the participants stop and talk with one another in this round. I like to use opposite emotional switches (e.g., happy then sad) to jolt participants into really stretching their emotional and physical range. Now tell everyone that you'll be having them think about how particular parts of the body literally lead the rest of the body as they walk around, starting with their faces. Ask them to start with their foreheads, imagining they are a person whose entire body is led by the forehead.[27] Make sure they keep walking around as they do so. As they engage in this process, encourage them to think about how this one simple change seems to be affecting the rest of their body, emotions, and the way they're looking at other people. The point here isn't to have participants go through a regular day doing any of these behaviors, but rather to have them experience what a profound difference even a simple bodily adjustment can make. Next ask them to have their entire body lead from their nose as they continue to walk around. What tangible changes are they feeling now? If anyone seems to be doing an extreme exaggeration, ask them to pull back a bit: there really are people whose entire bodies are led by their nose as they walk around, so this only needs to be a slight mental and physical switch to feel the difference. From there, work downward to participants' chests, stomachs, knees, and then ankles. You can have the participants also play with walking slower or faster than they normally do, or embody someone who swaggers as they walk, to discuss the idea of internal rhythms or tempos that people carry with them everywhere. I like to end by getting participants to behave like someone who takes up a lot of space wherever they go, and then someone who takes up very little space. You can ask them to imagine that they have a huge space bubble around themselves, or, in the latter case, a tiny space bubble. This is an interesting characteristic of everyday behavior. Again, emphasize that people really have these nonverbal habits in their lives, you can see them in the way individuals walk through spaces.

Debrief questions: How did you feel in making these switches? Which of the changes felt most like your own behaviors? Which of the changes were furthest from your own nonverbals? How did these nonverbal switches affect the conversations that you had? Did you find yourself getting locked into certain perspectives or attitudes that informed your verbal communication?

Applications: Many of the takeaways for this exercise should be clear from the instructions above, but you can also emphasize that being able to amp up or down at various times is critical to good communication (note: this is also a great precursor to teaching the idea of "managing your energy level," covered in the next section). Overall, these exercises should help participants see what their physical default settings may be, and stretch their range, even slightly, to grow in their communication skills.

Variations: Two advanced cues that I've also found work well involve asking participants to make their mouths small while speaking loudly (which makes them feel like tyrants), or expose their top teeth and grin or bite their bottom lip and giggle (which tends to make a person feel submissive).[28] Asking the question "How is my spine?" can be useful too, since the spine communicates different meanings through hunched versus straight postures.[29] If you're running a full applied improv course, you can further have your participants practice making these changes during the week (ask them to do so ethically; there should be no harmful impact on others) and write journal reflections about their experiences.

Nonverbal Meeting

Similar to the "Walk About" exercise, ask everyone to walk around the room in neutral. Tell them that we're first going to practice using "gibberish," a made-up language in which the words have no meaning. We're doing this to focus on all the other means of communication we have at our disposal (facial expressions, sounds, etc.) beyond verbal messages. Provide a demonstration of gibberish and then have everyone practice. Ask the group to imagine that they're at a party and to walk around greeting as many people as possible, using only gibberish.[30] Imagine you're seeing an old friend for the first time in many years as you meet each new person.

Make sure to correct anyone who is not speaking in gibberish, and watch out for anybody simply using a foreign language—these should be nonsense words. They also shouldn't get stuck talking to one person, they should try to get out and talk to as many others as possible. For a second round, they must now greet one another as people who do not like each other while maintaining their gibberish. You can go on with further rounds, having them imagine meeting their boss, their boss's boss, or even a homeless person on the street (this one is good for raising a moral discussion about how we treat each other nonverbally in public).

Debrief questions: What did you observe about your own and others' behaviors in this exercise? How were the interactions affected by using gibberish? What was more important, the words or how the words were said? What times in the past have you failed to be conscious of your non-verbals? Does anyone have any stories or experiences? Have you ever had an experience like this in another country, where you and someone else didn't speak the same language? How did you make communication work in that circumstance? Do you find your communication habits come mostly from your head? How can you better bring your physical, vocal, and emotional life to your communication with others?

Applications: The goal of this exercise is to awaken participants' emotional and nonverbal energies. Comedian Keegan Michael Key once said that one of the biggest lessons from improv is "Physically doing things a lot. Ten percent analysis, 90 percent do. Do, do, do."[31] Once participants are freed up physically by removing the verbal element, they will begin to engage in more multimodal ways of communicating.

Nonverbal Presentation

This exercise can take one of two forms.[32] One person at a time will come up in front of the class and, using nothing but gibberish, either teach about a topic or sell an object of their choosing. The participant giving the gibberish presentation will decide on either the topic they'll teach about (e.g., economics) or the object they will be selling (e.g., a toaster) by themselves without telling the audience. Let this go on for about one to two minutes at most. Once done, the audience should guess what was being taught or sold.

Debrief questions: Ask the audience what was clear and unclear. If anything was unclear, how could the speaker have made it clearer, using only gibberish?

Applications: This exercise is fantastic for forcing trainees to awaken their nonverbal communication skills. Where they typically may have just used words to talk about a topic or sell an object, you'll see them gesture more, using their hands to "show, rather than tell" (as the old adage prescribes) about what's happening. You'll see their facial expressions become livelier, with greater emotion communicated to those in the room. In this activity, Spolin advises that "if players stare or look over the heads of the audience, ask them to 'pitch' their sale, until the audience is actually seen. 'Pitching,' as practiced in carnivals or department stores, requires direct contact with others. Both audience and player will experience the difference when staring becomes seeing. An added depth, a certain quiet, will come into the work when this happens."[33] If you have a large class or workshop, you'll want to run this with four to five people at most before moving on.

Manage Your Energy Level

Let's say that you're about to give a presentation in ten minutes. It's been a hard morning, maybe you had trouble sleeping last night or the kids threw tantrums nonstop on their way to school. You may not have much energy as a result. Yet the worst thing you could do is start your presentation with low energy, which broadcasts a lack of excitement about the topic you're covering and a lack of care toward your audience. To be sensitive to the audience and to stand the best chance at persuading them that your ideas are important, you can't go on autopilot with your energy level. Maybe you'll smile or do some exercises to get yourself to a more energetic place, but regardless, you've got to make some physical or emotional change to let your topic shine and to meet your audience's needs.

You can demonstrate this idea quickly through the concept of "managing your energy levels" or, as improvisers sometimes call it, "energy manipulation."[34] The key is that you've got to *do* something to your energy, especially when first meeting someone or a group of people with whom you'll be communicating. Generally, this will mean raising your energy, but to be clear, I'm not talking about coming into every situation with a bouncing-off-the-walls kind of liveliness. That can be too intense and loud, and it often closes space for others to participate in your communication. Sometimes energy manipulation means having a quieter energy. We've all met soft-spoken people who act with poise and presence by speaking deliberately, making their words matter, and, most of all, making every effort to make sure they're connecting with others. That still takes energy. By practicing this skill, we're also following some current thought that energy management is even more important than time management.[35]

Theatrical improvisers put great stock in the first lines or "initiations" for scenes that they create on stage. Sometimes they'll run an entire training session on initiations, trying to get better at what happens in the first ten or so seconds, since these moments "contain the metadata for the rest of your scene."[36] The same should go for other contexts we face in life. I can't tell you the number of times I have interviewed job applicants and been amazed at the lack of energy exhibited in these situations. Despite having an incredible resume, sometimes interviewees arrive in their default settings, making you wonder if they've given any attention to preparing for the moment that will matter the most: the human encounter. Overall, creative people control their energy.[37]

The amount that's communicated between two people in the first moments of meeting sets a tone from which it's hard to deviate. As psychologists have noted, once meeting it can be difficult for us to break free from our "diagnosis bias" of others, or seeing them in any other way than our first impression, despite receiving further information that's contrary to our initial opinions.[38] In other words, we all want to be right about our diagnoses of other people and often cling too desperately to our first judgments. It's not fair, but it's a challenge worth doing all we can to manage. Good communicators should be strategic about what happens in the first part of an interaction, and that requires attention to managing one's energy.

Play Multiple Roles and Viewpoints

After four decades as a communication professor, Quentin Schultze finds that something has changed among his students over the past several years: "I repeatedly observed a lack of ability to empathize combined with an inability to 'switch codes.'"[39] Where empathy reflects one's ability to step into others' shoes and see the world from their perspectives, code-switching concerns the ease with which we can change our verbal and nonverbal behaviors to fit the people and circumstances at hand. Empathy and code-switching go together, as Schultze notes:

> When people lose their capacity to empathize with others, they don't properly adjust their communicative code (their verbal and nonverbal language). For instance, if interviewees can't imagine

themselves in the position of a job interviewer, they won't interview appropriately let alone effectively. They might even offend
interviewers. . . . The best human communication is partly a
matter of how we fit our message substance and delivery style
with particular people and contexts. What is most fitting for
conversation at the dinner table? What about for discussion on
national television? In a private versus a public speech? In the
bedroom or at church? At a job interview or with a mentor?[40]

Among other causes for these developments, I'd speculate that empathy
and code-switching are becoming harder for many people because of the
"context collapse" of social media.[41] Social media sites such as Facebook
and Twitter want us to broadcast one-size-fits-all messages to the audiences
in our lives. This is a new trend in human history. In the past, only at
events like weddings would we find all the different people and groups in
our lives in one space. As a result of context collapse, we risk becoming
less sensitive to the need to empathize and code-switch in the service of
adapting messages to various people and situations.

Given these challenges, the effectiveness of our communication ties
directly to our ability to play multiple viewpoints and roles. This skill also
connects with a need to develop expressive flexibility; it's easier to shift
among roles and viewpoints if we're more prepared to break out of static
verbal and nonverbal communication habits. These lessons become especially
relevant in teaching about diversity. Some of the most successful exercises
developed to teach about multicultural awareness and sensitivity use the
technique of "role reversal," where participants imagine that they were born
with a different skin color, or even go live with a family of another race or
ethnicity for a week.[42] I'm highlighting the same kinds of practices—that
playing multiple roles and viewpoints both enlarges our social worlds and
makes us better communicators. Many applied improv exercises teach and
train participants to experience this need in our lives. See the exercise in
box 3.4 for a primary example.

In my experience, there's one challenge that you may run up against
in teaching this communication skill. For many people, the idea of playing
multiple roles can be confusing. Don't we all have "core" identities, after all?
Isn't it duplicitous to maintain anything but our essential selves in different
situations? Multiple personality disorder is called a "disorder" for a reason,
right? In response to these points, it's critical to note that there are two
extremes here. At one end people run the danger of practicing completely

inflexible personalities that offer little opportunity to adapt and empathize with others. At the other end there's an equal danger of having no center to one's identity at all, merely being all things to all people and too much of a chameleon. I've found that most people struggle with the former rather than the latter problem, however. Neil Postman calls this problem "role fixation" and has an eloquent explanation for why it's a problem for everyday communication:

> We all know people who cannot transit from one semantic environment to another. Professors, for instance, are apt to remain Professors even in situations where none are required. And there are Political People who see Significance in someone's ordering scrambled eggs. And there are Comics who are always "on." And Moralists for whom there is no joy anywhere, only responsibility. And Cynics who will never let themselves be awed, or let anything be revered. Such people may be said to be self- or role-fixated, and, what is worse, they are apt to assert their fixation as a virtue. These people think of themselves as having strong character, but really it's impoverished, single-dimensional, lacking the courage to try out new selves and thus grow.[43]

You can't separate this issue from democracy building and civic skills, either. If two people meet and one defines themself as a "conservative" and the other as a "liberal," they're likely to get stuck in those roles and have problems communicating. But they'd increase the likelihood of finding common ground if they began by defining themselves in terms of the multiple roles they each play in their lives, such as "parent," "concerned homeowner," or even "customer at local businesses."[44]

This is what we should be trying to do in education, in general. Classes should help students embrace but also move beyond identity categories to practice "uncommon perspectives" and "to move from being subjects to being citizens."[45] Research also shows that the best educators themselves play multiple roles as lecturers, interlocutors, counselors, advocates, storytellers, observers, and more.[46]

The connection to one's "default settings" should be clear. Playing multiple roles gets us to break beyond our routine personality habits. Thorstein Veblen coined the term "trained incapacity"[47] to describe the limitations of being trained into patterned ways of thinking and acting. You see it in every organization. People in finance may only think about organizational problems in terms of numbers, engineers may end up seeing everything as like a machine that needs to be fixed, while lawyers can end up viewing every issue as an opportunity for a lawsuit. When individuals and departments become siloed from one another, they lose the ability to speak in terms that are familiar to other people, impeding communication. Like the "curse of knowledge," the more training we receive in a field, the more incapacitated we can become from seeing the world from other roles or viewpoints. In my experience, applied improvisation is one of the best methods for getting people to practice moving beyond such trained incapacities. The exercise in box 3.4 can take them a step in this direction.

Box 3.4
Flexing Roles and Viewpoints

Occupation Panel

In this exercise, three participants will sit up front. Have the rest of the class shout out suggestions of different occupations (try to make them as different as possible; don't have a nurse and a doctor on the panel, for instance). Each of these occupations should be different from those that the participants currently have; the purpose is to stretch their range and have them play new roles. Tell the participants to fully commit to being someone in that occupation. The audience should ask the panel questions, and the participants' goal will to be to filter their answers through their occupations. For example, as Alison Phillips Sheesley, Mark Pfeffer, and Becca Barish highlight, "if one person is a jeweler and gets asked what the meaning of life is, they could respond 'to surround yourself with as many beautiful things as possible.'" The instructor or audience can also ask follow up questions.[48]

Debrief questions: Did you have fun? What was it like to play these different roles? What did you find difficult? How do you think this exercise applies to our personal, professional, or societal lives? What do you think are its applications for people confronting difference and working across borders and boundaries?

Applications: This exercise is fundamentally about dealing with what's happening in the moment and playing with different roles. Go over lessons

about playing multiple roles, especially in their connections to communication outcomes. You can also discuss how being able to see the world
from different viewpoints is a critical skill for bridging differences with
diverse others. After running this exercise, I've found the following quote
by Gordon Phillips useful for the class to discuss in this context: "Acting
helps us live out our unlived lives."[49]

Variation: One variation is the "historical talk show," where participants
are asked to play an important historical figure and improvise answers to
questions asked by the audience or a host.[50]

Read the Subtext

Applied improvisation encourages people to develop greater sensitivity to the
two levels of communication that always occur in any interaction. There's
the "text," or what's spoken, written, or basically at the surface level of
communication. And there's the "subtext," which gets at the implicit messages and tone, nonverbal communication, cues about the relationship, or
essentially the deeper level of meanings present when two or more people
come together.

Take the simple greeting "How are you?" That's the text. But this simple question can be said in many different ways: curiously, angrily, happily,
fearfully, and so forth. We defer to the subtext to figure out what any text
means, but without the tone, nonverbal cues, and more that support it, *we'll
always read a subtext into a text* anyways. If a friend posts the message "Hi"
on your Facebook wall, you'll immediately read a certain subtext into it
(they're being playful, they're angry that I haven't been in touch in a while,
etc.). At the very least, your brain will go into overdrive trying to stabilize
what "Hi" (the text) means beneath that message (the subtext).

Communication scholars have called this the dual "content" and
"relationship" levels of communication.[51] There's the content that's said (the
what), but there's always a relationship that's communicated despite whatever's
on the surface (the how). In a meeting, two people communicating back
and forth in a tense fashion may think that they're only discussing what's
coming out of their mouths (i.e., the content), but it'll be hard to miss how
there's also a relationship level being communicated between the two with
each new utterance—in this case, perhaps that the two people disrespect
each other. Developing expressive flexibility and playing many roles and

viewpoints can help with this skill. When you become more aware of the range of emotional, physical, and mental commitments people can make, you'll start picking up on more of the subtexts at play in different situations.

Improvisers have long shared an investment in this skill. Anne Libera notes that "no scene is ever about the words that are being spoken."[52] Others teach improvisers that there's an electrical current going on between people before they even open their mouths: "words can be an avoidance of what is really going on in the relationship. . . . Words come from your head. The connection comes from your being."[53] This lesson comes from years of observing novice improvisers "overtalk" their way through scenes, thinking that the weight of what's happening comes from all the words being spoken. The words are important, but they'll lose meaning without sensitivity to the manner of communication. The vocabulary of "heat," or "the [emotional] intimacy and intensity of the relationship," and "weight," or "what is already in the room; what it feels like is going on" with the situational tone, lend substance to the idea of reading the subtext in any circumstance.[54]

As a result, one of the parallel skills that applied improv focuses is our ability to work with silence. Some people have no problem using silence strategically, but for others the impulse to always talk talk talk needs work (see the exercise "Working with Silence" in box 3.5 for one way to address this). Ultimately, this lesson demonstrates that "you cannot not communicate."[55] Even when we're not speaking, we're always communicating. Theatrical improvisers assert that "it's impossible to do nothing on stage," so silence can be one of the most powerful forms of communication.[56] When I give a presentation, this adage always comes to mind when I look out at an audience. Some audience members act like they're not communicating, since they're not the ones doing the talking. But, as a speaker, you can see almost everything going on—occasionally you'll observe people texting or chatting with their neighbors. We're always communicating when we're in the presence of other people. Even if you're alone in a forest, to build on the old saying, you'll still be communicating intrapersonally, to yourself. We can become more conscious of the subtexts that we're communicating by simply asking, "What am I communicating in this situation? What are my clothing, my demeanor and tone, and other behaviors broadcasting to others?"

One note of caution, however: we should all be humble about our abilities to "read" others. Despite the number of books out there that claim to help people read "body language," we live in a world where people from many cultures, with varying ways of acting, all complicate this picture greatly.[57] A nod in one country can signal agreement, and in another that the other person merely was heard. While the subtextual dimensions of human communication are real and worth attending to, remaining open to the possibility that our readings may be misguided or just plain wrong can prevent us from thinking that there's always a one-to-one correspondence between another person's behavior and what it means.

Box 3.5
Getting to the Subtext

That Means . . .

I first ran across this exercise as a student at the Groundlings Theater.[58] I like to demonstrate this with two volunteers first before having everyone break into pairs and do the exercise simultaneously (you'll notice that having everyone engage in exercises at the same time is a frequent feature of applied improv—we're not as interested in people performing in front of us as in everyone getting to practice each lesson). The format for this activity is essentially the same as the "yes, and" exercises. Two people should sit opposite one another, and one should make a statement of some kind (e.g., "I can't find any parking spaces at this mall"), but instead of saying "Yes, and," the other person will always begin with the words "That means . . ." and interpret what the statement may mean at a deeper level (e.g., "That means you're frustrated with how this day has turned out"). This response will explore and heighten whatever statement the other person made, getting the participants to practice looking for subtexts in textual remarks. The participants should continue back and forth after this initial exchange. Bill Lynn provides another example for how these conversations can play out: "Player One: I gambled in Vegas. Player Two: That means you risked a lot of money. Player One: That means I lost big. Player Two: That means you are staying temporarily in your ex-wife's house. Player One: That means I am under the thumb."[59] Once they've had a chance to play out this conversation for about two minutes, have the participants switch roles for another two minutes so each receives a chance to exercise the "That means" skill.

Debrief questions: What was the effect of saying "That means" in these conversations? What was highlighted in both the text and subtext (the what and how, or content and relationship) of your comments as you went back and forth?

Applications: The conversation may get a bit nonsensical, but it's a great way to get people listening and thinking about the different content and relationship levels of communication at play in their interactions. One limitation of this exercise is that it can sometimes focus the participants too much on the verbal exchange, so draw participants' attention to how nonverbal behaviors tend to communicate even more about subtexts in everyday life.

Variation: Another variation demonstrating how words are often less powerful than the subtext is to have your participants only speak one word to each other at a time, or only let them use the following four phrases as they have a conversation: "It's a beautiful day," "Not for some of us," "Stop, just stop" and "I wish I could."[60] Have participants and the audience discuss how the two levels of content and relationship played out with this language.

Working with Silence

Have two people come up front and start a conversation based on a topic suggested by the audience. Tell them that they're only allowed to speak when their partner makes physical contact with them. (Note: in my classes and workshops, I usually provide a behavior such as "touch them on the shoulder" only, to avoid inappropriate behaviors. You should also be aware that in some cultural traditions, human touching of any kind is perceived as inappropriate—so switch to touching an object like a table if needed.) This is a fascinating exercise to observe, with participants typically becoming far more observant, strategic, and weighty in their communication with one another.

Debrief questions: Have the audience share what they observed about this exercise relative to the idea of "reading the subtext." What did they learn? What are applications for their working lives? What could you do tomorrow to implement takeaways from this activity?

Applications: Quite simply, the subtext between the two people becomes tangible to everyone in the room. Every pause and every intonation carries meaning, highlighting the difference between meaningless versus meaningful forms of communication. This exercise brings into view how comfortable each of us may be with silence and how communication occurs even when we're not saying anything.

Variation: If you are running a class, you can also have participants carry out this exercise in everyday situations, such as with family or friends outside of the course, to see what they learn.[61]

Prepare for the Unpredictable

This may seem like a contradiction, but it's actually a paradox that expresses two truths. Great communicators prepare for both the predictable and unpredictable aspects of communication. Excellent speakers put a lot of work into researching and putting together the content and structure of a presentation. But if they hang on too tightly to what's been prepared in the act of delivering the speech, the results can be disastrous. There are always many more variables operating in a situation than it's possible to fully prepare for. The lighting in a room may be bad, the audience may be sitting much further away from the speaker than anticipated (creating a disconnected feeling), one's slides may fail to work, and so on. I once heard a story about a stand-up comedian at The Comedy Store in Los Angeles who fell prey to this problem. During the stand-up's performance, a waiter carrying several beers tripped, sending glass crashing to the ground. Instead of reacting to what was actually happening—and where everyone's attention in the room had gone—the comedian just continued telling jokes as if nothing had changed. That's failing to prepare for the unpredictable.

So how can we engage in such preparation? This is where applied improv exercises come in, almost all of which get people ready for the moments in life where honest responses and adapting to changes that have happened become paramount. The importance of this skill for communication practice is only beginning to be realized. For instance, what do you think affects an audience's judgment of a speaker more: how they give their presentation or how they handle questions and answers after? Two studies recently identified that "how presenters respond to questions and objections affects audience members' evaluations of speakers as much or more than the quality of delivery of the presentation."[62] Twenty-first-century communicators must be able to "manage ambiguity effectively,"[63] a concept that we're bringing down to earth through applied improv practices.

The mantra "follow the fear" trains improvisers to pursue rather than shy away from unpredictability.[64] As soon as someone standing on a stage begins to feel fearful, that's a good cue that there's something of interest to pursue. Rather than avoid the fear, we should go after it. In other words, "it is good to be uncomfortable; otherwise there is no danger, no excitement, no growth."[65] What does this look like in practice? Let's go back to the stand-up example. This individual was filled with a fear that his performance would be ruined by the unexpected event in the room. But what if he had pursued that fear and, among many choices that could have been made, told the crowd, "Everyone please make sure our stellar waiter is okay, they've been doing such a great job that I'm going to pay for another round of beers for everyone in that area. It's on me." Sure, it may have been a deviation from the jokes, but the response would have at least been more honest, humane, and fitting given what happened. Amy Poehler believes unpredictability can be the best part of communication, since "being slightly nervous means you care, and you're alive, and you're taking some kind of risk. . . . [So] substitute the word 'excitement' for 'nervous.' "[66]

Communicators who aren't afraid to take some risks and speak honestly will almost always do better than those who try to control every outcome in a planned fashion. There's not much in formal education about preparing for the unpredictable, so tell participants that they're way ahead of the curve in using applied improv to train for this critical skill. For more on these insights, I highly recommend viewing the Stephen Nachmanovich video "Improvisation Is . . ." on YouTube (see the endnote).[67]

React to Create

This concept takes the need to "push your focus outward" a step further. A lot of ink has been spilled about the need for creativity in education. What we really need at this point are methods for helping people put creativity into practice. It's amazing to think that the famous Bloom's taxonomy—a framework of six main educational objectives—was updated in 2001 with "creating" as its highest value.[68] Yet, despite being a way to promote deeper learning than lower-order objectives such as "remembering," it's still "the skill least taught and least assessed."[69] In fact, many educational systems put the weight of their pedagogical practices on the lowest rungs of the pyramid by, for example, promoting cultures of relentless testing.

Howard Gardner, a scholar at Harvard University's School of Graduate Education, has spent decades researching how education often misses the mark in attending to the diverse, multiple intelligences people possess. As a result, one of education's biggest victims has been creativity. But it's now clear that "people who enjoy taking risks, who are not afraid of failure, who are attracted by the unknown, or who are uncomfortable with the status quo are those likely to make creative discoveries"—all elements that applied improv targets.[70] Cornell psychologist Robert Sternberg further finds that most intelligence tests measure almost nothing of value (beyond the ability to take such tests) individually and professionally. Instead, "successful intelligence" consists of the kind of practical and creative intelligence we see top leaders exhibit in their everyday actions.[71]

All this leads Gardner to argue that we should favor forms of education that value "assessment" rather than testing. Where testing typically uses formal, neutral, decontextualized instruments that students will seldom encounter again once they leave school (showing how much our educational systems have been skewed toward linguistic and logical-mathematical intelligence), assessment applies and elicits information in the course of a student's very performance, "on the fly."[72] This is essentially what we're doing when side-coaching improv exercises: providing the impetus for participants to learn patterns, make immediate connections, and experience changes in the very moments that they matter.

So what does communication bring to these needs? Contrary to cultural expectations, communication specialists have long known that inventing is mostly a communal rather than individual enterprise, leading Deanna Dannels and her colleagues to ask, "What kinds of communication support creativity—in the classroom and broadly in the academic community? . . . Well, to answer this we could observe spaces that are *dedicated to improvisation* and try to see what they are about and how communication helps construct and activate creativity."[73] With connections to improvisation, they note that a communication and creativity curriculum would be filled with humor, "celebrate failure, praise and reward out of the box thinking, encourage nimbleness, be full of ambiguity, and uncertainty," foster divergent thinking, and encourage teachers to be vulnerable and move from competitive to collaborative models of learning. They also link this kind of teaching and training with a "community ethos" and "creative citizenship" that can incorporate many voices—underscoring the democratic work accomplished in this approach to education.[74]

Indeed, some believe the very strength of the communication discipline lies in its connections to creativity.[75] Johanna Hartelius notes that communication students "are ill-equipped to invent because they receive little instruction and even fewer opportunities for creative and productive innovation," which flies in the face of historical teachings from figures like Aristotle and Vico, who tied communication education to creativity, energy, dialogue, and civic engagement. For improved communication instruction, processes of collaboration, creativity, and working with ambiguity should be taught and sequenced prior to other communication skills that currently get the lion's share of attention in classrooms, such as criticism.[76]

With this important background in mind, applied improvisation has one specific tool that is great for jump starting participants' creative communication. I call it "react to create." Improv teaches that "honest discovery, observation, and reaction [are] better than contrived invention."[77] It is founded in "discovery, or realizing or uncovering what is already there. Its opposite is invention."[78] What improv offers the notion of invention is something different from its traditional image as creating something from nothing, starting with a blank slate and coming up with something new and brilliant. That's a hard task, and not how most invention or creativity works. In improv theater it's one of the hardest lessons to teach novice improvisers: you don't have to "make stuff up" so much as respond honestly to what's right in front of you. We don't think about invention so much as inheriting and working with what's already there. That's a big mental switch for many people.

This advice can be found everywhere in the improv world. Second City teachers argue that improvisers should learn to explore and heighten in their work; like surfers riding a wave, you don't need to make anything special happen once you're reacting to the moment in front of you.[79] Bruce Hunter tells improvisers that if their scenes stop working, the first place they should go is to their environment,[80] while Keith Johnstone admonished his students to "be altered by what's said,"[81] that is, be present and react to what's said or done by others to find inspiration.

This means that we should be ready to change by looking outward for our own creativity (connecting with the concept of "external focus" highlighted earlier). Acclaimed playwright David Mamet believes the center of all great theater can be found in the same idea: "here is the best acting advice I know. . . . *Invent nothing, deny nothing.*"[82] In improv theater, it's more honest for an actor to look at another actor at the beginning of a scene and respond to what they're seeing (e.g., "You look like you had a hard day at work, John") than try to invent something that doesn't exist out of thin air, which tends to have a forced, inauthentic quality (e.g., something random like "It's time to become a barista in Australia, John").

There's inspiration all around us. Great screenwriters, novelists, comedians, poets, and others all carry notebooks wherever they go for a reason: the world provides so many sources of inspiration, you never know who or what will act as tinder for that next great idea. It's easier to be a story collector rather than a story inventor.[83] If you run a business or a nonprofit, what's easier—spending your energies on gathering and building on clients' stories or always trying to invent your own about your organization? Which is more honest and observant? Clients' stories can not only provide a wealth of information for organizational communication, but once responded to can act as springboards to further creative ideas ("yes, and"). In essence, true "listening is attending to reality. It's the best antidote to superficial communication. All research and marketing are based on the idea of attending to reality."[84]

There are other applications. When giving a presentation, telling a presenter to "react" to the audience may spark creative moments that otherwise might have been missed. If Sarah notices that Fred is nodding in response to the material she is covering, she may suddenly find a creative, unplanned moment—for example, "Just last week Fred and I were talking about how our team could best use our current resources, and he mentioned that . . ." As discussed in the "Following Through" exercise in chapter 2, some of the best media interviewers use this technique for inspiration. By focusing intently on what their interviewees say, they find that everything they need to say themselves becomes apparent: they "react to create" content for the interview.

The final two ideas build on this concept. Applied improvisation shows us how invention and movement can't be separated in practice, since "when your body's loose, it unleashes your imagination" and "watching people *do* things and *discover* things is far more interesting than . . . verbal rantings."[85] These concepts underscore how communication and creativity can be affected by our thoughts, attitudes, and behaviors.

Practice Positive Communication

Before the turn of the millennium, some psychologists began noticing that their field had for too long put its stock in all that can go wrong with human beings. If you've ever watched television shows like Dr. Phil, you'll quickly get the gist. From Freud forward, psychologists have overwhelmingly talked about neuroses, complexes, denial, and all the bad patterns and behaviors that people can manifest to the exclusion of other aspects of human activity. Seeking to move the field beyond its grounding in negative, maladjusted behaviors, many began researching what might instead contribute to human flourishing. Thus began the field of *positive* psychology, which has grown exponentially and achieved extraordinary success in its short lifespan.

Similarly, communication experts have recently started wondering what might go into *positive communication*. These thinkers are even drawing our attention to the idea that "good communication" may be aiming too low. Why not aim for "superb communication" if that's a real possibility? Defined as "message processes that facilitate human needs-satisfaction," this new line of study is interested in humans' highest levels of need, especially "peak communication."[86] Julien Mirivel finds that seven behaviors encompass positive communication: disclosing, encouraging, greeting, listening, inspiring, asking, and complimenting.[87]

One useful way to talk about applied improvisation is in the context of positive communication. The "yes, and" standard alone gets participants to practice a positive and supportive behavior by seeking to build on others' thoughts and actions. That means approaching people with a common-ground orientation and quelling judgmental mindsets. But we can also link applied improv with each of the behaviors Mirivel identifies. When meeting people, how much do our greetings evidence that we're trying to create a positive interaction with them? Do we ever ask questions of others? (This also highlights the give and take principle). Do we ever compliment others or are we too quick to judge them? How much do we reveal about ourselves in an effort to establish rapport? (This is also akin to the "and" part of "yes, and"—we have to advance the communication by providing input ourselves). Are we encouragers? Do we listen well? And do we seek to inspire others and ourselves instead of negating possibilities at every turn? These are just some of the ways that we can ground applied improv with emerging work on positive communication.

There's another contribution that improv makes to positive communication. When participants are up on their feet and working with one another with movement and energy, there's a tangible improvement in the emotions, moods, and overall communication climate experienced. Sigal Barsade notes that people are "walking mood inductors," so much that when positive emotions are experienced within a group, outcomes such as "improved cooperation, decreased conflict, and increased perceived task performance" result.[88] These aren't simply what individuals and organizations need, they're what our public and political worlds could use.

These are no small matters. In my classes and workshops, often I find that participants express surprise at how much they enjoy the change in atmosphere. The positive communication climate couldn't be more different than what most people seem to experience in other classes, their workplaces, and the rest of their lives. Improv for comedy entertainment is a delight to watch when performers offer their audiences and one another good nature, warmth, and playfulness rather than calculated cleverness.[89] We can and should bring those behaviors into as many outside contexts as possible. Establishing a positive communication climate is built into the very DNA of applied improv teaching and training, showing us how much of a difference some simple practices can make in our lives, organizations, and societies.

From another perspective, applied improv also has something to offer our understandings of positive communication. Improvisers know what it takes to practice inspiration and encouragement, and this goes back to the "care and commit" fundamental. In essence, almost all improvisational training centers on the idea that people should generally make their communication clear, courageous, and committed. It brings out the default setting of "waffling," or stalling action and remaining tentative too much of the time. Like the adage to "follow the fear," in improvisational scenes taking risks and making "strong, bold, honest statements . . . are the best gifts of all."[90] The exercises in box 3.6 all get participants to practice this type of communication.

Educators and trainers can model positive communication in their classes and workshops through immediacy. Much is now known about what makes people more immediate to one another, or less distanced and more connected in practice. Communication scholars have long found that educators' immediacy behaviors such as smiling, making eye contact, using vocal variety, using hand gestures, and generally appearing relaxed all tend to improve participants' experiences in a classroom or workshop.[91] Good communication is also grounded in reasonable amounts of vulnerability and self-disclosure—research continually confirms that some reciprocal self-revelations can humanize and create liking for a communicator among different audiences.[92] From an effects perspective, educators who monitor their nonverbal communication reduce problems such as math anxiety and boost factors like intrinsic motivation for a subject.[93]

Box 3.6
Building Positive, Immediate,
and Confident Communication

The following four exercises are terrific for getting participants to practice positive communication and immediacy, and they typically help reserved participants feel more confident. In my experience, working with these in sequence provides a natural low-to-high-challenge learning curve.

Audience Support

Have one person at a time come up in front of everyone. Ask the audience to clap and cheer for this person with as much enthusiasm as possible. In my experience, running this with three to four people at the most is enough to demonstrate the point. The person standing up front should breathe without reacting or trying to do anything; they should just stand there and take everything in. For many people, it's quite an experience to be applauded in this way.[94]

Debrief question: Ask each participant what it was like to experience this level of support from the audience.

Applications: This exercise gets participants to engage in positive communication behaviors (e.g., encouraging) and helps individuals build more confidence in being in front of others. When people engage in good-natured, cooperative behaviors and feel comfortable making mistakes, a classroom or workshop will start to feel like a party.[95]

Heightened Speech

One at a time, have participants come up and count to twenty-five.[96] Each person should present as if there are hundreds of people in the room. By only being able to speak numbers, in order, the presenters will have to be as clear, committed, courageous, and muster as much vocal, physical, and emotional variety as possible. The idea of "peaks and valleys" is important here: sometimes being quieter and bringing one's emotional tone down, using pausing, etc., may be needed to keep the audience attentive and interested. Simply being loud from one to twenty-five will grate on the audience without such variety. To make this work, think about taking on an expert's confidence. This exercise can be practiced at home too.

Debrief question: What was it was like to communicate in this fashion?

Applications: This is a great second exercise for building positive, confident, and immediate communication. It also works the "expressive flexibility" and "manage your energy levels" skills emphasized earlier.

Question Blitz

I've seen this exercise performed in many different ways. For our purposes, the goal is to have one person a time stand in the middle of a circle and answer questions from those on the periphery with clarity and confidence as quickly as possible. Those on the outside of the circle should try to keep the person in the middle off balance by peppering them with questions on a suggested topic. You can also make the person in the middle a world-renowned expert on the topic to have them really take on this role (e.g., an expert on hairdressing, origami, cuisine from Chile, etc.). The content of the answers matters much less than the speed with which they respond. If you notice any hesitations, fear, self-consciousness, or any other stalling behavior, encourage the participant in the middle to "commit" or "play it to a ten." Tell the participant they are free to make up details or facts about their topic for the sake of committing more fully to their answers.

Debrief question: Did you fully commit to your answers? What was it like to communicate in this way?

Applications: Communicating with speed and confidence; unlocking spontaneity.

Variation: One variation is to play with the prompt "Why is . . . ," with those on the outside of the circle always starting their questions with "Why is . . ." (e.g., "Why is the sky blue")?[97]

Improvised Presentation

Have one participant at a time come up and give a one-minute speech on a topic suggested by the audience.[98] Tell the participant that they can say whatever they like about the subject. They can make up facts, statistics, examples, or stories as needed; we're not as concerned about the content as the delivery. Tell the participant to find ways to become more "immediate" with the audience. In other words, while they monologue they should read the room for how the audience is reacting and adjust and adapt their behavior to keep them interested. Side-coach the participant to smile or engage in other behaviors that show positivity toward the audience.

Debrief questions: What behaviors made this work well? What was difficult? What are the applications of this exercise for our personal, professional, and public lives?

Applications: This exercise demonstrates how we can build greater positivity, immediacy, and confidence into our everyday communication.

Find the Affinity

We've covered the fundamental of "yes, and" already, but let's zoom out for a moment to think about this concept from a larger, more advanced perspective. I'm one of the biggest proponents you'll find for debate, argument, and other modes of communication where critical thought and diverse, alternative viewpoints are taught and valued. I've been a teacher and researcher of argumentation and believe that complex societies more than ever need individuals with training in logic, who can link their claims with good evidence, and who can be critical of the many forms of persuasion all around us. History is replete with examples showing the dangers of "group-think" and social pressures in organizations and societies.[99] In essence, we need people who are skilled at not just following along with the crowd, but who can say "no, but . . . ," even when it's unpopular, to prevent getting locked into single ways of thinking.

Yet too much emphasis on debate can itself be detrimental to communication. We all know people who can't stop acting like defense lawyers any time they're presented with a new idea. In a meeting, someone can be so intent on shooting down others' thoughts that few or none get generated to begin with. The "no, but" mentality can even become embedded in an organization's culture, to the point where it's a chronic go-to behavior.

Without going too far down a philosophical rabbit hole here, one of the properties of human language is that it allows us to think of all the things that something is *not*. Kenneth Burke once wrote that "there are no negatives in nature" to point out the "unfulfilled expectations" that always pressure human beings when we're constantly in the "no" mode.[100] What does that mean? In nature, if rain "is" falling from the sky, it's falling from the sky. There's no "not rain" falling from the sky. But with language/words we can also think about what "is not" happening—there's not snow, not sleet, and definitely not locusts falling from the heavens. Where cats and dogs simply live in the world of what "is," we human beings can think of what "is not" and thus imagine all the ways the world could be. That's great for pursuing scientific and medical discoveries and building skyscrapers. Yet the "no" also creates difficulties in our relationships because it highlights all the imperfections in our lives. It makes us strive for perfections that can also be stifling, such as judging a friend's clothing choices because they don't fit with current trends. Dogs and cats just don't care about these things.

Closer to home, some communication scholars note that a "critical" orientation permeates typical university course offerings in communication, prompting the questions "Does our field exaggerate the utility of criticism as a habit of mind?" and "Does a heavy emphasis on criticism mean that we neglect to prepare students for creative and productive thinking"?[101] Critical skills are valuable, but also a potential problem when they become a "default setting" for communication.

This is where the foundational "yes, and" principle from improv comes in. I won't recite the core parts of this concept that were explained before. But, suffice to say, where the "no, but" orientation falls short, the "yes, and" skill fills the gap, and vice versa. Thinking about when agreement and disagreement can hinder or promote good communication gets us to be much more strategic about what we're doing.

For instance, think about how meetings might be improved by putting the "yes, and" principle in place during an idea generation period. If you're a nonprofit and want your group to come up with a name for this year's fundraising gala, you'll do a lot better by "yes, anding" one another first, rather than falling into the trap of only a few people putting ideas out and jumping to critique too soon. It's not that we don't want anyone saying no to ideas, but we can always put on our critics' hats at a later point when the need for some editorializing fits. To borrow Andy Eninger's phrase, we should "find the affinity" first, since starting from a positive platform gets us energized and ready to build with one another, and pushes our stories into the future.[102] For communication education, the order matters. Prioritizing the "yes, and" *before* the "no, but" also allows us to move to areas of disagreement without being disagreeable.

The importance of the "find the affinity" skill isn't a hunch. By encouraging us to look for ways to affirm others first before moving to areas of difference, applied improv follows decades of social scientific studies on how to best approach difficult or antagonistic people.[103] Improvisation can even act as a model for supplementing or replacing the language of war and adversarial argument that goes into so much public communication.[104] In a telling remark, a past president of the National Communication Association shared in an autobiographical essay how she early on "discovered that just about all I really needed to know about life, I could learn from debate and theatre."[105] Improv's roots in theater can be a yin to the yang of debate. Ultimately, a training in both "yes" and "no" perspectives helps us be more intentional communicators and better citizens. As your course or workshop participants head off into life, encourage them to "find the affinity" with others at every opportunity.

ॐ

I could share many more lessons about how to use improv to develop communication excellence. The goal of this and subsequent chapters is less to cover everything that might be said than to push this conversation forward. With these lessons and exercises, you can advance the communication skills of just about any group quite quickly. I've seen it happen everywhere I've been. As time goes on, participants start to practice greater confidence and creativity, and become more sensitive to the deeper layers of context and meaning in their lives. At the very least, they benefit from a new, behavior-focused vocabulary for making sense of these matters. Application and theory fuse, with every concept experienced before being intellectualized.

At the start of this chapter, I mentioned that I'm trying to recover some aspects of communication history that relate to this work. Early communication educators wanted communication training to move beyond speech situations to more informal communication behaviors—the ones that make up most of our everyday lives.[106] At almost any university in the nation you'll find a required class on public speaking, but few have the same level of support for courses that target behaviors we all engage in more, such as listening.[107] Elwood Murray wrote that methods that fostered "positive regard," "sociodrama," and "role playing" could especially help people become more sensitive and effective in their communication, with an ultimate goal of having them develop an "ability to communicate about communication."[108] As a methodology for accomplishing these goals, applied improvisation has these lines of thought and practice transfer to people's everyday communication habits.

As final reminders, don't forget to use side-coaching when teaching the concepts in this chapter. The lessons should work as close to the behaviors practiced as possible. Additionally, we still want to follow the best, researched practices for teaching in using applied improv for communication outcomes. Beyond creating a positive communication climate, we have to help our learners realize the relevance of this material to motivate them, and not only develop skills but know when they should apply them, with appropriate goals and feedback for each exercise and many opportunities to reflect and modify their behaviors.[109] If the participant-directed debriefs are not rising to this level, it's critical for the facilitator to step in and offer key lessons and further opportunities for practice. Simple asides can work well, such as "this lesson could be used when speaking to board members about raising funds for your nonprofit" or "think about how to use this at home when your family is stressed out by the start of the school year."

An applied improv curriculum is a laboratory for the communication habits our societies need. As teachers and trainers, it also acts back on us. Who among us doesn't need to work on the skills and perspectives covered in this chapter? In my own life, I have to remind myself to "manage my energy level," "read the subtext," and "find the affinity" in social situations. These take practice but make many situations easier to navigate. In the next chapter, we'll build on these teachings by turning to cutting-edge ways that improv can promote leadership development.

Chapter 4

Using Improv to
Develop Leadership Excellence

I've run a class called Improv for Leadership for many years with students in Executive Master's in Business Administration and Master's in Public Administration programs. There's always a great deal of tension in the room when I enter on the first day of class. Although this has changed in recent years, topics like improvisation have not traditionally been under the purview of educational curricula. To break through these barriers quickly, I have the students up on their feet and engaging in the "Working with Change" exercise described in box 1.1 as soon as possible. All they have to do is say the numbers one, two, and three back and forth to each other as fast as they can. That's it. Yet most students go into their heads, slow down for fear of making mistakes, exhibit nervous laughter, start judging themselves and their partners for not doing this exercise well, or find other ways to sabotage themselves.

In my debrief, I like to highlight that they are all students who have, to this point, passed graduate courses in subjects like accounting, finance, and statistics, but for some reason they can't count the numbers one, two, and three back and forth to each other well. What does this experience prove? To put it squarely, *there's a knowledge and performance gap that formal education has failed to provide them*, in improvising in real time, managing the unexpected, and leading adaptively—all skills that the class will address. What's most stunning, however, is how much alignment exists between improvisational training and the most supported ideas about leadership.

There's a lot to be said about the subject of leadership. A Google Books search on "leadership" returned an estimate of 191,000,000 hits. It's no wonder, since the future of our interpersonal relationships, our institutions, and our societies relies on the quality of our leaders and leadership practices. A running theme in contemporary leadership studies is the unpredictability and often chaotic nature of leading in and across organizations.[1] In a volatile, uncertain, complex, and ambiguous world,[2] there's now a broad recognition that applied improvisation has much to contribute to the development of leadership, especially in moving from theory to practice in the skills of adaptability and "getting thrown a curveball."[3] Suzanne Gagnon, Heather Vough, and Robert Nickerson make especially clear that "improvisational theater skills are directly aligned with those suggested in newer leadership theories—adopting an external focus, developing adaptability to changing conditions, optimizing curiosity and responsiveness, and honing abilities to listen, interact, collaborate, and co-create with others."[4] These are all skills that can be cultivated early in one's education, using many of the lessons and practices from prior chapters. Yet there are many more advanced applications to be made.

This type of training provides a cutting-edge, democratic approach to leadership development. Alfonso Montuori highlights how "the study of improvisation demands a profound immersion into (inter)subjectivity, emotions, time, aesthetics, performance, and social creativity, none of which have traditionally been the focus of organization and management studies, or the social sciences in general."[5] Tammy Tawadros finds that theater-based leadership development is experiential and provides an interactive form of education that "approximates to the contextual realities of contemporary leadership" and "affords learners a space to construct and project their developing identity as leaders, and provides them with an opportunity for behavioral experimentation and rehearsal in relation to others."[6] In fact, one study of applied improvisation training with sixty-seven leaders across different industries and regions revealed that "participants gained the highest benefits in working with others and their ability to lead."[7] To build democracies, it's critical to know the mechanics of excellent leadership and the practices that can get us there.

Exercise Adaptive Leadership

A wide base of research covering the best ideas about leadership will inform this chapter, which participants can apply in their lives to build relational and civic bonds. But I've found that applied improvisation connects the most with decades of field-tested theory and practice from "adaptive leadership," a hands-on approach to professional development for organizational and societal leadership that's taught at Harvard University. In fact, it's remarkable that these two clearly allied paradigms have yet to be brought together in a sustained fashion.

Works on adaptive leadership are replete with references to the essentially improvisational nature of leadership. Ronald Heifetz, Alexander Grashow, and Marty Linsky underscore how "what is needed from a leadership perspective are new forms of improvisational expertise," or "a kind of process expertise that knows prudently how to experiment with never-been-tried-before relationships, means of communication, and ways of interacting that will help people develop solutions that build upon and surpass the wisdom of today's experts."[8] They draw this conclusion from years of training emerging leaders, further highlighting how "The improvisational ability to lead adaptively relies on responding to the present situation rather than importing the past into the present and laying it on the current situation like an imperfect template. . . . [It] will enable you [to] practice experiencing and expressing particular emotions, and sensing and responding to shifts in your audience reactions. . . . Leadership is an improvisational art."[9] Leadership calls for the development of individuals who can stay focused and immediate in challenging circumstances, put their own philosophies aside when they get in the way of being responsive to others, and perform a range of emotions and actions that ebb and flow with audience feedback—all skills that applied improvisation targets. The need for such leadership skills has become so acute that some even argue that "our 'adaptability quotient' (AQ) will soon become the primary predictor of success," as compared to general and emotional intelligence.[10]

Leadership is not the same as management. Management is primarily about creating order and continuity (e.g., controlling procedures, organizing and staffing, and planning and budgeting). Leadership is about creating change and adapting well (e.g., motivating and inspiring, establishing goals and visions, and building teams).[11] While both management and leadership practices will always be necessary—and this division may be too stark for what actually happens in practice—the focus on leadership as a skill involving adaptation and multidirectional (rather than unidirectional) influence[12] remains at the core of this chapter's practices.

The connection between applied improvisation and adaptive leadership became particularly clear to me in reading about adaptive leadership classes where, for decades, graduate students have been asked to sing in front of the class as part of the curriculum.[13] You can imagine how many students are typically shocked at this request, thinking that the hard work of government, business, and other arenas for leadership has little to do with such behaviors. But the results over the years have been astounding in terms of getting students to exercise presence and being with an audience, to make their words count, to use silence strategically and to conduct their energies well, to reveal the role and power of their emotions, and overall to activate "layers of humanity previously kept hidden or simply unconscious" as they relate to the everyday exercise of leadership.[14] Sharon Daloz Parks says that "a key value of the singing session is that it cultivates an inner sense of permission to operate in uncertainty."[15] She finds that, unlike in many courses, these types of lessons sink in deeply because they emerge from what actually happens in the classroom.

I argue that applied improvisation provides a *means* for training toward the *ends* of being an adaptive leader in and across organizations. And through this learning, participants start thinking and acting more democratically, serving their clients or constituents in ways that better serve society as a whole. This chapter creates an advanced framework for using applied impro-visation to build adaptive and other forms of leadership. Since having the experience first and intellectualizing about it later is so important to this work, try the exercise in box 4.1 below, which begins the process of seeing how to apply this training to leadership.

Box 4.1
Making Adaptive Moves

Change in Motion

This exercise takes us back to many basic themes covered in this book, such as moving forward rather than dwelling indefinitely on mistakes, and getting people into their bodies and externally focused.[16] For the purposes of this chapter, however, this exercise provides a simple segue to issues of adaptive leadership and more. It's usually best carried out near the beginning of a workshop or course. Have your participants walk around the room without following any particular pattern. Let the group know that there are two initial commands, "walk" and "stop," which require them to either walk or stop walking. Once you've done this a few times, say, "We're going to reverse the order of the direction: 'walk' will become 'stop,' and 'stop' will become 'walk.'" Run the participants through this reversed set of commands a few times. Tell everyone to lift their heads up and look at each other; everyone will feel more connected and the energy in the room will pick up. Now add in two new instructions, "name" (they must say their first name) and "jump" (a little hop), and give them a few chances to practice these new moves. With the initial commands still reversed, say "We're now going to reverse the order of these commands: 'name' will become 'jump' and 'jump' will become 'name.'" The group should be struggling to carry out the task at this point, so give them a chance to practice all the commands for at least a minute. Finally, add in two additional commands: "clap" (everybody claps) and "twist" (everyone turns/shimmies with their hips). Once this last set of instructions has been practiced, tell the group that "clap" and "twist" are now reversed. Provide each of the six commands at random and make observations of what the participants do in response to each.

Debrief questions: What happened during this exercise? What insights about leadership skills do you think this exercise illustrates, in particular?

Applications: Once they've had a chance to share out a bit, draw their attention to the idea of being adaptive as a core leadership competency—adapting to the unexpected is a routine feature of leaders' lives. Participants often share that the idea of juggling multiple demands at the same time is highlighted in the exercise. You can also highlight the point already mentioned about leadership dealing with change and exerting multidirectional influence, rather than implementing the status quo and administering unidirectional influence (i.e., management skills). The analogy of an authority figure who has to meet with different people up and down the chain of command throughout the work day, or has a new person stop by their office every ten minutes, can bring these points home. Many of the lessons from the rest of this chapter will move participants toward more advanced concepts, but this exercise is a great primer for getting their feet wet in the adaptive leadership space.

Improvise Up and Down the System

This idea was mentioned in passing in the second chapter, but it's worth bringing more firmly into view due to its connections with democratic forms of leadership. Excellent leaders cultivate the practice of being on both the "balcony" (where they can get a systemic perspective of what's going on in an organization) and the "dance floor" (where they can be immersed in the everyday life and feel of what's happening on the ground).[17] Leaders who get stuck on either plane will not be effective. Looking at an organization from an enterprise perspective prevents getting locked into a narrow view, while understanding the pulse of an organization from a variety of locations keeps a leader in touch with the people and conversations at the core of organizational life.

The same is true of societal leaders. If political representatives become too distanced from their constituents' concerns, they'll fail. On the other hand, if they become too enmeshed in local needs, they'll also fail to address the larger problems that affect citizens across the board. I like to translate this in terms of improvising up and down the system, since most organizations don't necessarily involve only ground-level (dance floor) or top-level (balcony) perspectives. There are a variety of middle and other level perspectives that prove useful too.

Improvising up and down the system is an adaptive practice. Improv is all about getting unstuck from static perspectives and habits that prevent people from responding well to what's happening around them. From a leadership perspective, it's also not about ad hoc conversations here and there; it's a strategic commitment to improvise well between both the balcony and dance floor. It's about realizing that one has, for instance, spent far too much time with a senior executive team, but has failed to have sustained conversations with the building and grounds team or janitorial staff, who may see important aspects of the organization that others can't.

Drawing participants' attention to these concepts naturally brings out examples from their own lives. Once these are identified, you'll find that everyone has a wealth of stories they can share: the boss who never seemed like they were present (too much on the balcony, or neither on the balcony or dance floor), or the manager who always hung out with the IT folks and neglected the needs of other departments (too much on the dance floor). You can tell participants that the most basic takeaway here involves the act that they just engaged in: using this vocabulary to make sense of organizational and public life, and the need for all of us to improvise up and down the system to make accurate diagnoses of problems, to maintain a sense of presence and community with many people across an organization, and to make effective and ethical interventions in our work that truly address the needs of people and situations.

So that this vocabulary doesn't itself come across as a singular viewpoint, the basic concepts here can be linked to related fields and practices. Complexity science "suggests a different paradigm for leadership—one that frames leadership as a complex interactive dynamic from which adaptive outcomes (e.g., learning, innovation, and adaptability) emerge."[18] Additionally, compared to industrial models of organization and governance such as bureaucracies, "contemporary coordination issues often entail the need to deal with multiple stakeholder interactions involving varying degrees of interdependency as well as diverse and sometimes mercurial goal-seeking behavior."[19] The key is to find practices that cultivate more and better forms of interaction and adaptability in any organization. Karl Weick and Kathleen Sutcliffe explain that "when concepts and perceptions coevolve, fuller concepts produce more meaningful perceptions, which in turn fill out and fine-tune concepts, which further improves perception, noticing, and attunement to flux and incipient surprises."[20] In other words, a commitment to improvising up and down the system creates improved, evolving understandings of what an organization and its people need, making possible amendments and updates. See box 4.2 for two exercises that will help your participants begin putting these ideas into practice.

In its associations with issues of power and leadership, I also like to connect improvising up and down a system with standpoint theory. Standpoint theory has three basic premises: "knowledge is socially situated," that is, knowledge always comes from people living under certain circumstances (i.e., on the dance floor); "marginalized groups are socially situated in ways that make it more possible for them to be aware of things and ask questions than it is for the non-marginalized" (so those in silos or at lower levels of an organization often have more incentive to be aware of their conditions and what's going on than those at the top); and "research . . . should begin with the lives of the marginalized"[21] (so any attempt to effectively gauge or construct change in an organization or public setting should start with the perspectives of those who have the least power). The implications for leaders trying to improvise up and down the system should be clear: if you're out of touch with diverse people across an organization or society, you'll know less than you should.

Box 4.2
Leading Systems Change

The following two exercises are great ways to connect leadership with ideas about improvising up and down the system.

Systemic Universe

This exercise shows up in a lot of standard improv classes. This is my favorite version.[22] Everyone should stand in a circle. Tell the group that each person should select a "sun" (another person in the group) and a "moon" (a different person in the group), without letting the two other people know that they've been picked. On the word "Go," participants should try to position themselves so that the moon is always equidistant between themselves and the sun (they can either do this in a straight line or in a kind of triangle shape, with the sun and moon as the other two corners of the triangle). It's good to demonstrate what this looks like by asking one volunteer to play a person with a sun and moon (get two more volunteers to play each of these respectively) and just start moving around the room. The straight line version is like "creating a solar eclipse." Everyone should move around rapidly to adapt to the changing movements of the other people. Give everyone a minute or so to engage in the activity—you'll notice a lot of frantic movement in the room as everyone tries to maintain equidistance with their sun and moon—before calling stop. For the second round, ask everyone to slow down substantially (another option is to tell everyone to go in slow motion). They should carry out the same task as before by trying to achieve equidistance between their sun and moon.

Debrief questions: What difference did you notice between the two rounds? What do you think this exercise has to do with leadership or organizational life? What lessons could we transfer to our working lives?

Applications: The first round is defined by a frenetic, unfocused energy with everyone going about their own business (i.e., akin to getting stuck on the dance floor, or being in an organizational silo). In the second round, each individual becomes more perceptive, with a heightened awareness of both their own tasks and what others are doing. They start acting more strategically, with a broadened vision, simultaneously alternating between their own task and what others in the group are doing (i.e., oscillating between being on both the balcony and dance floor, or improvising up and down a system). Overall, you should see more of a systems perspective and reflective practice inform the second round. Direct students toward the idea that we're after "perceiving rather than preconception."[23]

Variation: One variation is to add a round after the first that involves the suns and moons switching places, to advance a sudden change to which they must adapt. You can link this new wrench in the process to the need for adaptive leadership.

Balcony Breaker

The previous exercise highlights the skill of getting on the balcony. In contrast, this activity underscores both why and how participants need to get on the dance floor to exercise leadership well. Overall, this is like a nonverbal version of the classic game "Telephone."[24] To begin, have about ten participants line up single-file facing in one direction. The person at the back of the line should choose three distinct gestures to communicate to the next person in front of them (who will need to turn 180 degrees in the direction of the person last in the line, so that they can see the gestures while the others can't). That person will then show those gestures to the next person, and so on. Inevitably, some of the original message will become distorted as the nonverbal message is carried on down the line. Once everyone has run the gestures through the line, the people at the beginning and end of the line should come up in front of everyone else and, after the facilitator counts down from three to two to one, show everyone what the three gestures are at the same time. Typically, the gestures turn out quite different.

Debrief questions: Why do you think we had these different results at the end? If we could do the exercise again, what could the leader who initiated the gestures do to make sure everyone is on board with the three actions? What did we learn about leadership? You can further ask the group if anyone tried to hijack the message and, if so, if this at all reflects what happens in organizations or society.

Applications: While the first and last person in the line typically exhibit different gestures at the end, even if they're similar the same point can be made. The person at the end of the line who initiated the gestures was the leader in this exercise and, as their message traveled down the line, that message became increasingly disconnected from the lives of the other participants. Imagine instead if that leader had gone down the line and improvised up and down the system. They could have clarified through feedback how to perform the behavior. This exercise can also lead to an interesting conversation about how leaders and managers can learn from their direct reports by being on the dance floor more often. By the time the message gets to person seven in the line, for instance, seeing that person's interpretation of the original message could lead to the leader modifying their own views or behaviors to develop more accurate and grounded messages.

Shift Your Status

Building on the advice in the last chapter to play multiple roles and viewpoints, there's a novel leadership practice that applied improvisation provides: the ability to shift one's status or power level skillfully. One of the most profound insights to emerge from improvisation is that status is often less something a person *has* than something that a person *does*.[25] That is, power is typically more about behaviors than one's job or position. Once this is understood as a leadership practice, it is usually quite a revelation for participants. I like to use the example of the president of a country. It's certainly the case that a president possesses power in inhabiting that role. But power is also a matter of perception so that, in a certain context, a president who walks with weak body language (e.g., shoulders slumped over or a dejected face) and is soft spoken might actually be perceived as low status. At the same time, status isn't fixed; it can be raised or lowered depending on one's behaviors.

Johnstone uses the example of teachers.[26] He says that we can probably all remember teachers who were ruthless in their discipline and played high status all the time, making for a miserable learning environment. Another teacher may play low status all the time, coming across as incompetent and creating an environment lacking any discipline at all. In this case, little learning may also take place. A teacher who skillfully plays high, low, and medium (medium involving messages that communicate "we're equals") status to adjust to the needs at hand will lead a classroom most effectively, however. When it comes to grading or giving feedback, high-status behaviors will be useful, but for establishing rapport with students, behaviors such as self-deprecating humor that lower one's status can also be valuable. The key here is adaptation. Using fixed-status behaviors is too "one-note" for the complexity and change in any situation involving people. The same could be said of any profession; we could imagine substituting doctor for teacher here, for example.

Applied improvisation intensifies this lesson, and the transfer of learning to participants' lives tends to be immediate. Some high-status behaviors include holding eye contact for long periods of time, keeping your head still, and slowing down, while low-status behaviors include putting "er" at the beginning of sentences, touching the face, taking up little space, and pointing one's toes inward, among many others.[27] See the exercises in box 4.3 for more. Try some of these actions; you should feel your status go up or down, depending on the movement. This bears similarities to messages that are "one-up" (trying to assert dominance over others in one's messages), "one-down" (trying to lower oneself or submit to others), and "one-across" (trying to establish equal relations with others).[28]

As participants become sensitive to what status is and how it works, you can draw connections to leadership practices. Using this technique, one can skillfully understand when others are making power moves and how conflicts can be defused quickly. For example, I remember one time when an acquaintance made a veiled insult toward another person (a one-up status move). The recipient of this message thought about what was being said, found it to be an accurate critique, and told the attacker that he agreed with the point (a one-down status move). The conflict went from competitive to cooperative in two moves. Had they played a game of one-upping each other, an indefinite struggle might have ensued. Those hoping to improve their leadership will also gain the ability to monitor their own status moves and see how other people are affected by how these power exchanges are always being negotiated.

In terms of adaptive leadership, the goal is to assess the width or narrowness of one's roles and to practice "broaden[ing] your bandwidth."[29] In effect, "the more roles you can play, the more effective you will be. As with bandwidth, you will have a wider repertoire to draw from in different situations, and you will be less predictable and less readily pigeonholed. And the more roles you play, the more factions in which you will be a part and the more people with whom you will have connections as you try to make progress on tough issues."[30] The ability to work well with others across society requires expanding one's genuine selves in interactions with others, raising or lowering one's power in different circumstances. For instance, someone with a disability can let that part of their identity overshadow all others, whereas expanding one's roles to include "empathic friend" or "confident person" can open up new possibilities; similarly, someone switching from a career in medical practice to the business world will need to play new roles to operate effectively.[31] Leaders can also explicitly tell others what roles they're employing so that all can "take things less personally if the role doesn't work out."[32]

Training in status further links with operating beyond one's cultural default settings. In a world where leaders are increasingly expected to work globally, status shifts become a core competency to develop. Keith Grint argues that "a real danger is that we become prisoners of our own cultural preferences—hierarchists become addicted to command, egalitarians become addicted to collaborative leadership, and individualists become addicted to managing all problems as if they were all tame [or simple]. In effect, we become addicted to elegance, when we ought to be cultivating a clumsy approach if and when our approaches prove inadequate to the task."[33] By clumsy, Grint means adaptive. One's cultural background affects how partial we are to variables such as hierarchy (for example, Mexico tends to be a hierarchical culture) or collaboration (as in Sweden), and operating effectively across cultural boundaries requires expanding one's perspective and behaviors to adapt to different situations.[34] Even practices such as "public speaking" are cultural forms of expression specific to largely Anglo-American speech communities; other communities place different values and meanings on the practice in ways that are far from universal.[35] Status negotiations are an inevitable part of traveling across borders and boundaries, so the skilled leader should be as comfortable commanding attention as acting with deference. Similar to how "improvisers have to be actors, directors, and editors all at once,"[36] effective leaders shift their roles and status seamlessly.

Many students have spent their lives in social worlds where comparing, competing, tearing others down, or acting defensively are habitual. So status training can bring into being transformation that "comes to everyone when they act out of their humanness without need for acceptance, exhibitionism, or applause."[37] Moreover, as an activity in and of itself, "in many organizations, maintaining one's status is more important than getting anything else done."[38] Researchers Robert Kegan and Lisa Lahey forward this argument by noting that in many organizations people carry out an enormously wasteful second job: "spending time and energy covering up their weaknesses, managing other people's impressions of them, showing themselves to their best advantage, playing politics, hiding their inadequacies, hiding their uncertainties, hiding their limitations. Hiding."[39] In contrast, improv offers people an opportunity to step into spaces where hiding is no longer an option. It aims to peel off the layers of guardedness and distance that keep one safe from growing or exhibiting vulnerability with others, developing a greater capacity for expression and connection to the humanity that we all share. Improv invites individuals to move from only inhabiting "safe spaces" to what John Palfrey terms "brave spaces," where necessarily uncomfortable learning and development can occur.[40] If the opposite poles of status seeking and status minimization become fixed behavioral defaults for so many in organizations, improv provides leaders with the skill of status pliability.

At its heart, status training promotes a healthy respect for oneself and curious and caring relationships with others, without absolving either need. Paul Sills says that his mother, Viola Spolin, saw "approval/disapproval" or "authoritarianism" as obstacles to directly experiencing what's happening, especially through her idea that, "categorized 'good' or 'bad' from birth (a 'good' baby does not cry too much), we become so enmeshed with the tenuous threads of approval/disapproval that we are creatively paralyzed. We see with others' eyes and smell with others' noses. . . . We function with only parts of our total selves."[41] When individuals fail to shift power levels they indicate little need to adapt to others. On the other hand, only adapting to others may forgo the need to make a choice or exert assertive leadership. Overall, status brings these skills into focus, ultimately cultivating what adaptive leadership theories have long called for: "a more effective deployment of self, especially as a consequence of a wider range of choice."[42]

Simply because someone is in a position of influence does not mean they are exercising leadership well. Through improvisational status training, facilitators can focus the distinction between "leadership" and "authority."[43] Someone at the very bottom rung of an organization can be applying many leadership skills—having conversations with colleagues at all levels of the institution, building coalitions, helping an organization adapt to needed changes, and more—while the head of the organization may not. Participants usually find this distinction enlightening. It also serves a democratizing function, showing that everyone is capable of exercising leadership in organizations and across societies, not only those at the top.

Box 4.3
Leadership Behaviors

Freezing Roles

This exercise provides a quick way to introduce everyone to the need to operate beyond default settings and engage in more varied behaviors in the exercise of leadership. Ask everyone to walk around the room, being careful not to bump into objects or others. Tell the group to "freeze" (i.e., stop walking), close their eyes, and pose as statues created by the cues that you'll provide.[44] The first cue is "You're a leader telling another employee to do something." Give them a few seconds to quickly pose in any position that comes to mind, with their eyes still closed. Then ask everyone to open their eyes. Many in the group will end up in the same positions, pointing their fingers or engaging in a similar behavior. Ask everyone to walk around the room again, say "Freeze" and "Close your eyes," and have them pose as statues for other roles that leaders typically play, such as coaches suggesting an improvement, colleagues sharing a story, or negotiators making their first request in a negotiation.

Debrief questions: For this one, let the participants simply share what they got out of the exercise first.

Applications: General points for discussion should include how almost everyone engages in similar poses and has some collective default settings when we think about leadership. For leaders to broaden their roles and perspectives and shift their status skillfully, they must think about what the most productive body language and approaches may be instead of getting locked into common and potentially unproductive habits.

Status Shifts

This exercise is similar to "Walk About" (in box 3.3), but it gets participants working on more advanced practices involving status and leadership.[45] Ask the group to walk around and blink a lot more than they normally would. Now ask them to never blink. In the former practice, they should feel low status, and in the latter, high status. Ask everyone to notice how working on only one status technique tends to affect other behaviors and one's overall outlook or attitude. It's best to introduce participants to a number of these moves so that the effect of particular behaviors on the feeling of status is experienced. Have participants utter phrases and move their heads around (or touch their heads or faces with their hands) (low status) and then have them keep their heads absolutely still, with no touching (high status). Now have participants stop and get into pairs for conversations in which one person will be A and the other B. Ask the A's to move slowly and deliberately and take physical and verbal delays before responding to the other (high status) and ask the B's to make small flinching movements and respond quickly to the other (low status). Have a variety of these conversations so that some are between A's only, B's only, and a mix of A's and B's. You can also have them hold eye contact (high status) or look away a lot (low status). Other high-status behaviors to play with include gesturing precisely, expanding the middle of one's body, getting in other people's space, being comfortable with pausing and silence, not reacting much to others' presence, and placing one's feet a bit wider than usual and not moving them.[46] Other low-status behaviors include nervous touching, breaking up one's speech into fragments or rambling, minimizing the middle of one's body, keeping distance from others, not making eye contact (but wanting to), nervous giggles, shifting feet and making distracting gestures with one's hands, and crossing one foot over the other.[47]

Debrief questions: Each step of the way, ask participants how they feel and what outlooks and attitudes arise from these practices.

Applications: Thread in the lessons from the prior section on status shifts, particularly about authorities who play a chronically low or high status, as differentiated from those who shift their status adaptively.

Facilitate Co-creation

"Co-create" has become a buzzword for professionals, but the term shouldn't fall into disrepute. It arose from a valuable set of concerns about the need to get beyond top-down models of leadership to engage many people and ideas in the development of new products and initiatives. Just as adaptive leadership recognizes that leadership is defined by moving beyond the sole administration of authority to engaging multiple stakeholders in change efforts,[48] applied improvisation positions creative activities with the group.

In contrast with the myth of the lone creative genius, applied improv connects with evidence showing that co-creative approaches generally bring about better results. Research confirms that this is how creativity mostly works, since "an idea or product that deserves the label 'creative' arises from the synergy of many sources and not only from the mind of a single person."[49] Creativity is participatory, contextual, and complex.[50] Whether it's coming up with a name or plan for a nonprofit program, inventing a new product line at a business, or thinking about top-level government strategies for a meeting between international delegates, leaders should facilitate co-creation at every opportunity.

A two-year study of co-creation found that having more and diverse people in such processes fares considerably better than status quo approaches. Community developments, health advances, and technological breakthroughs can come about through five practices of co-creation: sharing power, prioritizing relationships, leveraging heterogeneity, legitimizing all ways of knowing, and prototyping early and often.[51] Further research finds that "compared to a leader who advances personal interests, a leader who advances the interests of a collective is (a) perceived as offering more authentic leadership and

(b) more likely to inspire followership."[52] Consistent with the idea in this book that communication, leadership, and civic skills should be put in verb form, co-creation establishes how "the phrase *high reliability organization* can be misleading because it suggests a static container rather than a dynamic activity," so instead we should advance "*high reliability organizing* to describe ongoing, collective efforts to improve and maintain reliability."[53] Applied improvisation highlights the importance of co-creation as an activity rather than the co-creator as the locus of leadership.

This is generally the direction the leadership literature has taken too. Concepts such as "distributed leadership" highlight the benefits of inviting participation, realizing that the synergies of the whole are greater than the parts, and expanding knowledge beyond one's own expertise, while recognizing that this type of mobilization still requires individual leadership.[54] Damien O'Brien, a global chairman of an international executive search firm, summarizes this perspective: "the new generation of workers is looking for different types of leaders. Out is the autocratic, top-down approach. People are looking for leaders who are inclusive and can inspire their creativity."[55] Participants often feel the most impetus to address these differences from trainings. A support manager for the organization World Vision in the Philippines noted that before taking an applied improv workshop, "I felt that 'because I'm the boss, you need to listen to me' and 'I am fully experienced, you should do it this way.' After the workshop I feel this must be changed—let it go, follow the flow, recognize others, build relationships."[56] Each of these practices embody the skills of facilitating co-creation, and can be emphasized as part of applied improvisational lessons.

This isn't wishful thinking. The concept of "transference" that originated with Sigmund Freud spotlights how many people basically want "to be taken care of by a superior being," and that what starts with transferring power to parents early in life can easily lead to too much dependency on authorities later in life.[57] Leaders can easily get caught up in this craving for security too, minimizing the power of other's voices. In essence, the ability of leaders to relinquish control and especially to exhibit humility creates organizational teams that are more effective, humbler, and mentally and emotionally stronger.[58]

In terms of adaptive leadership, facilitators can draw attention to several concepts with relevance to applied improvisational exercises. The distinction between short-term "technical problems" that are easily solved by an authority figure and longer-term "adaptive challenges" that require broader stakeholder input and support should be at the forefront of this learning.[59]

Failing to distinguish between these problem types can be disastrous. For instance, if a partner in a law firm thinks that continuing to hire graduates from the top law schools will solve all the problems that their organization faces (a quick, technical fix),[60] while the legal industry continues to change (the adaptive challenge of new online and low-cost, pre-paid forms of legal support that are changing the industry, etc.), they are sticking their head in the sand. Indeed, to some the difference between "tame" and "wicked" problems (or problems that require simple solutions and those that defy common logic) is the difference between simple management and more complex leadership practices.[61]

Leading through these challenges will take time and collaborative work through tough processes and decisions. The related concepts of "carrying other people's water" (leaders taking on the load of too many others, given the temptation of transference), "giv[ing] the work back" (delegating the work outward, helping others not avoid the difficult work that needs done), and "nurtur[ing] shared responsibility for the organization" can further clarify this leadership practice.[62] In the end, all these ideas support the need to train people in the skills of co-creation.

James MacGregor writes that one of the biggest failures of the leadership literature is a too-stark separation between leadership and followership.[63] In fact, one study found that organizations and authorities that support creative role identities for their employees get what they ask for; creativity between leaders and followers tends to be heightened simply from perceptions that creation is valued.[64] Applied improvisational approaches collapse these boundaries, demonstrating the reciprocal nature of leader and follower interactions. The "Campaign" exercise from chapter 2 is a perfect illustration of co-creation in action. See box 4.4 for another way to bring this practice more firmly into view.

Box 4.4
Co-Creation on the Fly

Incorporation

Ask participants to get into groups of two or three.[65] One person should begin telling a story. Any story will do: an origin story for a company, a personal experience, or even a fairy tale. While this person tells a story, their partners should intermittently say words that are in no way related to the story (e.g., "fish," "towel," "Taj Mahal," etc.). The one or two others hearing the story may want to says lots of words, but tell them to hold back (every thirty seconds or so interject a new word is a good rule of thumb). The person telling the story must then incorporate these words into the story in a way that makes sense. As the story is co-created, each group will be surprised at the creativity and turns that the story takes.

Debrief questions: Have everyone share about what surprised them with specific examples (this'll usually lead to laughter). What does this exercise show us about co-creation?

Applications: This exercise is fairly simple, but supports the point that leaders need to facilitate co-creation with their stakeholders, demonstrating how much easier it is to lead with a story while incorporating suggestions from others. Make sure to underscore some of the other core lessons about co-creation detailed earlier.

Perform Resilience

Erika Marx says that you should "play when the stakes are low so you can perform when the stakes are high."[66] Nothing better captures how the means of applied improvisation can train for the ends of adaptive leadership. Research on "resilience" finds that it's "the skill and the capacity to be robust under conditions of enormous stress and change," suggesting that resilient people have three qualities: "a staunch acceptance of reality; a deep belief, often buttressed by strongly held values, that life is meaningful; and an uncanny ability to improvise."[67] Applied improv's focus on observing at a heightened level, being present and connecting with others, and using the "yes, and" principle to affirm and build on offers all support an acceptance of reality, acting with purpose, and an ability to pivot on the fly. Best of all, applied improv transports participants from intellectual beliefs about the need for resilience to a laser-like focus on what it takes to practice this interdisciplinary leadership concept.

A major part of developing resilience is managing surprise and leading one's colleagues through the volatility that exists in any organization or public setting. The previously mentioned leadership concept of "high reliability organizing" works with and builds on these tensions in organizations, especially in being preoccupied with failure (i.e., not to repeat it, but to adapt and move forward well), being reluctant to simplify in complex environments, having a continuous sensitivity to operations (i.e., a "watchfulness for moment-to-moment changes in conditions"), making a commitment to resilience, and pushing expertise down and around the organization—all goals in which "relationships and continuous conversation" are essential.[68] In Weick and Sutcliffe's terms,

> Greater skill at improvisation is a way to increase one's commitment to resilience and to act on a greater variety of surprises. If a limited action repertoire limits perception, then increased skill at improvisation enlarges the potential actions available in one's repertoire, which should broaden the range of cues that you can afford to notice and handle. For example, medication errors were reduced 66 percent when a pharmacist was added to a team of doctors and nurses making rounds in an intensive care unit. By expanding its repertoire of capabilities, the medical team was able to notice more mistakes and correct them before they became catastrophes. . . . If [a leader] is not at once *improvising* and improvising *warily,* he is not engaging his somewhat trained wits in a partly fresh situation. It is the pitting of an acquired competence or skill against unprogrammed opportunity, obstacle or hazard.[69]

These should be familiar themes now. Improvisation trains for resilience as a performed behavior; or at the very least, participants can be introduced to and inspired by what resilient leadership feels like. Any number of surprises specific to a field can be used to talk about how improvisation develops resilience. Whether it's the accountant who realizes that they fudged some numbers for a client, the medical assistant who receives a letter in the mail detailing that they failed a required job test, or the head of a government agency who has to deliver bad news to a thousand staff, anyone can learn to improvise better at such moments.

Although it's a mouthful to say, the adaptive leadership concept of the "productive zone of disequilibrium" stresses why resilient leadership needs to be practiced at a larger, organizational level.[70] People will often treat adaptive challenges with technical solutions or simply avoid the tough work that needs done. To lead people through this difficult period of work, which can't be solved overnight, you have to apply enough fire to keep them centered on the work, but not so much that everyone freaks out.[71] Parallel to this concept is the idea of the "holding environment," or a temporary place with "the cohesive properties of a relationship or social system that serve to keep people engaged with one another in spite of the divisive forces generated by adaptive work."[72] I like to highlight that applied improvisational courses or workshops are themselves a productive zone of disequilibrium and holding environment for learning to perform resilience. Each exercise is intended to push participants out of their comfort zones and learn to lead through moments that demand the full attention of the body and mind.

It's important to make known what structures you're using to build resilience. After all, "skilled improvisation involves creativity within a structure."[73] One of your roles as a facilitator is to help your attendees engage in high-level sense making, providing at least some perspectives, joined with participants' own, about this work's value. To have your participants perform resilience, repeatedly refer to concepts from this chapter and invite them to transfer this learning to their organizations. To put performing resilience into practice, see the exercises in box 4.5. The second is one of my all-time favorites.

In running improv for leadership classes, one additional reaction I often receive is that these sessions provide a surprising benefit that participants hadn't expected: they feel much lighter, engaged with the world, and freer from stress. This feeling shift is no small matter for leaders, as "stress has been implicated as an important determinant of leadership functioning," and sets an imitative tone in organizations, such that "leader stress influences leader behavior," with leader-follower interactions and leadership behaviors as determinates of burnout and stress in direct reports.[74] From organizational relationships to societal networks, one has to wonder how much harm is done by leaders who feel overwhelmed by their daily demands and turn anger and other emotions into regular, expected communication patterns that are mirrored repeatedly throughout institutions. Applied improvisation is no panacea to this problem, but it does provide one significant way to de-stress and promote resilience by bringing the whole body and productive patterns of interaction more clearly into practice.

Box 4.5
Leading with Resilience

Problem Junction

I've seen this exercise run in a number of different ways. The most basic version can quickly focus one's ability to perform resilience in a demanding situation and serves as an excellent segue to the next, more challenging exercise. Have participants sit down in groups of three. One person, in the middle, will pull out an imaginary photo album and start describing some of the people and places in the album. The person to the right should have a conversation with the person in the middle to continue prompting their thoughts about the album's contents (e.g., the person could say, "Now show me what's on the next page," or "It looks like you had quite a vacation in Cancun there"). Both participants should keep "yes, anding" one another. Here's where it gets fun: the person to the left should intermittently provide the participant in the middle with straightforward math problems to solve (at least ones that wouldn't require a calculator, e.g., eight plus five or eleven times seven). While continuing the conversation with the person to the right, the participant in the middle should provide answers to the math problems as quickly as possible. Keep this going for about a minute and then have each of the three members rotate roles until each has had a chance to play all three positions.

Debrief questions: Did you enjoy this exercise? What surprised you? What did you find challenging?

Applications: Connect the exercise to the concepts of moving through disequilibrium and performing resilience amid difficult circumstances. This is also a great exercise to return to the idea of default settings and how we can all learn to improvise better given piling pressures and changing conditions.

Managing Disequilibrium

For this exercise, ask your participants to sit down in chairs in groups of four to five.[75] One person in the group will stand up and play the leader. As the boss, they will need to think of bad news that they will have to deliver to the others. This can be bad news of any kind: "We're cutting everyone's pay by twenty percent," "We're merging with another organization," "We're consolidating jobs so that you're now in charge of two jobs instead of one," etc. This should be an adaptive challenge that will require the support of stakeholders. It must be news that will be difficult to deliver, and you can tell the recipients of these messages that they will not like what they are going to hear. Once the news is delivered, everyone who's seated in each group should start peppering the standing leader with angry questions and comments; make life as difficult as possible for this bearer of bad news. It's the leader's job to hold their position while taking the group adaptively through the change that will happen. At the same time, the leaders will need to maintain an open, receptive stance toward their groups to make this work. At the end of this first round, I find it useful to highlight the "productive zone of disequilibrium"[76] again to show how those who hope to lead others effectively through organizational changes have to improvise well over time, rather than avoid the adaptive work that needs carried out. Have at least one more person in each group practice this exercise with new bad news to deliver.

Debrief questions: How did you handle this challenge? What insights emerged about managing disequilibrium? What did you learn both as a leader and as a participant? What can you take away from this exercise in your practice of leadership at work tomorrow?

Applications: After getting participants' reactions, make sure to connect the exercise to the core skills at the intersections of leadership and applied improv covered in the chapter to this point: improvising up and down the system, shifting your status, facilitating co-creation, performing resilience, and more.

Variations: After one or two of the group members have performed this exercise, I recommend changing the focus for each of the other group members to keep everyone slightly off balance. For practice and a lot of fun, have the leaders deliver more nonsensical bad news, e.g., "Everyone must shave their head," "No more lunch breaks," or "All employees must master the Portuguese language by this year's end to keep their jobs." Despite the laughter that will ensue, tell both the leaders and the groups to play this version of the exercise deadly seriously—everyone should imagine that this will be a real policy and work to defend their position and concerns with it. I've found that there's more gut-level reactions and emotional interest and intensity in this version that actually reflects the way that people feel when monumentally bad news is delivered in organizations. Another variation involves having the leaders go out of the room and then asking the groups to come up with their own bad news; when the leaders walk in they will discover the bad news that has already happened and need to improvise responses to it.[77] Just when subsequent group members start planning what their bad news will be, this variation requires them to switch gears. A final variation that I use involves asking the leaders to rotate to different groups (a simple prompt such as "please rotate to the group to your right" will suffice). Everyone who is sitting should stay seated in their own groups; it's only the leaders who will rotate. Just when the leaders start getting used to interacting with their group's styles, this variation replicates the real life condition of having to communicate across organizational silos, or of being a new leader who has to earn the respect of a team.

Line Shifts

This final exercise shifts everyone's attention toward the entire group, replicating the dynamics of a day in the life of an average organization. Have everyone get into teams of four and have them line up one in front of the other, much like a bobsled team.[78] The people in positions two, three, and four should put their hands on the shoulders of the person in front of them and, when ready, the entire team should start walking around the room, with the person up front leading the team around. Have them start slowly until they can work up to walking speed, and direct them not to bump into any other groups while staying in motion. Then introduce the first command, "change," in which the player at the front of the bobsled should go to the back (the person formerly in the second position will now be at the front leading the team forward). For safety, make sure that the person up front does not run backward at this command, but rather turns and walks forward to the back of the line. Do this a few times until all the teams get used to the prompt. Emphasize that the teams should continue walking forward around the room, be careful not to bump into the other teams, and simply adjust to the commands as they keep this up. The second command is "rotate," in which all in each team turn 180 degrees (so that, for example, the person who was now at the front is at the back, and vice versa). The third prompt is "switch," in which the people in positions two and four in each team switch places. Continue to run the other prompts until everyone becomes used to the format. The last command is "trade," in which the third person in each team trades places with the third person from another team. This one will take some getting used to, so run it a few times. You can then use all four prompts so that the teams are constantly on their toes in managing the change. Finally, tell everyone that you'll be abdicating your role in shouting the commands. From here forward the person at the front of each line can shout out the rule that everyone in the room will need to respond to, introducing some negotiations between all.

Debrief questions: What does this exercise highlight about our lives in organizations? What does it show us about working in teams? Finally, what does it demonstrate about leadership?

Applications: This exercise is great for underscoring many of the concepts in this chapter, particularly adaptive leadership that relies on a give and take between people and collapsing boundaries between leaders and followers. The final round, when those in the front may shout the commands, can lead to an interesting discussion about co-creation, or even what happens when there are too many people trying to lead at the same time. Practices in listening, fixing mistakes, and taking action can also be discussed.

Act Charismatically

The largest study of leadership ever conducted looked at over 17,000 people across sixty-two countries and found that some specific attributes of leadership are universally desirable across cultures: charisma, integrity, and interpersonal communication skills. Universally undesirable qualities include being nonsocial, malevolent, and self-focused.[79] Although this book isn't an ethics manual, it's certainly the goal of improv for democracy to improve the integrity of individuals and groups across societies through applied improvisational training. It's clear that societies with globally oriented leaders who have high and ethical performance standards "tend to be more economically prosperous and competitive, have governments that better follow the rule of law and are more organized and transparent. They also have a happier and more satisfied citizenry who have more confidence in their public institutions."[80] Such goals can partly be reached through exercises emphasizing excellent interpersonal communication skills that invite participants to be more other-focused.

The remaining challenge is clear: how can one develop the leadership skill of charisma? Contrary to popular views of charisma as an ethereal quality that one either has or not, work in this area has been conclusive for some time: individuals can be taught to behave more charismatically, with an impact on leadership outcomes.[81] Even brief glimpses of charismatic nonverbal behaviors "can be valid indicators of leadership."[82] Olivia Fox Cabane finds that "charisma is the result of specific nonverbal behaviors, not an inherent or magical personal quality," breaking down along three dimensions that can be improved: warmth, presence, and power.[83] These findings correspond to extensive research in the social sciences showing that two dimensions are always assessed in our interactions with other people: warmth and competence.[84]

Using improvisational training on status helps individuals exercise the practical leadership skills of raising and lowering their power. Many of the teachings and exercises to this point have also focused on getting individuals to practice more presence with others. As Ann Lamott writes, "there is ecstasy in paying attention. . . . Anyone who wants to can be surprised by the beauty or pain of the natural world, of the human mind and heart, and can try to capture just that—the details, the nuance, what is. If you start to look around, you will start to see."[85] Similarly, charisma involves paying attention so that others feel truly listened to and accommodated. Charismatic leaders practice empathic observation.

That leaves us with the critical concept of "warmth," a subject that few have ever likely received instruction in. Yet we all know the difference between individuals who behave warmly and those who don't. The feeling is instantaneous. If you walk into a bank and a teller makes no eye contact, looks downward, and says "How can I help you?" in a low, uninterested tone of voice, you can feel the chill. As a result of these types of experiences, it's easy to think that warmth is a quality that one either does or does not possess, a deeply psychological characteristic that just can't be changed. Nothing could be further from the truth. I've found that in improv training sometimes just asking participants to hold a smile, even if they don't feel like it, can teach them to suddenly feel more warmth toward others. Conversely, holding a frown on purpose will automatically cast a pall over one's vision.

Some teachers of improvisation believe that much of the damage to one's ability to project warmth can be traced to educational systems where values such as competition, perfection, and aggression have played a large role in people's experiences. In essence, "many teachers think of children as immature adults. It might lead to better and more 'respectful' teaching, if we thought of adults as atrophied children. Many 'well adjusted' adults are bitter, uncreative, frightened, unimaginative, and rather hostile people," so "instead of learning how to be warm and spontaneous and giving, they've become armored and superficial, calculating and self-obsessed."[86] Improv can reverse these longstanding tendencies: first by making participants aware of myths about charisma, second by having them feel the differences between one behavioral choice and another in projecting warmth, and third by repeated practice in alternative behaviors. It's hard to argue with one's own experience of feeling open and warm as a result of a particular nonverbal behavior.

MIT's Media Lab has been doing research on charismatic behaviors in recent decades, and has come up with one additional finding that's in line with the ethos of adaptive leadership, co-creation, and applied improvisation.

"Charismatic connectors" have a way of speaking that demonstrates "high levels of listening, more even-handed turn-taking, and high levels of engagement, trust, and cooperation," and "the more charismatic connectors a given team had among its members, the better the team performance was judged. . . . It was not simply one charismatic individual, but rather a charismatic team, that pushed them toward success."[87] Given the many myths that people hold about charisma, one implication is that those looking to practice high-level leadership skills must think about the subject in terms of specific behaviors within group development. Training individuals to act charismatically should be a matter of organizational citizenship and growth more broadly.

Ultimately, when teaching or training about charisma, emphasize performance. Something as simple as videotaping participants engaging in an impromptu presentation before and after improvisational training on warmth, status, and immediacy will support this work's relevance. Some inspiration for how to carry this out can be drawn from a class on improvisational leadership at the University of Southern California. Students are taught that creativity and courage go together (in this chapter's terms, co-creation and acting charismatically), and they build leadership skills through assignments that require them to take risks—mustering up the courage to find a mentor, going out of their way to learn a subject that they don't understand, or being asked to pull topics out of a hat and then having only five minutes to prepare a speech.[88]

To act charismatically, tell your participants that they have to make a choice to be bold and take action when they'd rather not. In essence, "frightened improvisers keep restoring balance for fear that something may happen."[89] Rules and fear can get in the way of good improvisation (see the "That Is . . ." exercise from chapter 2), which requires us to make a choice and do something, rather than to pull back into a state of inertia.[90] In essence, "the message underlying all the lessons of improvisation is to be courageous, to go out there and take risks—to use the natural fear of failure as the fuel for success."[91] As has been a theme throughout this book, "If we treat confidence as something we do rather than as an inner quality we 'have,' we can achieve extraordinary results in our everyday interactions."[92] Along these lines, for an interesting new program that uses improv to help girls develop leadership skills and act charismatically, see The Harnisch Foundation's video "Funny Girls—Improv for Leadership Skills" on YouTube (the link is in the endnote).[93]

Reframe the Game

There's a negative connotation to the idea of playing "games," as when someone says "stop playing games" in a conflict situation. That's not the definition of game that we're after here. It's too narrow and misses a key leadership skill that improv supports: the ability to see that almost all human interactions and experiences have game-like qualities. Throughout our lives we enter into a series of closed systems that have patterns, rules, and expectations. These become habits in the workplace, in our family lives, and even when walking through supermarket aisles—you're not allowed to climb inside the frozen meat section and lie prostrate among the ground beef, after all.

In this respect, our behaviors are always framed or contained within structures. The game being played can be positive or negative, but they're all around us and always there. In a meeting with colleagues, the game of "who can critique the new policy proposal the most" may play out time after time or, after a typical workplace presentation seeking feedback from everyone, a game of "let's never share our opinions" may play out between two staff who consistently retreat from making contributions. Roger Callois confirmed that even in spheres such as the military, law, and religion, games are enacted through certain rules of play.[94] When leaders develop an ability to see the game being played, they can more effectively intervene and improvise in a variety of situations.

Improvisers and comedians use the concept of game to focus on the patterns and habits that develop within systems. When you watch a great comedic sketch on a show such as *Saturday Night Live*, you're essentially watching a game being played that reflects how some human beings act in certain situations. A character may have a behavioral tic such as blurting out sensitive information at inopportune moments, or a family might play out a scene where all the communication is passive-aggressive. Comedy writers and performers call the game "a theme or pattern in the character's lives that repeats and escalates for comic effect."[95] Some scholars refer to a similar concept, arguing "the term 'game' . . . refers to sequences of behavior which are governed by rules."[96] For fans of the show, the founders of the improv comedy juggernaut the Upright Citizens Brigade share how "Kenneth's relentlessly positive attitude in every episode of 30 Rock is an example of Game."[97]

This concept has many applications for our professional lives. Applied improvisers note how "one of the biggest shortcomings for aspiring entrepreneurs and managers is that they get stuck playing games that are not as productive as other games would be"; for example, being territorial and hunkering down in one's department, engaging in relentless judgment, or perpetually joking in a way that avoids dealing with topics of importance to an organization or staff.[98] More productive games could be "Go Big or Stay Home," which involves "making a big splash with your moves," or "Mutual Interest," which involves listening for what one has in common with clients.[99] The idea of expanding options is central to each of these examples.

Paul Watzlawick finds that human beings play many games with the past—for example, when someone glorifies bygone times so much that they filter out all but the greatest moments. Cycles of sinfulness, guilt and repentance, a continuous raising of one's wounds, or even the stubborn use of solutions or conclusions that once worked well but no longer fit the nature of current problems are all games that wreak havoc on the world.[100] There are even patterns of "games without end"; for instance, "two persons decide to play a game consisting of the substitution of negation for affirmation and vice versa in everything they communicate to each other. Thus 'yes' becomes 'no,' 'I don't want' means 'I want,' and so forth." Ultimately, "to stop the game it would be necessary to step outside of the game and communicate about it,"[101] which is precisely what the improvisational leadership competency of reframing the game is all about.

After explaining these concepts and before engaging in any exercises that hone this skill, I like to ask participants to spend some time thinking about the games that currently play out in their personal and professional lives. A few minutes of silence and personal written reflections can help each person identify how and what this concept means. It's impossible to see all the games in our lives, but bringing at least a few into awareness is all that's needed to start the process of applying this leadership practice. After that, make the connections between framing the games of our lives and improvisation explicit. For many adults, there's a shock that comes from improvisational exercises that pull into view the games that each participant has been either willing or unwilling to play (for example, the status level that feels normal or not in the previous status exercises can be considered games).

This idea links with the ability to improvise up and down the system. Through embodied game-playing, participants begin to see the hidden structures and habits of their lives play out in different improvisational acts, while rising above those acts to see the broader range of choices available. Essentially, "a creature that plays is more readily adaptable to changing contexts and conditions," and "improvisation is not breaking with forms and limitations just to be 'free,' but using them as the very means of transcending ourselves."[102] To make this a leadership practice, participants should become more aware of their personal games, their games in interaction with others, and higher-level organizational games. It's worth underscoring how "every team in trouble is poisoned by something. Sometimes it's cynicism, sometimes it's fear, sometimes the team is just demoralized," but "playfulness defeats all three."[103] Overall, urge everyone to switch from negative to positive game-playing.

One related trope is Rosamund and Benjamin Zander's metaphor of "being the board."[104] Imagining that any situation can be compared to a chess board, we can see any situation from the perspective of ourselves (an individual chess piece), or we can choose to be the board, thinking about the situation from the perspective of the entire playing field. It's a recognition that our thoughts and behaviors are always situated, that a larger perspective is there if we try and see it. From the board's viewpoint (not our own), we get to inquire about our assumptions and understand more about how we got to where we are and what previously unseen possibilities lay before us. The idea of a chess board having boundaries is also a nice way to illustrate that systems have constraints; options for action, while plentiful, may not necessarily be limitless.

How does this all contribute to the idea of leaders needing to "reframe" games? Human beings frame every moment of their lives. Frames are "constructed meanings," and in the absence of a frame, we'll come up with our own as we search for coherence.[105] Frames always include and exclude details, so an ability to reframe the words and symbols we become attached to helps us to see beyond our limited perspectives to more accurately gauge events.[106] At its heart, this lesson focuses how attached we become to our messages and understandings. Can we hold our opinions tentatively and generate alternate views, or do we hold on to particular explanations at all costs? Weick and Sutcliffe underscore this need to maintain an ambivalence about one's past experience and understandings in moments where leadership is needed: "You've seen lots of messes, but you've never seen quite this specific mess. This means that your past experience is both partly relevant and partly irrelevant. . . . you're attempting to engage in simultaneous belief and doubt, admittedly a difficult exercise. Your goal is to act simultaneously as though the unexpected situation you face is just like every other situation you've faced and like no other situation you've ever faced."[107] Consistent with improvisational practices, adaptive leadership takes place in the liminal present, highlighting the necessity of "generat[ing] multiple interpretations" in one's head simultaneously.[108]

Games and framing thus go together. Where framing draws our attention to the picture an individual draws around a scenario (e.g., "an illness is punishment from God"), games reveal the persistent frames applied to circumstances (e.g., when a political figure sees all events in terms of a "crisis"). To break a pattern, reframing can help. To make that change in the longer term is to regame. Thinking in this fashion also means thinking critically about the frame and game metaphors too. I use them to get participants thinking in these directions, but there may be times and places where other metaphors might be more fitting.

Box 4.6
Regaming

The following exercise hones the skills of reframing and regaming an existing challenge. After running through these ideas with participants, it provides a great way to bring a variety of leadership skills from this chapter into view.

Improv Prototyping

The liberating structure "improv prototyping" is a method for identifying and addressing chronic problems and "a playful way to get very serious work done."[109] It's also a means to co-create the new by having everyone act charismatically (with the full involvement of their minds and bodies) in the service of reframing the game. Everyone should first identify a persistent challenge at work. You can create a list of these and choose one. Multiple issues can be addressed across many rounds, but for now just pick one that seems to resonate the most with the group. You'll then split everyone into observer and player roles. You'll only need three or four players, who will improvise a scene in front of everyone that demonstrates the challenge. Give them three or so minutes to act out the scene. Directly after, have those in the audience "identify successful and unsuccessful 'chunks' from the scene that they just observed," first by talking out their reaction in pairs, then in groups of four, and then by sharing out with the larger group to make sure all are engaged and included.[110] Putting together elements of the chunks deemed successful, everyone in the audience who observed the scene should then get into groups of three to four and act out a new prototype within their groups. Participants from each group will then come up in front of everyone to improvise this new prototype, and this process can continue for as many rounds as it takes to collectively arrive at one or more prototypes worth putting into action. You can have participants replay scenes if they don't seem to connect well with the audience, invite role changes beyond each participants' typical jobs, or even have someone play creative director.

Debrief questions: What parts of the scenes were successful or unsuccessful? What new choices might be made? What elements from these scenes (or newly prototyped scenes) should we put into action?

Applications: As researchers have found, we need this kind of "contained chaos" and "white space" for creativity and innovation to thrive.[111] Some examples of how this exercise helps participants lead adaptively include "hospital trainers [who] have substituted Improv Prototyping for conventional courses," "for sales reps to invent new ways to interact with their customers," "for managers to make their interactions with people who report to them more productive," "for health-care providers to practice end-of-life and palliative-care conversations with patients and family members," and "for teachers to discover effective responses to disruptive classroom behaviors."[112]

Fuse Tasks with Relationships

Many ideas about management and leadership point toward how focused individuals are on either tasks or relationships in their working lives.[113] Some people work better by themselves, such as many computer engineers who write code or have a knack for fixing technologies. On the other hand, some people can't imagine a working life without interactions with others, such as salespeople. With a recognition of how integral tasks and relationships are to leadership and our professional lives, applied improvisation teaches us to fuse both. In fact, without a strategic concentration on both people and tasks, effective leadership is impossible. Applied improvisation follows leadership studies that, for instance, exemplify needs for "three task-oriented behavior categories (enhancing understanding, strengthening motivation and facilitating implementation) and three relation-oriented behavior categories (fostering coordination, promoting cooperation and activating resources)."[114]

To lead well, an individual must cultivate strong organizational performances. At the same time, stewarding the relationships for bringing about that kind of performance takes conscious effort.

Improvisation contributes to this leadership practice by showing how tasks and relationships are always happening at the same time. Relationships form the inner circle of this pairing, while tasks are at the outer core, however. If you put two human beings together, the question of "who are we to each other" is always present. It's the starting position. A manager who has to advise a direct report about the need to use a ten-point checklist when they are on the phone with a constituent may think that this message is all about the task to be accomplished. Yet the recipient will always implicitly assess the relationship with the manager in this request. From past experience, if the manager isn't found credible, has acted inconsiderately, or has invested little time in building rapport with staff, the chances that the task will be carried out grudgingly or with minimal effort are heightened. This takes the idea of reading the subtext (identified in chapter 3) to the level of organizational development.

Why aren't tasks at the core? If you ever watch excellent improvisational theater, you'll notice that at the center of what makes scenes electrifying to watch are the unfolding relationships between the actors. The two improvisers' tasks are important to the scenes, but they aren't the chief engine for engaging an audience. Two improvisers pretending to bag groceries at the supermarket isn't enough fuel for a scene. But two improvisers bagging groceries who are secretly in love but haven't had the gumption to tell the other yet, well, that's a scene worth watching. The point is that whatever tasks we're engaged in will necessarily take on the relational character that forms the basis for those tasks to begin with. You can support this idea in a training by having two individuals come up and improvise a short scene in which only a task takes place (e.g., stapling papers), compared to a replayed version where a specific relationship has been formed between the two improvisers (e.g., a boss and employee stapling papers and expressing how much they like being part of an organization with little hierarchy).

Great relationships form the basis for outstanding achievement, so leaders should be working on their relationships with as many people as possible across an organization (parallel to improvising up and down the system), while holding those relationships to the highest standards of achievement and performance possible. Yet above all, as leadership studies confirm, "leadership is necessarily a relational phenomenon."[115] One analysis even determined "that effective communication and relations-oriented leadership were the best predictors of satisfaction, motivation, and organizational commitment" from staff.[116]

At the same time, it's important to consider tasks and relationships as matters that can be changed, so a distinction between the overall culture that may be hard to change and the development of micro-climates that are subject to leadership interventions is helpful. Caitlin McClure argues that these climates must be created, since "an organization shares one culture—traditions, values, history—and multiple climates, each the result of individual team leaders. Culture is typically inferred and difficult to change. Climate, however, is easily observable, can be readily changed, and a positive climate directly correlates with productivity and innovation," where employees feel safe emotionally, get the organization's purposes, share control, and interact authentically.[117]

I've heard many coaches over the years prompt improvisational performers with the question, "What does this scene need?" This question is intended to get improvisers to switch from a mindset of "What can I add to this scene?" (working from the self outward) to "What do the other actors and what's happening in this scene need from me?" (working from what's externally happening to provide fitting, adaptive responses). To fuse tasks with relationships, start with the "external focus" highlighted in the last chapter, scanning the environment for opportunities to address what's there, rather than starting from one's own perspective. The tasks that need accomplished should arise from focusing on people (prioritizing relationships), but leaders should also keep tasks and relationship in an improvised dialectic, never losing sight of one or the other in their day to day work. An organization with great relationships but where little is accomplished will fail, after all.

Box 4.7
Leading Tasks and Relationships

World's Worst Leader

In this exercise, participants will improvise bad employee performance reviews.[118] Ask for two audience volunteers to come up front, and then ask the two participants to improvise a conversation for one minute or so illustrating terrible leadership practices with the ideas of "tasks" and "relationships" in mind. The person giving the feedback may choose to be only task- or relationship-focused, for example.

Debrief questions: Use concepts from this chapter to ask questions about how leadership could have been practiced more adaptively and productively—using the task and relationship distinction to generate ideas for how the observed actions could have been different. Segue to a longer discussion about participants' own experiences with good and bad leadership.

Applications: Like improv prototyping, this type of exercise is, as Steve Kakos says, "a way to exaggerate the things we do wrong to unlock what works."[119] This goes hand in hand with creativity research highlighting how "creative individuals alternate between imagination and fantasy at one end, and a rooted sense of reality at the other."[120]

Variation: You can also ask the audience for suggestions of other situations between a leader and subordinate where bad leadership practices can be observed (such as a presentation on a new policy, crisis management, and more).

❧

Applied improv gets participants to transcend their physical, emotional, and intellectual boundaries, moving them beyond their typical default settings into the territory of adaptive organizational and societal leadership. If, as Peter Drucker said, "leadership is lifting a person's vision to higher sights, the raising of a person's performance to a higher standard, the building of a personality beyond its normal limitations,"[121] then applied improvisation provides a path to these ends. And as Paul Newton writes, since "changing circumstances require the ability to adapt immediately," "improvisation is the development of a skill set that allows for exactly that type of automatic adjustment. Those interested in leadership should pay close attention to the pedagogy of improvisation."[122] The calling is toward a moral, dynamic flexibility. Such "ethical leaders are people dancing over ever changing terrain to often changing music while trying to balance community, individualism; freedom-justice-equality-order and compassion; competency with cold bureaucracy; ambition with tyranny; and conscience with dogmatism and inaction."[123] The lessons explained in this chapter provide an advanced vocabulary for threading improvisational leadership practices into our lives.

The astounding number of connections between applied improv and extant and emerging leadership research only raises the stakes for this kind of work.

Overall, this is a type of leadership education that finally pushes learning into the body. Scholars have lamented how "one of the outcomes of academic education is a fear of the body, or at least a detachment from it. Academics tend to be disembodied. Academic education is focused on developments from the neck upward."[124] Using applied improvisation toward the ends of creating adaptive leaders engages the mind and the body to create an experiential form of education that forces individuals to confront their practices in process.

By repeating core exercises and inviting dissonance between one's baseline practices and other ways of operating, learners perceive the transfer of learning as immediate and memorable. Since "leaders learn more from their challenging leadership experiences when they are in learning mode, defined as intentionally framing and pursuing each element of the experiential learning process with more of a growth than a fixed mindset,"[125] applied improvisation invites participants to examine their habits and stretch. Pedagogical research underscores that for learning to be effective it must provide some motivating discomfort joined with opportunities to engage with diverse contexts and practice cognitive flexibility.[126]

To this point, everything that has been said about communication and leadership in this book applies equally to the development of skills in democracy and citizenship. In this day and age, education guru Ken Bain says that learners need to become "adaptive experts" who "enjoy and know how to improvise, invent, and overcome unexpected obstacles. Our society needs adaptive experts, whether it is to address the ravages of climate change, fix a sagging economy, or end wars."[127] To bring this overarching goal of this project firmly into view, the next chapter will cover how applied improvisation can be used to train participants in civic skills, building a vocabulary to scale improv for democracy in our local and global communities.

Chapter 5

Using Improv to
Develop Civic Excellence

A remarkable number of improv-based programs have sprung up nationally and internationally to build civic and communal bonds between citizens, often under the most vexing conditions. In Michigan, for example, the Detroit Creativity Project has been "helping Detroit youth transform their lives by teaching them to improvise, a tool that fosters collaboration and respect for others, builds literacy, and encourages taking risks in a safe, supportive setting."[1] Through a wealth of after-school and other programs, the project has had an incredible impact on students and the public school system. Beth Hagenlocker, who sits on the program's board of directors, shares how "one of our improv classes is held during the last period on Friday at the high school in the Southeastern Detroit neighborhood. There is 98% attendance for our class, compared to 60% attendance school-wide. . . . Student improvisers have had two-fold growth in their overall academic achievement at one of the middle schools."[2] Once students encounter the full range of intellectual, emotional, and physical powers that improvisation unleashes, it's hard to turn back.

Similarly, in Massachusetts, after years of escalating violence, a program called Urban Improv has used an improv curriculum to teach young people violence prevention, empathy, conflict resolution, self-awareness, and collaborative decision-making. On its website, Urban Improv describes how "professional actor/educators lead interactive workshops that offer students the opportunity to explore their own solutions to challenging, real-life situations."[3] After a multi-year evaluation, researchers determined that "the program has been proven effective in preventing increased or new-onset of aggressive behaviors with elementary school children, while also increasing pro-social behaviors."[4] As mentioned previously, it was the original vision of Spolin and others that improvisation should move outside its associations with acting and entertainment to have applications in non-theatrical contexts. With measured success, that vision has reemerged.

Beyond improv as an individual and organizational practice, it's time to start thinking about the larger ways in which applied improvisation can be scaled systemically as a societal contribution. Some international examples are already leading the way. Working on the US–Mexico border, the Institute for Improvisation and Social Action's mission is to "use performance and improvisation to empower communities through programs, workshops, classes and performances in El Paso, TX and Ciudad Juarez, Chihuahua, Mexico." The Institute seeks "to promote artistic and social development by bringing professional artists and art educators together with at-risk populations to build collaborative spaces where we can create new performances, allowing participants to see alternatives to the way they live and relate to others and the world."[5] After one of these experiences, one participant from Juarez related how "I am taking so many tools to build with people in my community. You gave me a different perspective on what we are," while another participant noted that "this workshop teaches [us] how to live in harmony with others."[6] Using improv to find novel ways of connecting people, these types of programs are breaking beyond boundaries, fashioning new forms of civic engagement.

In another global context, on the forty-fifth anniversary of martial law in the Philippines, the improv theater SPIT in Manila developed performances of "protest improv" to speak to political events in the country. Through these experiences, SPIT actor Happy Feraren shares how it's "important that this is something that's happening outside the online realm where everybody is so vicious, [where] there's so much misinformation and disinformation. . . . There's so much hate online, so I think it's also good that we get out of this bubble and be with other people physically." Fellow actor Ariel Diccion further notes, "I think joining these kinds of events, *inaangkin mo na* (you're owning them) I am an individual person and I am interacting with different people, different bodies and individuals. The physicality I think is very important."[7] Whether it's constructing public outcomes for violence reduction or creating separate spaces for citizens to do new political work, it's now critical to build on (yes, and) this emerging work.

This chapter takes up the task of creating explicitly civic connections with applied improvisation. Improvisation can contribute to the efforts of countless groups around the world promoting dialogue, deliberation, and other forms of civic participation. As argued throughout this book, excellent communication and leadership skills are civic competencies—these concepts can't be separated in the practice of building democracy from person to person and organization to organization. Martín Carcasson highlights that "citizenship skills in this country are practically in a state of crisis," so following the pattern I've laid out in this book, a first step is to foster the "improvement of communication skills to address differences."[8] But for the sake of pushing applied improvisation more firmly into the realm of civic engagement, I will thread together the lessons, exercises, and examples in this chapter with literature on politics and the development of democratic communication and communities. A civic context can guide contemporary learning applications, determining the "what, and how, to teach."[9] In particular, I'll focus on how improv can be used to bridge differences with others as its central contribution to civic engagement.

Box 5.1
From Competitor to Collaborator

Adversarial Supporter

This exercise is based on the classic game of "Rock, Paper, Scissors," but with a surprising twist.[10] It's worth running simply for the incredible energy that it unleashes in a group at the beginning of a class or workshop, yet it also makes a point about civic skills quickly and effectively. Have everyone in your group pair up. Let them know that they will face off in the game of "Rock, Paper, Scissors." Demonstrate what this process should look like with one participant, saying the words "rock, paper, scissors, shoot" together at the same time. On the word "shoot," each person will pick one of the three options (rock breaks scissors, scissors cut paper, paper covers rock). For large groups, have everyone only play one round to determine who wins. For smaller groups, I like to have everyone play the best two of three rounds to determine who wins. Whoever wins the first round should then find another person in the group who won their round to face off in the next. The person who lost—and this is the most important part—should become the biggest fan of the person who won. They should clap, cheer, and continue shouting that person's name as the winner faces off against the new opponent. Everyone after the first round will have a fan who cheers for them. In the second round, the winner will now have three fans moving forward (the person who lost, their supporter, and the fan who carried over from the first round). This process should continue until there are two final participants who have an equal number of fans cheering for them on both sides. Ask everyone to give a big round of applause for the final winner.

Debrief questions: What did this process feel like? How has the tone in the room changed?

Applications: Since it's the first exercise where I try to point everyone toward civic skills, I like to draw my conclusion explicitly: the key moment here was the turn from an adversary to supporter, which is a fundamental skill for society. Great improvisation relies on overriding our competitive and egotistical impulses to see others in a new light. That decision is ours and can be improvised in a split second. Not only did the energy and interest of engaging with one another pick up palpably in the room when this turn was made (for most, a playful spirit followed), but those continuing in the competition likely felt emboldened and connected with others in subsequent rounds as a result of that choice. The takeaway is clear: think about how many everyday encounters we have with others that, whether consciously or not, are framed in an adversarial fashion, and how we have the power in any one of those moments to quickly improvise support. The laughter that emerged in the room in this exercise has significance too. When we're in a joyful, collegial mindset it's hard to engage in unproductive forms of conflict.

Inquire Openly and Earnestly

One of the hardest skills for many citizens to cultivate is the ability to inquire about others' beliefs, values, and attitudes openly and earnestly. To do so, every human being faces an uphill battle. In its default position, the human brain likes the feeling of superiority, seeks to reduce dissonant information at every opportunity, and tends to have a hard time going against group repetitions.[11] People can become so wedded to their own views and ways of operating that any point of difference can automatically serve as a mechanism for excluding others. In addition to cognitive biases that make us want to filter information through the frames of what we already believe, we each come from particular backgrounds, with particular crowd and familial loyalties, and with many unexamined commitments that make it incredibly hard to step into others' shoes and try to understand the world from their perspectives. This is an area where applied improvisation can do some of its greatest societal work.

As just some examples, whether working with a group of students, with public workshop participants, or in an employment training focusing on organizational citizenship, the skill of inquiring openly and earnestly is about improvising with a learning orientation. Approaching others first and foremost with the idea that "I stand to learn something from you" changes the nature of all relationships. In a demonstration of a youth and police dialogue that applied the "yes, and" technique to inquire openly and earnestly between differing sides, Omar Ali and Nadja Cech describe a key moment when

> to shut down the police officer with a "no, because" response would have been to stop the conversation and miss out on an opportunity for growth and development of the group. Keeping the conversation open to multiple perspectives (rather than one "right" way of seeing things) allows for the possibility of a deeper understanding for all involved. And while deeper understanding may not lead to justice (or perceived justice) at the macro- or institutional level, in an immediate sense, it helps to diffuse tensions. As importantly, it builds a relationship between participants that might make all the difference, at a later time, if they are confronted either directly with each other, or with officers or young people who remind them of each other.[12]

Note how the authors of this passage position open and honest inquiry with learning to stand in different subject positions that can have a bearing on future situations. To inquire openly and earnestly doesn't mean letting go of one's dearest beliefs and values, but rather doing all possible to start from and recognize others' viewpoints before moving to one's own. That order matters for building civic bonds. Benjamin Barber argued that "at the heart of strong democracy is talk,"[13] so any activity that can act as a precursor to or have participants engage in robust forms of conversation contributes to society. David Mathews, too, relates how "citizens in communities that are accustomed to interactive public talk will not tolerate panel discussions and speeches. They insist instead on engaging one another."[14] In my experience, once people get used to this way of operating with one another, they don't want to go back. The concept of inquiring openly and honestly builds on the kind of external focus and give and take that are improv's hallmarks.

Box 5.2
Performing Civic Engagement

Performing Curiosity

I learned this remarkable exercise from Cathy Salit, who created it to help people break through a key performance barrier in their professional lives.[15] It gets to the heart of what it means to improvise with an attitude of open and honest inquiry. First have everyone break up into groups of three. One person will be the questioner, one will be the talker, and one will be the coach. Give everyone a moment to choose who will play each role. Next, each group should pick a controversial topic, or you can bring some prepared controversial topics that they can choose from, such as abortion, gun control, or drug legalization. The questioner should tell the talker what their true viewpoint is on that topic. The talker must then take the opposite viewpoint and begin making statements and expressing opinions about the topic from that position. The questioner should ask questions in response to the talker's statements. Each coach will make sure that the questioner is only, as Salit puts it, "performing curiosity" with the talker as the conversation continues. There are three rules that the coach must enforce: the questioner should only perform authentic and curious questioning (as opposed to leading questions, questions with a judgmental tone, or statements—the coach can say "Try again with more curiosity" if the questioner goes off track), only ask open-ended questions, and make sure that the questions are always related to what the other person last said. Put these three rules on a flip chart or screen so that the coaches can refer to them throughout the exercise.

Debrief questions: Have each group of participants share what they experienced in the conversation. What was challenging about it? How could these practices be applied in your own lives? How does this exercise relate to current societal problems and potential solutions?

Applications: Draw your participants' attention to the skill of inquiring openly and earnestly. Salit underscores how everyone in this exercise is performing; in fact, almost of all life's situations can be viewed through the lens of performance. I also like to link this exercise with what Jay and Grant call "dynamic authenticity," or the ability to get unstuck in relationships by operating with a genuine willingness to change.[16]

Paraphrase Connections

This exercise is excellent for getting two people with different viewpoints to find common ground and build together.[17] Have your participants get into pairs and ask them to find something that they truly disagree about. This must be an authentic point of disagreement (this is the most important part for the exercise to work) that they actually have. It doesn't have to be about a monumental issue; for example, they could disagree about their preference for dogs versus cats, or being a morning or night person. One person should make a statement about the topic from their own viewpoint, for example "Dogs are better than cats because they're always more excited to see you." This participant should not try to go longer than ten to twenty seconds in their statement. The recipient should then paraphrase back what the first person said (the paraphrase doesn't need to be exact, but must maintain the essence of what the other person said). At the end of the paraphrase, they must say "Is that accurate?" The first person should say "Yes" if so. If not, the recipient must try to paraphrase the other's statement again, until the first person agrees to its accuracy. Then the second participant should make a statement about their views on the topic for no longer than ten to twenty seconds. This process should go back and forth for a few minutes.

Debrief questions: Ask the participants how they felt and what they noticed in conducting this exercise. How was this different from the way conversations about points of disagreement usually go?

Applications: By being forced to paraphrase the other person's statements each step of the way, you'll notice that participants take on the kind of learning orientation that's the basis for inquiring openly and earnestly. They'll be listening to one another with more intensity and interest, and not going into their heads and rehearsing their arguments, since they can't state their own view without first getting the other's. Every group that I've done this exercise with finds that they're not used to conducting charged conversations in this manner, but find this different process much more satisfying. Most of the time, one of the best parts of this exercise is that the participants find themselves gradually coming together and finding common ground as they articulate their differences. To finish out this exercise, I like to raise the poignant Mahatma Gandhi quote: "Three-fourths of the miseries and misunderstandings in the world will disappear if we step into the shoes of our adversaries and understand their standpoint."[18]

Transcend Your Physiology

The body plays a role in the development of civic skills. A lot has been covered to this point on the connections between improvisation and body language, status, and more. Yet one of the chief contributions that improvisation can make to civic discourse is the capacity to shift talk of democracy only as a matter of ideas (this bias is built into terms such as "ideology," for instance) to the role of physiology in maintaining or changing political positions. Lerner argues that "stimulating peoples' sense[s] is essential" for "preparing them to participate meaningfully [in society]. . . . Once people get used to moving, speaking, listening, and looking carefully, they are more likely to carry over these habits into later activities."[19] Improvisation certainly awakens these capacities.

Yet improv can also train for what I call "transcending your physiology." As detailed earlier, our default settings often prevent us from improvising well. Improvisers have long known that much more is often communicated via actions rather than dialogue, so that "much of what you do is determined by what is *not* said. In fact, most of what you communicate in life and onstage is determined by your behavior, not by what you say. A grunt can communicate much more than a poetic speech. A shrug can be more meaningful than a witty one-liner."[20] In terms of civic skills, these understandings teach us to that we have to rise above our standard ways of operating to bridge differences with others. As right or entitled as we all are to our political opinions, if the only emotion we ever express when someone raises a divisive political topic is rage, then we're going to have a difficult time making friends. On the flip side, if a person only withdraws or plays neutral in political discussions, then they may be failing to raise their voice about a topic that really matters.

The point here isn't about reducing one's political orientations to, for example, being civil or not (there are times when civility can get in the way of important advocacy[21]). Rather, the civic skill of transcending your physiology invites us to recognize how wrapped up our physiology gets with certain political orientations and to skillfully rise above them to connect with others. Bodily responses such as disgust, anger, or pride are automatic, and we're often right to feel such responses. But they can also keep us bound and unable to practice social flexibility or to express different emotions. Ultimately, then, the goal of transcending your physiology is to function with greater freedoms that promote better relationships.

No one has done more work on the connections between our moral psychologies, deep emotions, and politics than Jonathan Haidt, who finds that many of our civic problems arise from the entrenched positions our bodies form in particular communities around contentious issues.[22] Arabella Lyon also conceives of democracy in terms of "performative deliberation," situating the body, relationships, and speech acts at the very center of what it means to make practical decisions and exist in communities (over and above traditional understandings of democratic decision-making as about procedures or persuasion).[23] Under these terms, civic apathy stems from a "lack of possibilities to perform, express, and maintain relevant identities."[24] Finding ways to transcend these responses is critical to working with others in a democratic fashion.

Applied improvisation helps us get in touch with the performative aspects of our political selves and opens up spaces to think about alternative possibilities for acting. This lesson ultimately achieves what Boal argued should happen in education: citizens should realize that being passive in the civic realm is itself a political act, so finding methods for liberating both the mind and body is critical to civic engagement.[25] The first two exercises for performing civic engagement in this chapter demonstrate how to transcend one's physiology, especially in overriding certain impulses so we can show others that we are truly there: present, engaged, and willing to bridge differences.

Play to Engage

Jesuit priest Gregory Boyle, who has worked with former gang members in Los Angeles for decades, says that his services are about not "helping" but "finding kinship" with those he serves, fulfilling our "our common calling to delight in one another."[26] Boyle's programs demonstrate that finding delight in and cultivating playfulness with others are more than nice add-ons to life—they are core civic virtues. Indeed, research shows that people like one another more after playing games with each other.[27] In a political world where rancor and divisiveness reign, where people hunker down in their social media enclaves and often don't venture beyond the confines of their groups and communities to experience new ideas or people, these findings are significant.

When it comes to thinking about civic skills, it's easier to imagine serious people sitting down and saying serious things to one another than it is to imagine how play or joy could have any connection to what they're doing. This range of what's thinkable about the role of play in our lives needs to change. Play expert Stuart Brown confirms that "when we play, we are engaged in the purest expression of our humanity. . . . Is it any wonder that often the times we feel most alive, those that make up our best memories, are moments of play?"[28] If play can get people to approach one another in productive ways, it should play a central role in the development of civic engagement.

I've found repeatedly that rooms filled with tension, bitterness, and negativity dissolve instantaneously under the guidance of applied improvisation. Participants find themselves laughing and creating joy together in a way that's difficult to argue against. This has wider applications for society above and beyond helping people in organizations do their work with one another. In this book's opening story of police and youth clashing in the Netherlands, remember that it was only after playing improvisational games with one another that the police officers found themselves relinquishing their negativity toward the boys. Even Spolin asserted that "Play is democratic! Anyone can play! . . . Play touches and stimulates vitality, awakening the whole person."[29] Play functions to equalize the statuses constructed in our day-to-day lives in a fun way. Games are also more intuitive and accessible than many rationalistic forms of political discourse.

There's broad support for this idea, which can be used to frame an entire class or training, or can simply be referenced to get people thinking about the applications of play to learning and communal development. Mihaly Csikszentmihalyi's concept of "flow," or "the mental state in which a person performing an activity is fully immersed in a feeling of energized focus, full involvement, and enjoyment in the process of the activity,"[30] has applications for playing to engage. According to the psychologist, good societies foster forms of expression that serve the needs of people and proliferate options for their lives, so "the most powerful effect flow theory could have in the public sector is in providing a blueprint for how institutions may be reformed so as to make them more conducive to optimal experience." In other words, learning to enjoy life can't be disconnected from humanity's evolution.[31]

A political environment in which people feel devalued, demoralized, and incapable of exerting agency over their lives is a setup for civic failure. Chris Barker and Brian Martin note that we must "increase opportunities for people to experience flow in their roles as citizens—what might be called citizen flow—[so] creative ideas are needed for ways to enable people to gradually improve and exercise their participatory skills."[32] Reforming organizations and societal structures to build infectious, positive energies that advance humanity and joy can set the conditions, attitudes, and desire for continued involvement in civic life.

Playing to engage is one way to build these kinds of approaches, with a ready-made set of exercises and games that can act as precursors to headier forms of civic engagement. Both scholars and practitioners underscore how "improved democratic attitudes" and "improved democratic skills" are first-order goals of civic engagement, and have begged for the building of micro-level, ground-up approaches to address these issues, especially through activities that are "specifically designed to create different forms of interactions that avoid simply pointing fingers and spouting cynical frustrations."[33] The connections with playing to engage should be clear. At the same time, there's a paradox about play, which is that "the more importance you place on an improvisational experience, the less likely you are to play"—in other words, "it's the unrestrained, carefree playing around that leads to funny and exciting choices."[34] So letting go and giving oneself the freedom to "just play" (advice I've heard constantly in the improv world: drop the rules for the sake of "just playing") means that critical civic work does not always have to follow instrumental functions.

Although I've separated the trajectories of improv for comedy entertainment from improv for communication, leadership, and civic skills in this book, these boundaries collapse when it comes to the topic of humor in public affairs. As a by-product of play, humor can connect with civic engagement. Postman once said that "a sense of humor is at the core of all our humane impulses,"[35] and there's certainly a great deal of support to back up this idea. In the previously mentioned Urban Improv Workshops, contrary to a perception that "students who are laughing and having fun are out of control," in an overall evaluation of the effects of its work, fourth-graders in the program "showed less aggression and were more engaged in class" and "the participant group showed more cooperation, self-control, and engagement in class than the control group."[36] These findings beckon a shift in many teaching and training paradigms.

Play, humor, and laughter can serve civic purposes by building empathy and setting a positive tone that frames conversations and subsequent actions. Indeed, "a staggering amount of data, emerging from biological research and from imaging technology, provides compelling evidence linking humor and learning," especially to attention, comprehension, memory, and creating a nurturing environment.[37] Some studies identify humor as an important component in creating social trust.[38] Comedian John Cleese summarizes this perspective perfectly: "When you have a lot of warm, friendly, funny faces coming at you, you respond very naturally . . . I'm struck by how laughter connects you to people. It's almost impossible to maintain any kind of distance or any sense of social hierarchy when you're just howling with laughter. Laughter is a force for democracy."[39] To implement these ideas, look for opportunities to have participants in classes or other events play with one another before or during civic teaching and work.

Affirm the Negative

Politics has always been filled with negativity between those of differing beliefs. But negativity doesn't need to lead to animosity; it can be used for creative inspiration. Given improvisation's roots in theater and comedy, the idea that negativity should be affirmed might initially seem perplexing. Improvisers view the world through the lens of "offers," however, so that any remark, move, or event is seen as something to build on or "yes, and"—at its heart, this is all about respecting what others do first. That includes negative information. Rather than avoid what has actually happened, improvisers can affirm the negative by recognizing that such offers are always made to express some motivation and create reactions in others.

For example, in a political discussion a Democrat might say to a Republican "Republicans don't care about the poor." A bitter feud could certainly follow such remarks, with the Republican pushing back with "That's not true, and all Democrats are idiots," and so on. To affirm the negative, these discussants don't need to agree with the opinions of the other person, but they can at least *first* signal a recognition that the negative statements mean something and aren't coming out of nowhere. The truth or falsity of the belief doesn't need affirmed, but that person's humanity and need for affirmation can be. The Republican in this example could respond with

"I hear you, I've heard many remarks from others like this too," "It's true that there are Republicans who don't care about the poor (just as there are Democrats who don't care about the poor either)," or even a genuinely curious question such as "You've probably seen too many examples of this, what are one or two that best illustrate the point?"

The idea is to affirm that the negative statement happened and, before retreating into instant divisiveness, make a joint attempt to build on what's been said. Don't get the impression that what you're doing is ceding control completely to the other person, though. Far from it. By affirming the negative you'll take the initial offer and build on it with an expectation that further responses are needed. In the process, if you "yes, and" the other person's information, inevitably you'll be adding your own information in a way that'll end up transforming the initial offer into a new, shared reality. What started as an attempt at division will turn into mutual exploration. Choose to respond rather than judge. You may still end up fundamentally disagreeing about the issue at stake, but the attempt to build on the negative viewpoint offered will likely change the tenor, direction, and productivity of the conversation.

The adaptive leadership principles of finding and cultivating connections with unlikely partners in the opposition also relates to affirming the negative. Forcing yourself to spend time with those resistant to your views has the following benefit: "You will never seem as evil in person as you can be in people's imagination. Simply spending time in their presence can help take the edge off their hostility and thus soften their determination to block your efforts."[40] If anything, treating the other person's opposition with respect can be so unusual that it's disarming. The two exercises below illustrate this concept in practice.

Box 5.3
Transforming the Negative

Conflict Defaults

Variations of this exercise show up in a lot of conflict management or negotiation trainings, but my favorite version is Tammy Lenski's.[41] Do this demonstration with one other participant so that everyone can see how this works. As the instructor, put your hand into a fist shape and hold it out in front of the other person, as if you're going to fist bump. Ask the other person to also make the same fist. Rather than do a fist bump, though, ask them to "put" their fist against your own (Lenski says using the word "put" is important). Once your fists touch, add some slight resistance to their fist. You should notice that they'll push back equally in response. Ask them why they're pressing back against your fist (that wasn't part of the instructions, after all). Their response should be that you pressed against their fist so they pressed against yours. Now increase the pressure and you'll notice theirs automatically increases too. Ask again why they pushed back and they'll often respond with some version of their previous response. Decrease the pressure now and you should notice an equivalent decrease from their end. Ask them why they decreased their pressing against your first.

Debrief questions: In addition to the questions you ask the participant about why they increased or decreased their pressure, ask the audience what they think this exercise highlights about social or political conflict.

Applications: Lenski notes that she has never met anyone who failed to increase or decrease their pressure in response, and that's been my experience too. She relates, "I don't like someone to feel duped or stupid, so I always make a point of highlighting that every single person does the same thing they did. I tell them that it's like we're wired to deliver exactly the amount of force we feel like we're receiving and that's why, in conflict, things can get so stuck. We push, they push back. They push, we push back. And since so much of the pushing happens subconsciously, resistance builds stealthily until we grind to a frustrated halt."[42] Along these lines, introduce participants to the idea that affirming the negative isn't pushing back against the other person's offer ("negating the negative"), but could include other choices such as pulling back with less resistance against the fist pressure, or something entirely different such as opening one's hand and offering a high five to the other person. More often than not, affirming the negative involves breaking a pattern with an unexpected move that first affirms and then attempts to transform the initial offer. Affirming the negative involves any other choices that attempt to work with the offer and build on it toward a new reality. This exercise also illustrates how we have to transcend our physiology to practice excellent civic skills.

Obstacle Inspiration

In this exercise, participants will practice novel ways to confront obstacles and other challenges.[43] Have everyone get into a circle. One person should turn to the person to their right and say "I'm finally going after my big dream of _____" (e.g., learning to speak a foreign language), to which the next person on the right will respond with a line that turns the dream into an obstacle, such as "Well, you can't do that because _____" (e.g., learning foreign languages has been banned by the government). The next person to the right will then create a third line that uses the obstacle as inspiration for a productive melding of the two prior lines, such as "Well, it's a good thing I have _____" (e.g., a special membership with the ACLU and they are fighting that ban!).[44] Continue around the circle until everyone has had a chance to play all three roles.

Debrief question: What do you think this exercise has to do with the concept of affirming the negative?

Applications: Where the exercise began with an exciting initial offer, the second response constituted a negative block. The critical moment is the third person's role: this person could have chosen to engage in a negative block in response (e.g., "No it didn't"), but instead chose to affirm the negative response and build on it, offering new ground in the conversation by working with rather than against what was offered. Negative or critical information can be used as a means of inspiration.

Exercise Narrative Flexibility

The stories that we tell create the worlds that we live in. If you consume lots of media filled with violence and conflict, the world will likely become a mean and scary place to you.[45] If you learn to tell different stories about the possibilities for compassion and respect, the world will take on a different cast. It's critical to tell our personal stories and try to create narratives that lead to productive futures for us all, but a critical part of democratic life involves respecting, building, and sometimes even outright rejecting a range of different stories.[46] This can all be summed up through the skill of exercising narrative flexibility. Assuming that no person is all-knowing and all of us have to rely on other people to learn and grow, flexible storytelling is at the heart of what it means to be humane. The capacity to edit or add to old stories, create new ones, and engage with stories beyond our own can't be separated from our civic lives and the need to stretch beyond the boundaries of living in small, limiting worlds.[47] Even in the hard sciences the ability to amend and update stories has been crucial to modern research breakthroughs.[48]

Fixed stories about the world that brook no dissent or alternative interpretations become self-sealing and communally destructive. John Burtis and Paul Turman write that "citizenship is the obligation to help your group to thrive. This includes engagement in the co-constructions and reconstructions of your group's story/experience: past, present, and future."[49] Similarly, James Carse argues that "*Evil is the termination of infinite play.* . . . Evil is not the inclusion of finite games in an infinite game, but the restriction of all play to one or another finite game."[50] Politics becomes evil and our communal lives become squelched when restricted to only one way of operating. Totalitarian regimes seek to restrict citizens' views to only one story or game for a reason—they want to pursue the fantasy that it's possible to forgo all of the incredible differences in human experience to only one consuming vision. This is why book burning (destroying the availability of other stories) is all the rage in fascist governments.

Restricting stories makes improvisation impossible. You cannot improvise if there's a set template from which you're always meant to perform. Improv shows us how scripted our lives can become and offers opportunities for unscripting and rescripting.[51] Barnett Pearce finds that "most of the stories humankind has told itself feature the importance of maintaining deep enmeshment in the local system," so much that anything that creates a rupture from these systems can help citizens break out of patterns and think from a larger, societal standpoint.[52] We are temporarily taken out of our narrative enmeshments through games, which transport us into alternate worlds or spaces, even for only a moment, to play with and view our stories anew.

In this sense, improvisation and propaganda are polar opposites. The ability to exercise narrative flexibility keeps one open to surprise and innovation, which often comes through fictional storytelling or role playing in improvisational teaching and training. Different than propagandistic forms of communication that limit thought and action at every turn, "fictionalizing is a form of play that allows us to stage an endless number of ideas about the human condition."[53] Playing with different scenarios, roles, and stories shakes us out of rigidified patterns.

To be clear, I'm not suggesting that any narrative is as good as any other, and this isn't to reject stories that you may hold dear, such as life-altering personal experiences or faith narratives. Instead I'm arguing for a greater recognition that our stories are necessarily partial and prone to biases, and that there are always selections being made in the language and framing of any story. Brian McLaren brings this point home in describing how even a figure like Jesus was always selective in his language—he quoted particular portions of the Old Testament in the sayings attributed to him in the New Testament, leaving certain words and phrases outside the scope of his selections.[54] An essential aspect of being human is that we're always selective in our communication and the stories that we tell, and improvisation brings out these truths in both ideas and practice. Overall, "in improvisation, intersubjective truth is negotiated, and experience is mediated through language,"[55] fostering what some call an attitude of "ironic enmeshment."[56]

Improv for comedy entertainment gets interesting when change happens. If you do the same thing for too long on stage audiences get bored, but if an actor starts crying the audience will look "not because crying is interesting, but because change is interesting."[57] Transferred to other areas of experience, people who expect their life narratives will change and who prepare to improvise well for such turns are practicing a civic skill. The Second City improv theater provides a great example, where military veterans have been taking improv classes to transition back to civilian life; having been changed by new narratives of military experience, for many veterans reentry into society necessarily involves living in an updated story. One student, James Taku Leung, shared how he "wished courses like this were taught when he was first getting ready to leave the military. It would have made that transition a lot easier," since "we came from a place where we had purpose and pride and suddenly we're in a world where we don't have direction. . . . Learning how to give yourself direction without a set of directions is a very powerful tool."[58] One's ability to amend, update, or replace stories becomes a crucial competency for individuals at major turning points in their lives.

Exercising narrative flexibility partly has to do with democracy being a process, never an achieved fact, with creativity and playfulness playing a key role in that achievement.[59] In Stephen Asma's terms,

> meeting life with unbending expectations is a recipe for disaster. Those who expect the world to conform to their preset calculations and predictions are destined to be frustrated. They are uncomfortable with spontaneity, and rail against deviations. . . . The bad improviser makes moves that are maladaptive. And the single greatest predictor of quality improv is simply experience. But there's nothing simple about experience. A great jazz improviser such as Miles Davis had thousands of hours of practice and problem-solving underneath every one of his improvisational flights. . . . Muscle memory is loaded with this kind of intuitive wisdom.[60]

Improv forwards narrative flexibility and practices that support democratic deviations and, paradoxically, adaptations to many narratives that allow for more unity than inflexible stories. In the following two exercises, your participants will have a chance to exercise this critical civic skill.

Box 5.4
Improvised Narratives

Story Lines

For this exercise, have eight to ten participants form two lines in front of the audience (so that there are two straight lines of four to five people, each line with one person up front and the rest lined up behind that person).[61] Ask the audience for the name of a famous person (e.g., "Bill Gates") and then ask for any household object (e.g., "a hammer"). Join these to create a story title, "This is the story of Bill Gates's hammer." The two people at the front of each line will be the first to build the story, only one sentence at a time. Do a practice round with both of them to demonstrate to everyone what the exercise looks like. The person in the line to the left should both state the first line of the story and perform one accompanying, memorable action that will go with it (e.g., "One day, Bill Gates woke up," and in saying this, the participant may stretch their arms up high and yawn to signify Bill Gates waking up). Coach your participants to put their statements in terms of actions that can be performed. This gets them out of their heads and into their bodies. The first person will then go to the back of their line while the next person in that line will step to the front. Then have the person at the front of the second line do the first statement and behavior, and add to it with their own statement and behavior to advance the story (e.g., "One day Bill Gates woke up [with yawning motion], and picked up the hammer at his bedside [with picking up motion]"). They will then go to the back of the second line and the person who was behind them will step forward. The story and accompanying motions will then continue with the person at the front of the first line performing both of the original actions and accompanying motions, and then adding their own new line and action. This will continue until someone in one of the lines can no longer remember a part of the preceding story or actions. That person will be eliminated and the story will continue with the next person in the line on the other side. Note that the story should continue from the beginning of the already established narrative. Don't start a new story each time a person is eliminated. The last team/line standing wins.

Debrief question: What do you think this exercise teaches us about storytelling?

Applications: There's a slightly competitive element to this story build between the two lines, but you can emphasize that ultimately the two teams are trying to work together playfully to co-create a narrative that's never been told before. I like to underscore how this game has participants exercise both narrative and expressive flexibility in a way that's conservative (you have to retain elements of the story that came before you) and progressive (you have to create a story that pushes the narrative in new directions).

Narrative Polarities

I have had much success with this simple exercise.[62] Have two participants come up front and face the audience. Ask the group to come up with a title of a story that's never been told before (e.g., "Sara's Journey to Jupiter"). Tell the first person that they will always advance the story with one sentence, and that this information will always be positive. The second person will always advance the story after the first person with another sentence, but their information will always be negative. The first person will then begin one line of this story, similar to the last exercise (e.g., "Sara finally made it through the asteroids and could see Jupiter from her spaceship"). Whenever the first person delivers a line, the audience should always yell "yay" in unison after. The second person will then advance the story with their line (e.g., "But her spaceship was about to run out of fuel"), to which the audience should always yell "boo" after. The two participants should continue going back and forth to build out the story. Reinforce that the first person's line will always make things better, while the second person's lines will make always things worse. Shout out "yay" and "boo" to prompt the audience to repeat the pattern.

Debrief questions: What do you think this exercise teaches us about the stories that we tell? What about the stories that communities, nations, and societies tell?

Applications: Several lessons about narratives can be advanced through this exercise. You'll notice there's an ease with which the participants—

bolstered by the audience's expressions—craft a story. You can underscore how we all create the worlds that we live in through stories, and we have the capacity to craft and recraft the stories we tell each step of the way. We're often unaware of how much of a positive or negative frame we put on our stories, but we have the potential to make these choices and not simply accept the stories we've inherited or that we're currently telling ourselves. There's an endless number of directions these stories can take, and forwarding actions with others allows us to build indefinitely into the future, exploring and taking a number of different paths.

Perspective Shift

Depending on your group size, ask five to seven participants to come up in front of everyone.[63] Two participants should take seats at the side facing the audience. They'll pretend that they are showing the group a slide show of a major event in which they took part (e.g., a vacation, wedding, an international work trip). The other three to five participants will get into different freeze-frame positions of photos in the slide show, which the two individuals on the side will provide commentary over. You can ask the audience for a suggestion of a major event that these two people experienced. The three to five people in the middle should then get into different positions (e.g., one person sitting on the floor, another with their hands in the air, the other pointing and looking like they're yelling at the others). In other words, they should improvise a freeze-framed scene without using any words. You can give them a countdown from ten to get into position. The two commentators should then tell the story of what happened in the scene, providing interpretations of who the people are, where they were, what was going on, and more. Once this has run its course (usually after thirty seconds to a minute), tell the improvisers to "advance the slide," then give those in the frame another ten seconds to get into an entirely new scene/image, which the other two participants will then provide commentary over, and so on. Coach everyone through the first few examples until they get the format.

Debrief questions: What does this exercise teach us about being citizens in society? What practices does it forward for our public and political lives?

Applications: I use "Perspective Shift" to reinforce the lessons of the previous narrative exercises, but also to talk more about the possibility for many different interpretations in any situation. The participants have to exercise narrative flexibility in each slide by remaining open to the emerging commentary and different directions each person contributes to the scenes. Clarity is arrived at through the joint effort of the group. No one person can start with a complete story at the outset. As each slide advances, the overall story will continue to emerge and develop in a co-created fashion—as all narratives do.

Repeat Trust

I've been part of several improvisational groups that have a ritual before every performance. After warming up and trying to focus the body and mind, every performer will pat every other performer on the back and say "I've got your back." This saying sets an expectation that no matter what happens in that performance—perhaps we don't feel like performing, someone screws up (although some people believe there's actually no screw-ups, only offers to build on in improv), or we're not sure what to do—every player will be there to provide support and help out at any point. Even performers sitting on the sidelines during any scene will be prepared to jump in and provide extra bodies, sounds, or scenic elements if it seems like the performance needs it. Carried over to our societal lives, this idea translates to the need for repeating trust with others at every opportunity.

Why the emphasis on "repeat"? Rhetorical scholars (academics who study how persuasion works) have established that repetition is one of the greatest influences on what human beings believe, and these repetitions are more than simply ideas: they manifest themselves deeply in our bodies and actions.[64] It's hard to separate what we think of as "truth" from what's simply been repeated many, many times in our lives. If you live in a society where the mantra "it's a dog-eat-dog world, so you've got to face every situation as a battle" has been repeated to you since childhood, it'll be hard thinking and acting in ways that belie this "truth." While repetition as a technique has certainly been used to do great harm in the world, especially when used toward propagandistic ends, the other side is that we can use repetition for good. Communities that create sustained forms of trust prosper.

Improvisation comes with a ready-made set of structures designed to build trust. Participants might not know that this is happening in the process of engaging in improv, but the architectures of each of the exercises introduced in this book (and the many more games available outside of it) build trust between participants. In the "Story Lines" exercise above, the game can't take place unless a platform of trust is built between the two teams. Although there's some competition at play, the game is constructed on a foundation of others' listening to and advancing what came before.

The applications of this idea to society can already be seen in initiatives like the Detroit Creativity Project. Another noteworthy example is the All Stars Project in New York and other states, which has a program using "performance, improvisation and conversation to help inner-city teenagers and police officers develop a positive relationship." These sessions "give teens and cops the chance to step outside their usual roles and responses and discover new ways of relating."[65] What's clear in the All Stars Project is that the unspoken, existing structures many young people and police use to relate to one another aren't working. On the other hand, applied improvisation builds trust by offering novel ways for such groups to listen to and respond to one another.

Let's not lose sight of the key idea here, though: *repeating* trust is key. Simply having a one-time workshop that builds some trust can showcase how different an improvisational mindset is from an adversarial mindset, hence my argument that these types of structures need to be embedded and scaled in our educational systems and beyond. Improvisational exercises are designed with a long-term process in mind, where "you can see [the] 'armour' peel off layer by layer."[66] When participants practice new positions and roles repeatedly, it's easier for these differences to permeate. This is also why, for instance, Japanese companies often start their work days with collective exercises, because "synchrony builds trust."[67]

One important concept that connects with the idea of repeating trust is creating a "shared reality." For many years, I have taught a course in global communication. There are countless books written for such classes about the need to respect the reality of others' cultures, such as one cultural group's preference for always being on time to events and another cultural group's preference for looser conceptions of time in which being late is just fine.[68] What's lost in a lot of these teachings is that, once two human beings start interacting a great deal, they actually come to create a new, shared reality or "third culture."[69] In other words, over a period of conversing, an alignment between interlocutors occurs that blends both of their perspectives to create something new.

When you've known a good friend for a long time, you often develop your own unique, shared language with that other person that's hard for those outside your interactions to understand. There may be special terms you both allude to or insider references that you've developed. I did this with my late Scottish mother for years. In conversations, we'd perform and repeat scenes that exemplified Scottish–American cultural differences (I'd give you an example, but you won't understand it and that's the point). And in doing so, we were always brought closer together. For me this illustrated a teaching I'd heard at the Groundlings improv theater many times, that "you become what you pretend to be." There's nothing disingenuous about this remark. It gets at the idea that in performing novel realities and pretending to be our better selves with others, we bring into being those very realities and, as a by-product, more trust-filled relationships. See Rich Hollman's TEDx video "How Improv Training Can Create Compassionate Behavior" (link in the endnote) for how improv can create this kind of affirmative behavior.[70] The exercise below illustrates a process for repeating trust.

Box 5.5
Crafting a Shared Reality

Term Repetition

In this simple exercise, have participants get into pairs.[71] I've found that it's best to demonstrate this in front of the group with a volunteer first. Standing a few feet apart and facing the other person, explain that you will both say the numbers one, two, and three together at the same time, and then each say any word after that at the same time. Neither participant should pre-plan their word, tell the other what word to use, or delay to try to hear the other person's word and then say it (that's basically cheating in this exercise). Rather, everyone should say any word at all instantaneously after the numbers. For example, one person in the pair could say "one, two, three, orange," while the other might arrive at "one, two, three, bridge." The pair will then say "one, two, three" again and say a new word after that. This process should continue until both participants land on the same word. Walk around and have anyone not abiding by the basic rules start over again. I've found that participants get engaged with and enjoy this exercise tremendously. Eventually, most should come to the same word. Tell everyone to give one another a high five if and when they land on the same word.

Debrief questions: For those of you who arrived at the same word, how do you think you were able to do this? For those who didn't arrive at the same term, what do you think prevented you from getting to the same word?

Applications: Discuss how repetition is one of the most powerful forms of persuasion and how the only way that trust is built is one word or behavior at a time. You can also explain the idea of coming to a "shared reality" or "third culture" described in the section above. The process of coming to and landing on the same word was a joint accomplishment in which participants' frequent communication got them on the same wavelength and created a mini-culture between themselves.

Advance the Ensemble

The improvisational notion of a community-oriented "ensemble," as distinct from a competition-focused "team,"[72] has a number of applications for civic engagement. I like to use the phrase "advance the ensemble" to try to get everyone on the same page with this idea. Whenever a participant is thinking about how they can shine at the expense of others (which none of us are immune to), bring the ensemble to the forefront of their thinking. Although one of the skills highlighted in the last chapter was about attending to our levels of status or power as behavioral choices, ultimately the goal of improvisation is to create spaces for equality and friendship. Improv flattens hierarchies. Getting a group of people to affirm and build on one another's ideas and actions, and laugh a lot together, creates the kinds of equalizing spaces many people are not used to inhabiting in public and political life.

All the exercises in this book have participants construct spaces where both group cooperation and individual expression and responses are heightened. Hal Saunders writes that "the paramount political question today is how spaces can be created in which citizens can discover their capacity to respond to or generate change."[73] Scholars have noted how spaces for "civic friendship" can address the need for "spirited intellectual diversity" and "training in citizenship."[74] Sara Evans and Harry Boyte, too, find that democratic change is best fostered by "free spaces," or "public places in the community . . . in which people are able to learn a new self-respect, a deeper and more assertive group identity, public skills, and values of cooperation and civic virtue. . . . Free spaces are settings between private lives and large-scale institutions where ordinary citizens can act with dignity, independence, and vision. These are, in the main, voluntary forms of association with a relatively open and participatory character . . . grounded in the fabric of community life."[75] Although these authors probably write these comments with forms like dialogue and deliberation in mind, every one of these standards also arises in improvisational training. Improvisation comes with norms such as "yes, and" and "give and take" that not only have an "open and participatory character" but forward civic associations and new ways of perceiving others with dignity. In essence, advancing the ensemble has a Wikipedia-type mentality to learning and living, with multiple people and groups working and building common spaces together.

As I've mentioned throughout this book, a lot has been written about what democracies should look like, but far less has covered how to actually train citizens in democratic skills. Replete throughout literatures on politics and society are calls for better forms of engagement founded on evidence-based, core principles for interaction. Some believe the goal is to advance "a principle of reciprocity" that is "at odds with behavior that has been observed in political campaigning and policy making where advocates of competing positions talk past one another."[76] Much of politics is about functioning as either a lone wolf or part of a tribe; very few politicians seem to work with an ensemble mindset in their approaches to civic life. Partly, this derives from how people are trained to behave and what models are offered up as worth emulating in the first place.

The antithesis of democracy is isolation. Without working in ensembles, there's much research showing that our bodies and minds atrophy too. National Public Radio reporter Angus Chen tells us that "loneliness has been linked to everything from heart disease to Alzheimer's disease. Depression is common among the lonely. Cancers tear through their bodies more rapidly, and viruses hit them harder and more frequently. In the short term, it feels like the loneliness will kill you. A study suggests that's because the pain of loneliness activates the immune pattern of a primordial response commonly known as fight or flight."[77] Among the many other factors involved in such incidents, it's also relevant that those who commit some of the most heinous acts in society (like mass shootings) are almost always described in news reports as lonely individuals who had no friends and kept to themselves. All this raises the question: what if we *don't* advance ensembles throughout our lives and societies? The need to build civic skills has many different offshoots all underscoring that we must find more and better ways to create democratic connections between citizens from an early age forward.

From another standpoint, anything that advances turn-taking in conversations and "psychological safety," or a "shared belief held by members of a team that the team is safe for interpersonal risk-taking," is good for groups.[78] These ideas are at the center of what it means to advance an ensemble. Yet building robust ensembles takes the idea of contributing well in groups or teams to the level of the public interest. To use this concept, when they're in doubt, when they hesitate, when they want to focus on themselves, or when they want to express hostile or similar actions toward others, continually coach participants to "advance the ensemble."

Box 5.6
Group Build

Ensemble Support

Form a circle and have one person step inside and say "I am a tree." Then a second should step in and add to it, e.g., "I am the branches."[79] A third could add "I am the fruit," with each acting out their part physically. The first person then selects one person to stay in the circle (for example, the one who said "I am the fruit") and leaves the inside of the circle with the other participant. The sole remaining person in the circle will repeat their phrase and action ("I am the fruit"), and then two people should step into the circle and add to this information with new phrases and actions (e.g., "I am the wheelbarrow collecting the fruit" and "I am the farmer who is glad this process is only seasonal"), and this process keeps going.

Debrief question: How did this exercise highlight the idea of advancing the ensemble?

Applications: This exercise teaches quick thinking, making agile decisions, and, most of all, the need for everyone to contribute and support one another.[80]

Improvise in Liminality

Longtime political strategist Steve Ayscue believes that improvising is a critical skill for politicians to learn. He says that improv can help them tell more authentic stories and connect better with their constituents.[81] Many public figures are so afraid of unpredictability that they try to script everything, whether giving speeches or providing television commentary. For example, a previous representative in the district that I live in lost the support of his constituents by never holding town hall meetings where people could interact with him. Because he never held forums with those he served, citizen resentment began to build through social media, reaching a tipping point on Election Day. The representative's message to our district was clear: "I'm afraid of anything spontaneous that could happen in these situations." Public relations firms add to this mess by often advising their political clients never to go off script.

On the other hand, there are political figures who engage in pure improvisation that's unmoored from others' perspectives, best practices, and the need to adapt to and talk with people. I wouldn't want any reader to walk away from this book with the impression that all forms of improvisation are good. There can be bad improv. A blowhard leader who just monologues extemporaneously at every opportunity will alienate people. There's no skill in that. Improv that's self-focused and airtight won't build relationships and certainly can't bridge the differences necessary to our societal lives.

Contrary to these approaches, improvising in liminality focuses the skill with which a person can operate in a place of uncertainty and ambiguity, where the existing scripts may not fit, or at the very least may need to be adapted to the emerging present. In Victor Turner's terms, being in a "liminal" space betwixt and between the certainties of the past and the uncertainties of the future is a critical part of human and communal development.[82]

To advance this argument, I like to put up on a white board or flip chart Victor Frankl's proposition: "Between stimulus and response there is a space. In that space is our power to choose our response. In our response lies our growth and our freedom."[83] When juxtaposed against our default settings, this is really what all applied improv training is about. All day long each of us is presented with a variety of events. Rather than operating according to set scripts in a determined fashion (with only singular responses to stimuli), the goal is to improvise in liminality, extemporizing responses that help us alternate between different options, adapt our behaviors to meet the needs of different situations, and ultimately liberate our minds and bodies from prior constraints. A society in which people become more comfortable in liminal spaces is one in which knee-jerk political responses are reduced and measured political actions become more possible.

The idea of "relational dialectics" supports this approach.[84] Fed up with overly prescriptive approaches to building good relationships between intimate partners (if you walk into any bookstore you'll see lots of titles such as "The Five Principles of Marriages that Last"), Leslie Baxter and Barbara Montgomery kept finding in their research that great relationships aren't wedded to any one principle, but rather oscillate between different poles, such as independence and interdependence, or change and stability.

For instance, we all have a need for both time to ourselves and time with others. To have a great relationship you have to keep improvising between one pole and the other, without getting stuck in either approach. That means extemporizing in a liminal space, always making adjustments while respecting the needs that each pole expresses.

To improvise in liminality, we have to be willing to examine and possibly undo any fixed ways of knowing, being, and acting that we've inherited. Lois Holzman calls attention to "how organized our lives are by *the ideology of knowing and its institutionalization,*" for instance.[85] With a direct connection to civic matters, she underscores that we are in a world awash with knowledge, testing, and "diagnoses, assessments, evaluations, predictions and pontifications," but asks a compelling question about the ultimate effects all this prioritizing of fixed ways of knowing in so many of our educational systems and professional institutions has had on society: "are we any closer to peace within or between nation states, to bridging what educators call the achievement gap between white middle class children and minority and poor children, to eliminating poverty and hunger, to ending violence, to stopping the destruction of the planet?"[86] Instead of emphasizing fixed *products* of knowledge (as well as fixing people with one-dimensional educational labels such as "smart" or "average" or litanies of fixed psychological types like "extraverted" or "introverted"), one solution lies in tapping into the improvisational, interactive, and networked *processes* by which human development, the capacity for identity transformations, and many forms of knowing come to be in the first place. Gregory Bateson called it "stamping out nouns."[87] Knowledge is powerful and needed, but shouldn't blind us from our inherent possibilities for growth and capacity to move beyond fixed positions and fixed knowledge—and that requires dancing mentally, emotionally, and physically in liminal spaces.

From improving the experiences of neurodivergent young people to creating empathy between police and youth,[88] applied improvisation asks people to step into liminal spaces for democracy's sake. In the courageous settings of applied improv, we step into these spaces to see and act upon the humanity in one another.

༄

In all of these ways, improvisation can be a means for training citizens toward civic ends. It's the kind of teaching and training that's infectious. Once participants experience better ways of relating to one another, backed up by the enjoyment of play and laughter, it's hard not to see the world differently. The play and laughter are political acts in and of themselves. Alan Alda says that "when people are laughing, they're generally not killing one another."[89] What the world needs are bridge builders who can perform their politics with both joyful and serious purpose. Among the many other excellent efforts taking place around the world, applied improvisation can be part of giving everyone an opportunity to expand their skills in citizenship.

When we start acting in more civic ways, we model what a better world could look like for others. Improvisation has us let go of our anxieties to shine forth as improved people. The following passage by Marianne Williamson vividly captures how this deep need for personal liberation connects with our civic lives:

> Our deepest fear is not that we are inadequate. Our deepest fear is that we are powerful beyond measure. It is our light, not our darkness that most frightens us. We ask ourselves, Who am I to be brilliant, gorgeous, talented, fabulous? Actually, who are you *not* to be? You are a child of God. Your playing small does not serve the world. There is nothing enlightened about shrinking so that other people won't feel insecure around you. We are all meant to shine, as children do. We were born to make manifest the glory of God that is within us. It's not just in some of us; it's in everyone. And as we let our own light shine, we unconsciously give other people permission to do the same. As we are liberated from our own fear, our presence automatically liberates others.[90]

With this in mind, and the tools to now put a curriculum for democracy into practice, I'd like to turn to some final implications for what these methods for improving our communication, leadership, and civic skills ultimately offers our futures.

Conclusion

Developing for Our Global Futures

In 2014, people across the US watched a video of a police officer choking a civilian, Eric Garner, in Staten Island, New York. During the struggle, Eric lost his life. New Yorkers took to the streets to protest the barbarism and injustice that Eric and so many black people have faced at the hands of police brutality. Seeking to make a different kind of contribution to this issue, Terry Greiss, the executive director of the Brooklyn-based theater company the Irondale Ensemble Project, contacted police commissioner William Bratton to tell him, "You need what we do. As actors, we train ourselves to really look, to really listen." Within a week, he received a call from the department.[1] A program followed, "To Protect, Serve, and Understand," bringing together seven civilians and seven officers to engage in improvisational theater games, with the goal of "develop[ing] empathy" between the groups.[2]

Inspired by these examples, this book has sought to develop new ideas and ways to teach the skills our world most needs. Each step of the way, I've focused on bridging differences to craft outstanding relationships. Similar to the example of police-community relations in the Netherlands provided at this book's outset, the parallel emergence of improvisation as a tool for building empathy in New York and other parts of the world underscores a need to find new tools and practices to address our biggest problems. As demands for social and racial justice rightfully only grow louder around the globe—especially in light of the historically rooted obstacles to progress and horrific losses of life those in black, brown, and other marginalized communities continue to face in the US and beyond—the need to change the structures of our societies and do politics differently cannot remain suggestions; they must be imperatives for everyone. Among many other efforts to support individual growth, organizational development, and societal improvement, applied improvisation has a role to play in developing for our global futures.

In writing this book, I've tried to use the very practices advised: taking an external focus, looking outside myself for creative inspiration, and "yes, anding" that knowledge to co-create new concepts and practices. Admittedly, when I sat down to put this research project together, my first big surprise was all the incredibly innovative work that has emerged all over the planet. Just as the question "What does this scene need?" should guide the improviser's actions, my task became easier the more I looked outward. I found myself not only drawing from my own experience and all the data I had collected on this subject across the last two decades, but simply needing to point at so much of what has transpired and been said out there.

Take the extraordinary Prison Project now operating across California prisons, which a former US attorney general called "the kind of innovative initiative that legislatures on all levels should support."[3] Although initially met with skepticism, the expanding program has used improvisational performances to reduce recidivism rates from 50 percent to around 10 percent among incarcerated people, and "has led to a nearly 90 percent reduction in behavioral infractions for participants, one of the unexpected effects the program has had outside of class."[4] Using theatrical performance as a means of behavior change among inmates is not the first thing many people would think of when presented with this subject. Yet as Christopher Bisbano, who was incarcerated for eighteen years, reports, "There were no racial boundaries in class. The African-Americans, the whites, Mexicans, Hispanics, we were all playing together. It's very rare in prisons, especially in California. When we had our presentations, we would invite other inmates to come watch. Then they would see that their homeboy was up there dressed up like some character, acting like a fool. It started to break some boundaries. We had something special in common." As told by one of the program's creators, another participant shared how "I didn't realize until I took this class that I've been wearing a mask on the yard for 20 years. That angry face, that tough guy, that's not the total of me. That's just a part of me that I do for survival. But there's another part of me that is capable of feeling and expressing other emotions other than anger."[5] In completing these improvisational performances, many participants found common ground, new emotional choices, and most important, expanded civic spaces and selves.

As I ran across these stunning examples, what became clear is that a complete analytic framework of higher purposes and practices for applied improvisation was needed, and that the next step would be to push this movement further in the direction of the societal contributions already being made. As I have argued throughout this book, it should be a goal of every educational system to find ways to embed and scale this work at greater levels. My hope is that this book can be a starting point of lessons, practices, and exercises that others can use in whole or part, and that can be built upon to fit the nature of differing contexts and needs.

Before moving to some final implications, I want to make one point that emerged during the course of this project especially clear. Some people may think that improv is about playing games and having fun, as differentiated from the realm of serious work and other important matters. Nothing could be further from the truth. All the exercises in this book show that what goes on in the regular course of politics, business, and other fields is as much about games as what happens in applied improv. When an individual shows up in the workplace, they are playing a game with objectives, challenges, and formal and informal rules. In interacting with others, patterns of thought and behavior with game-like qualities develop. What applied improvisation gets us to do is to step into spaces where different and more productive games can be played, such as a personal conversation where heightened listening takes place, a meeting where a leader raises and lowers their status to motivate staff, or a political discussion where participants exercise some narrative flexibility with each other that opens rather than closes space for learning. As one of the participants in the Prison Project said, stepping into an improvisational space broke the game of "putting on an angry and tough mask" with which he had been functioning for so long. Framed in these terms, applied improv is not some separate realm from life, but rather puts into perspective and offers greater choices over the core activities we engage in every day. In the interest of moving this conversation forward, let's concentrate on a few final themes that reflect and extend the territory mapped throughout this project.

Improvisation, Communication, and Cosmopolitan Citizenship

Improvisation helps people become more global, cosmopolitan citizens. Our life together requires preparation for the unpredictable, the ability to play multiple roles and viewpoints, a capacity to be inspired by and find affinity with others, and the capacity to work across systems in a co-creative manner and with a liminal mindset. As so many of this book's examples have illustrated, improvisation provides one way of teaching and training for all these skill sets.

The stakes for developing cosmopolitan citizens have never been greater. Kwame Anthony Appiah writes that cosmopolitanism has two components: "One is the idea that we have obligations to others, obligations that stretch beyond those to whom we are related by the ties of kith and kind, or even the more formal ties of a shared citizenship," while "the other is that we take seriously the value not just of human life but of particular human lives, which means taking an interest in the practices and beliefs that lend them significance."[6] Even a technique as basic as "yes, and" shows that we each have responsibilities to one another, that we can see others from the perspective of offers, and that we should respect and value the contribution of the group, distributing leadership where possible. In doing so, improvisational practices lend weight to the second idea: that particular people and lives have intrinsic worth. William James once wrote, "I am done with great things and big plans, great institutions and big successes. I am for those tiny, invisible loving forces that work from individual to individual, creeping through the crannies of the world like so many rootlets, like the capillary oozing of water, yet which, if given time, will rend the hardest monuments of human pride."[7] Grand theories of democracy and social change can be important for imagining more cosmopolitan futures, but we can't forget to forward the one-to-one orientations and practices that can get us there.

At the core of leadership and civic excellence lie communication skills, which is why this book has prioritized communication as the primary competency for societal improvement. Yet communication is more than a skill, it's also a perspective to apply to any situation or event. Arthur Jensen argues that we must find "our way in the 21st century by taking forms of communication as seriously as we do health and happiness; by giving up certainty and embracing curiosity, living in the tension between being scared and being awed; rediscovering that conversation is about expanding horizons rather than being right or convincing."[8] Applied improvisation positions participants in these spaces, where they learn to inhabit ambiguities while stepping out courageously to connect and create with others.

At the same time, while parsing communication, leadership, and civic skills can be useful for viewing certain ideas, in practice, they all go together. When we build productive relationships with others, we are stringing together and leading alliances; when we're leading, we must communicate well to bridge differences and create clarity and motivation; when civic skills are exercised well, excellent communication and leadership practices are involved that alternate between local and more global viewpoints. These ideas have a past: many ancient figures saw the building of skills with social and civic knowledge as at the core of a liberal education—meaning an education that liberates the mind and body by making possible greater freedoms and choices.[9]

At the heart of becoming a better citizen is building trust. With all the risks and crises that threaten to undo life on this planet, we don't need to add forms of distrust into the mix. We need all the tools that we can get to foster useful language and frames, positive ways of relating to one another, and repeated behaviors that engender individual and collective resilience. Some improvisers even believe all the principles of improvisation are superseded by the need to "behave and respond honestly."[10] In essence, then, applied improvisation trains for the practice of "cosmopolitan communication."[11] Jesse Sostrin notes how such perspectives are necessarily improvisational, since "the world of improvisation can also teach us important aspects of communication" and "what this suggests is that people know how patterns are made, how they are enacted, and how they play a role in making sense of what we see. The interesting thing about improv is that it is not random. . . . We make our experience at work from the same kinds of patterns of communication and interaction that we just 'whipped up' during the improv activity."[12] In other words, every person is involved in world-making. Through our words and actions, we bring worlds into existence, moment by moment and day by day. Life is, in this sense, one long improvisation, so the skill with which we improvise with one another should be a central concern for building new scripts, scenes, and patterns that forward cosmopolitan citizenship. This also touches on leadership. Leaders who see themselves as stewards of the type of improvisation and communication that support cosmopolitan perspectives build organizational worlds in which dynamism, opportunity, and engagement thrive.

If there's any central value for cosmopolitan citizenship that's stimulated through the ideas and practices described in this book, it's flexibility. Without some flexibility and adaptation to the needs of our fellow citizens, it's impossible to have a democracy. A world in which everyone is stuck in their "default settings," with little ability to have a regard for others, would be a world constantly at war. We've already seen versions of that world play out too many times in human history. A society in which skilled improvisation is a core value, on the other hand, invites citizens to keep asking "what's needed here," and remain flexible, open to possibilities, and wary of all forms of cognitive, affective, and behavioral closure.

Closing the Gap in People Skills

As addressed throughout this book, the training of people skills remains an underdeveloped area throughout much educational programming. After three years of research at the University of Southern California, nearly two thousand executives said that the skills they most want from employees include a hunger to grow and experiment, to see patterns and "make imaginative leaps," an ability to work well across organizational and cultural boundaries, the use of emotional intelligence, and adaptability, or a "mental agility, comfort with ambiguity, and the capacity to change old behaviors in light of new evidence."[13] While these expectations are often seen as meeting the demands of an emerging society, there's nothing new about them. Two millennia ago, one teacher wrote that "the all important gift for an orator is a wise adaptability since he is called upon to meet the most varied emergencies."[14] Even prominent modern philosophers have advocated for citizens to develop a "moderation of expectations, adaptability, presence of mind, [and] attention to what the moment offers."[15]

From the past to the present, these types of findings lead us to the question of what kind of teaching or training can help people best cultivate these skills. Among other emerging approaches, applied improvisation provides answers. One remark I hear repeatedly from students in my executive MBA improv course (and these are people with at least five years of work experience) is that they wished they'd had the class sooner in life. From resolving conflicts to managing the unexpected to getting more in tune with one's energy levels, every day skilled improvisation is needed to meet the demands of our institutions and communities.

Increasingly, organizations are seeing the results of putting a value on closing the gap in people skills. The use of improvisational training advanced a realization that more staff than ranking officers should be involved in decision making at the US Office of the Secretary of Defense, promoted better ideation at a public relations agency, and forwarded a more positive culture and communication at the Inter-American Development Bank.[16] Aside from these types of examples, another way that I like to showcase the value of this work for participants or clients is through a reverse question: what if we don't place a premium on developing these types of skills? Think about the number of organizational and community problems that might have been prevented had people had the tools and practices to improvise well with others. Think of the number of meetings that could have been more about building and connecting than posturing and critiquing as default settings. Think about the email chains that have gotten out of hand because employees spent too little time establishing relationships and cultivating presence up and down the system. Or, with a smartphone in our pockets pressuring us to be anywhere else, think about all the information sharing and rapport lost that's impacting the outcomes we most care about in our institutions and communities.

From any snapshot of political discourse, what's clear is that many of our politicians have placed little weight on developing people skills (or do little to build bridges with others beyond their own tribes), proving the point that more and better forms of sociality are needed. Imagine if every incoming member of congress were required to receive training in and commit to the practices of applied improvisation. Can you imagine how different interactions in our highest political institutions would look?

It's also time to drop any and all pretense that schools and organizations are doing enough to address people skills. In a provocative article titled "What Students Know that Experts Don't: School Is All about Signaling, not Skill-Building," Brian Caplan says that certification has become more important than learning.[17] Putting aside continuing debates about whether education should promote the liberal arts, technical training, or other labors, Caplan raises a point that's worth taking seriously: too many schools and students are playing a game with little value, a game that's more about indicating one has an education than actually learning and applying it to personal and professional contexts. As highlighted in the previous chapter on leadership, we need to "reframe the game." When education becomes a static possession rather than a dynamic, lifelong process to become a better human being and contributor to society, there's little room for people skills to improve. Even when it comes to classes that theorize how to become a better communicator, unless those skills are practiced and observed, it can all matter very little.

We should stay attentive to evidence that a transfer of learning has taken place—that people are applying the lessons and exercises in their everyday lives. Formal measures such as pre- and post-testing can be applied; many of the studies highlighted earlier in this book certainly use and support these approaches. But I've found it best to hear from people who have gone through these lessons and trainings themselves about what kinds of meanings they have created. While many of the categories and applications in this book and others will come in handy, I've also found it critical not to assume you know what meanings participants will construct. As mentioned previously, you'll want to give participants plenty of space to debrief, listening for what improvements they say they have discovered through improvisation.

Upright Citizens Brigade co-founder Matt Besser says that improvisation has the effect of "making you an easier person to be with, whether it's in your personal life, your business or wherever. And there are certain listening skills that you think are just obvious or should be self-evident, but they're not. People do the opposite of it and [there are] easy exercises to help people not do that."[18] Through the repetition of exercises and commitments, intellectual reflection, and embodied activities that go deep into muscle memory, improv for democracy is relentlessly focused on closing the gap in people skills.

Performance-Based Teaching and Training

If cold, dull lectures that speak entirely to people's heads stand at one end of the teaching and training spectrum, applied improvisation stands at the other. Speaking to the mind and body, applied improvisation asks us to perform our way to better selves and social worlds. Don't get me wrong, I'm a big fan of using a diversity of teaching methods, depending on the subject and group. Sometimes lengthy lectures are called for and, in skillful hands, can be electrifying and inspiring experiences. But to balance out the overwhelmingly heady experiences that most people have had in modern educational systems, especially given continuing budget cuts and the subordination of arts-based programming in favor of other subjects, it's time to place greater heft on performance-based teaching and training.

At its heart, improv for democracy is all about experiential education. Countless observers have called for more of this approach to human development, and the unique contribution of applied improvisation is that it provides a sustainable means for actually putting these visions into practice. Alan Alda summed up these sentiments perfectly: "If you're going to play piano at Carnegie Hall and never had a lesson, it doesn't help to tell you 'Here are three tips.' "[19] The same goes for the development of communication, leadership, and civic skills. Further expounding on these ideas,

Donald Bligh underscores how, "if you want to teach a behavior skill, at some stage the student should practice it. If you are training athletes to run 100 meters, at some point in that training they should practice running 100 meters. . . . You might think this principle is obvious. And so it is to ordinary people. But it is quite beyond some of the most intelligent people our educational system has produced."[20] Teaching and training in this way may require a significant shift in thinking for many people. Yet the simple idea that, at some point, we have to move beyond readings and discussions to show evidence that these competencies can be performed should be beyond dispute. There's also a difference between drilling a skill to experience a concept and deciding to apply that skill in other circumstances.[21]

In years of doing this work, I've observed many participants bringing more of their bodies into these processes. Sitting on the sidelines and analyzing everything can be much easier than engaging with and bringing one's whole self to daily tasks. Overall, as Adam Blatner puts it, "active physical involvement adds to the warming-up to spontaneity because active involvement opens up a corresponding flow of intuitions, images, feelings, and insights that are otherwise distanced and blocked by more passive modes of exchange."[22] It's both jarring and liberating to view anew the ways in which human beings' bodies are often not involved enough in their approaches to the world.

In Lev Vygotsky's terms, improv is a process-based activity that manifests both tools and outcomes at once.[23] Holzman writes that there is far more going on here than simple skill-building. She sees "improv as bridging education's cognitive-emotive divide with its simultaneity of action and reflection and socially produced and shared thinking-and-feeling."[24] What's more, there's a challenge (or at the very least an update) to entire educational systems built into this conception of performance-based learning:

> As I understand it, the downside of our culture is that as children perform their way into cultural and societal adaptation, their potential for continuous development becomes limited. What they have learned through performing becomes routinized and rigidified. By middle school . . . many children become so skilled at acting out certain roles that they no longer keep creating new performances of themselves (that is, developing). By the time they are adults, most people have an identity as "this kind of person"—someone who does certain things (and does them certain ways) and feels certain ways.[25]

Contrary to the way these reified selves play out in education and society, improv performance offers an opportunity to expand one's roles and horizons: an opportunity to both be and become more than the status quo has afforded. And this ties directly to democracy; it's citizens' rigidified orientations that prevent them from speaking meaningfully and productively with one another, having the potential to re-author or revise stories, collaborate well, and move beyond culturally generated binaries, despite differences.

Going further, performance-based teaching and training also ties to diversity, equity, and inclusion. Providing opportunities for people to express themselves, to be part of decisions that affect their lives, and to develop to their best potential all relate to the possibilities for voice and growth. What else are such things as racism, segregation, and classism than the keeping of people within small worlds that prevent them from having opportunities to expand beyond boundaries and develop the potential to be more than current definitions of their lives suggest? On the other hand, performance-based approaches to teaching and learning give "children and adolescents opportunities to do what they rarely can do in school, which is to engage in social performances of caring, interest, curiosity and passion (performances that give expression to the unity of intellect and affect) . . . incorporating the other," and moving beyond the narrowness of their individual experiences.[26] Moreover, as Annalisa Dias highlights in her work using applied improvisation to advance diversity and decolonize college campuses, "improvisation techniques like accepting offers, lowering status, and valuing silence eliminate structural social hierarchy when in conversations, which allows dialogue participants to share their voices and represent their perspectives more freely" and "on an equitable footing."[27] Improv puts these critical values into action.

In participant-centered applied improvisation, the focus becomes learning rather than teaching, and fully immersing oneself in education rather than simply being housed in an institution. Similar to some of the examples highlighted in this book, Michael Golding works with at-risk students who "Show up expecting a lecture course. Instead, they are exposed to my learning by doing approach" that "keep[s] the students out of trouble and from being targeted by gangs. It also instills the idea that college is a possibility for them. Being exposed to a different approach in learning has a ripple effect on the students that enhances their academic and social skills. Attendance improves as well."[28] The surprise of learning in this way stems from a deeper recognition that students wanted to learn in this way all along.

Of even greater significance, this kind of performance-based teaching and training is not at odds with cognitive academic work, but rather appears to enhance scholarly study and commitment through a kind of spillover effect that Golding and others have discovered.

This all suggests that much of education has aimed too low in building expectations for engaging experiences. I often think about why, in so many courses, students are tempted to turn to browsing the internet or texting friends. Yes, technology is making it more difficult to resist these pressures, but where participants are often blamed for lacking the willpower to suspend diversions, an equal argument can be made that we educators sometimes don't do enough to fully engage them—to the point where technological distractions become a poor substitute for the presence offered when whole bodies and minds are engaged in experiential learning. The direction of modern science has been to underscore that "the brain-body connection is more important than we think,"[29] so we're swimming with rather than against the tide in training for human development in these ways. Much research has also confirmed that we are working with rather than against the nature of our minds when we promote a plasticity that's already there.[30]

It's not just experiential learning, but affirmative, playful experiential learning that expands the self in society. Affirmation is incredibly important in classrooms,[31] and the "yes, and" foundation of applied improvisation supports this orientation as a way to build better behaviors. Where meaningful, motion-filled, playful engagement occurs, citizens can learn to thrive well in a variety of circumstances. And contrary to some views that serious work and entertainment stand in opposition, Douglas Thomas and John Seely Brown highlight that "the ability to play may be the single most important skill to develop for the twenty-first century."[32] Again, this is a good place to ask: what if people don't learn to take an affirmative, playful orientation toward others? Not all of life needs to be fun and games, of course, but compared to many unproductive alternatives—inflexible minds and attitudes, chronic anger and humorlessness, and so on—an affirmative, playful stance becomes a civic skill in its own right. If everyone of us, at multiple points in our schooling and professional education, were to learn and relearn the lessons of improv, we would become immeasurably better communicators, relational partners, leaders, and citizens. Overall, the shift to performance, experience, play, and the building of better norms for human interaction positions improv for democracy in a unique and needed space.

Transparency in a New Key

When people start to create better connections with one another and peel off many of the self-imposed layers that have stifled their performances, they become more honest. Perhaps the highest contribution that applied improvisation can make to democracy is the building of transparency within the self and between people. In a day and age where misinformation fills the airwaves, hit-and-run political attacks have become a mode of operating online, and people often hide behind snarky or ironic masks in their social commentary, communities must find ways of training for transparency. Transparency is central to our social and political life. For instance, "think about political scandals. Was there ever a scandal in which the cover-up or response wasn't worse than the original transgression"?[33] As a solution, "there's a strong sense in which Improvisation equals honesty. The games we propose invite you to inhabit the moment and to strip away artifice."[34] In a paradox, when we start to see each other improvise better, relationships become more grounded and stable. By creating inclusive and engaging processes for human development, skilled improvisation provides "liberating structures" for our lives.[35]

Artifice often begins with the restrictions that individuals place on themselves, especially through self-imposed rules and habits. Transparency and vulnerability open up possibilities within the self and create space for undertaking the hard work of listening to others. In fact, according to surgeon and otolaryngologist Charles Limb, once you've been improvising for a while the inhibitory part of the brain starts to quiet down.[36] As your self opens up, your expressive capacities are expanded, generating transparent communication.

At the same time, transparency is not merely a matter of what one broadcasts. It's a relational phenomenon. In improvisational theater, it's the give and take between actors that fosters candor, responsiveness, and truth. Participants in improvisational training continually return to these themes in their reflections on the applications of this work to the rest of their lives, highlighting "let go of your own agenda," "don't hog the spotlight," "listen for the word 'no' and see if it comes up too much," "failure is a chance to grow," and "switch to being a helper, not a hindrance" as core learnings.[37]

At the center of this are acts of *recognition*: recognizing others' offers rather than avoiding or denying them, recognizing a need to shift one's styles and status at any moment to be a leader or follower, and recognizing how much human potential is expanded when people are truly heard. We could call improv for democracy a politics of hearing, since, as David Ausburger puts it, "Being heard is so close to being loved that for the average person, they are almost indistinguishable."[38] And these are the hard skills: even science only progresses through a great deal of give and take between people.[39] No important human endeavor can come into being without transparent social engagement.

Toward Bold, Sustainable Public Possibilities

Everything that I've discussed and applied in this book has been intended to contribute to the building of a courageous, charismatic, and innovative citizenry. A lot of talk about politics and community-building takes place in a rather somber register, which accords with the serious nature of public issues and their instigating problems. But we need to switch to the other side too. Creating democracies should be as much about constructing resilient and agile citizens as focusing on what to avoid, lambaste, or negate. Among many other ways that this can be carried out, applied improvisation relieves stress and builds motivation and character. It gets us to try out small acts of courage, in the hope that we can make skillful choices when bigger decisions and actions are required.

Preparing individuals to work well in groups is at the heart of a democracy. Even the highest-level interactions of government authorities draw on individuals' abilities to perform well with others. Applied improvisation is all about spaces for possibilities, where energy and novelty emerge. Sara Bender argues that "It is about imagining being in a situation, with no predetermined need or vision for how it will go, taking what comes and allowing the offer to grow and develop into something. . . . it's not just about listening, it's not about paying lip service, and it is not about being clever. It's about being present, noticing more, living in the moment, finding a space of non-thinking, holding things really lightly and being open to what comes. Possibility emerges in the space, if we allow it to."[40] Individuals who approach the world with the mindset that each day is about emerging possibilities will bring into being remarkable feats. They will see opportunity where others don't, and reframe, regame, and reimagine events with an intent to bridge differences. Given the lack of civic education and opportunities for engagement that people across our planet face, at a minimum this book has been a call simply to do something different. It is time to make some new and surprising choices that can lead us into a more adaptive global future that collapses the borders and barriers that have held humanity back at so many junctures.

Earlier in this book, I mentioned the general decline of public places where civic engagement can take place. Many researchers have written extensively about the lack of public gathering places across areas, especially in the US.[41] This raises the question of *where* improv for democracy can sustainably be practiced. I've highlighted throughout this book that my goal is to see improvisational teaching and training embedded and scaled across all of our educational systems, as part of professional development programs, and in communities writ large. Having stand-alone classes and workshops as a permanent part of K–12 and higher educational or organizational training curricula (or simply integrating in this work to existing instruction in areas from communication to leadership) certainly constitutes one way in which improv for democracy can have greater reach and effect. The goal here is to advocate with decision makers for across the board policy changes that make improvisation a core course and competency—not just ad hoc or one-off programming but a regular feature of students' educational experiences. Following the Detroit Creativity Project's lead, one first step could be to get this work in after-school programming, let the effects speak for themselves, and then make a case for greater inclusion in curricula from there.

Yet there are other places to sustain the public possibilities of improv for democracy. One is public libraries that exist in just about every community and that opinion polls show are highly respected as "a safe place, a source of educational opportunity and trusted information, as well as a place to ignite creativity in young people"—a description that matches the objectives of improv itself.[42] Most libraries have community rooms that are used for all kinds of purposes (and where people don't have to stay quiet). Nowadays, just about every city has an improv theater or improv group that, in addition to comedy performances, also runs trainings with corporations and other entities. These groups could play an integral part in building sustained programming at such venues.

At base, integrating this work into already existing infrastructure would be the most effective way to make improv for democracy widely applicable and easily accessible for the greatest number of people. For instance, just about every city has at least one Toastmasters club, which anyone can join to practice their public speaking skills, usually meeting at a local community venue.[43] Since the goals of this organization and others like it are already so aligned with developing citizens' communication skills, chapter leaders could use the concepts and exercises in this book in Toastmasters meetings to advance an already existing goal while forwarding higher-level leadership and civic competencies in the process.

Improv for democracy should also be integrated into spaces where the work of civic engagement is currently being practiced, such as community conversation initiatives. Take the dialogue- and deliberation-based National Issues Forums, where groups of citizens (usually of varying political views) are brought together to discuss three policy options on a contentious political issue such as immigration, healthcare, or gun control.[44] At the beginning of a forum, facilitators establish group norms and have everyone share a story about their connection to the issue at hand to help participants tap into their personal journeys and connect with others. In this respect, perhaps improv could be used in these spaces as a means of "pre-dialogue" or "pre-deliberation" to get everyone into a shared space that emphasizes the listening skills the event will abide by, or to depolarize participants through laughter and empathy building before the serious discussion. This is by no means an exhaustive list of the public possibilities for improv for democracy. I put these ideas forward to "yes, and" the amazing work that already exists out there,[45] and in the hope that others can "yes, and" other ways this work could play out.

An improvisational orientation also most addresses actual human needs in public places. Ray Oldenberg writes that amid a need for more "third places" (outside the first place of home and the second place of work, as a space where community and contact with diverse others can arise), "it may be well to point out that the fundamental motivation for this kind of belonging is neither personal advantage nor civic duty. The basic motivation; that which draws people back time and again is *fun*."[46] With all the emerging and extant efforts to get citizens to engage with each other in productive ways around the nation and world, the fundamental human needs for playfulness, laughter, and fun should not be lost here. From diseases to environmental disasters, nature's cruelties against human beings are enough to deal with on their own terms. We don't need to add any more humanly created problems such as racism, war, or other forms of anti-fun to this mix. While we often have no choice about what happens to us, what is within our capabilities is our response to such events and, more so, the ability to fight entropy by co-creating social worlds of joy, hope, and possibility.

Overall, what's been offered in this book should translate into new attitudes and orientations to life through a liberating form of teaching and training. In doing so, we're joining together longstanding calls with present needs. Over 100 years ago, in a section of *The New State* titled "The

Training for a New Democracy," Mary Parker Follett wrote that courses in government and current events cannot be the sole foundations for civic education. Instead, a training for democracy can be "acquired only through those modes of living and acting which shall teach us how to grow the social consciousness. . . . Every cooperative method conceivable, therefore, must be used in our schools for this end."[47] Through the present, scholars have argued that the best forms of learning should have "a political aim, a *democratic* aim," creating "environments that both invite and promote democratic participation."[48] That's the central message of this book, too, a lead that I hope you will follow in applying this work across different contexts.

And that, dear readers, brings this book to a close. In the spirit of improvisation, I hope you take what's written here and evolve it further in the direction of improv for democracy. In the interests of building better relationships, organizations, and societies, let's advance the inherent democratic potential that exists within applied improvisation. The most important point is to now move this form of learning from the page to people. Start with working on just a few lessons and exercises from the beginning of this book and build to more advanced versions from there.[49] You'll find that once you start teaching and training in this way, you won't want to go back. Please also feel free to contact me and let me know how you're using improv for democracy. I love to hear stories of people from around the world using these ideas and practices to improve their lives and communities. If there's anything I've learned in doing this work, it's that it will take as many of us as possible to improvise our way to better futures.

Notes

Introduction

1. iDebate NL, "Second Wave 'My City Real World' in Gouda," *IDEA Debate Exchange*, August 26, 2015, YouTube video, 8:02, www.youtube.com/watch?v=6NTThMO2ufo.

2. Ibid.

3. W. Barnett Pearce, *Making Social Worlds: A Communication Perspective* (Malden, MA: Blackwell, 2009).

4. See Wayne C. Booth, *The Rhetoric of Rhetoric: The Quest for Effective Communication* (Malden, MA: Blackwell, 2009).

5. Although there are certainly positive effects of social media on people's lives, studies on such negative effects are now legion; for examples, see Cass R. Sunstein, *#Republic: Divided Democracy in the Age of Social Media* (Princeton, NJ: Princeton University Press, 2018); Claudia Marino, Gianluca Gini, Alessio Vieno, and Marcantonio M. Spada, "The Associations between Problematic Facebook Use, Psychological Distress and Well-Being among Adolescents and Young Adults: A Systematic Review and Meta-Analysis," *Journal of Affective Disorders* 15 (2017): 274–281; Hunt Allcott and Matthew Gentzkow, "Social Media and Fake News in the 2016 Election," *Journal of Economic Perspectives* 31 (2017): 211–236.

6. Dustin Stephens, "Civics Lessons: Justices Sonia Sotomayor, Neil Gorsuch on Promoting Education in Citizenship," *CBS News*, November 4, 2018, www.cbsnews.com/news/supreme-court-justices-sonia-sotomayor-and-neil-gorsuch-promote-civics-education/, par. 6. Andrea Gabor further spotlights how "a civics revival is long overdue. As of 2018, only eight [US] states required students to take a yearlong civics and government class, and only 19 required students to take a civics exam to graduate. Even the National Assessment of Educational Progress, which is considered the nation's report card, dropped its 4th- and 12th-grade civics and American history exam, in 2014. The ostensible reason was to save money, but the NAEP then adopted a new technology and engineering literacy test a year later. Indeed, civics

fell victim to the narrowing of curricula under both Presidents George W. Bush and Barack Obama, and to the standardized testing regimen that focused on math, science and English. Worried about economic competition from China, neither Democrats nor Republicans anticipated the recent populist and authoritarian threat to Western democracies that civics education is meant to forestall. The reality is, schools need to do both: prepare students for a global economy and to be engaged citizens in a democracy." Andrea Gabor, "Bring Back High School Civics (With a Twist)," *Bloomberg*, September 17, 2019, www.bloomberg.com/opinion/articles/2019-09-17/high-school-civics-is-on-the-way-back-with-a-twist?srnd=opinion, pars. 4–6.

7. National Task Force on Civic Learning and Democratic Engagement, *A Crucible Moment: College Learning and Democracy's Future* (Washington, DC: AAC&U, 2012), aacu.org/sites/default/files/files/crucible/Crucible_508F.pdf, 69.

8. Tatiana Suspitsyna, "Higher Education for Economic Advancement and Engaged Citizenship: An Analysis of the U.S. Department of Education Discourse," *The Journal of Higher Education* 83 (2012): 51.

9. J. Michael Hogan, Jeffrey A. Kurr, Jeremy D. Johnson, and Michael J. Bergmaier, "Speech and Debate as Civic Education," *Communication Education* 65, no. 4 (2016): 378.

10. Brooke Gladstone, William Gibson, David Brin, and Anne Simon, "The Science in Science Fiction," *NPR*, October 22, 2018, radio program, 50:23, www.npr.org/2018/10/22/1067220/the-science-in-science-fiction.

11. Tom Yorton, "Using Improv Methods to Overcome the Fear Factor," *Employment Relations Today* 31 (2005): 7–13; Suzanne Gagnon, Heather C. Vough, and Robert Nickerson, "Learning to Lead, Unscripted: Developing Affiliative Leadership through Improvisational Theatre," *Human Resource Development Review* 11 (2012): 299–325.

12. Aidan Daly, Stephen J. Grove, Michael J. Dorsch, and Raymond P. Fisk, "The Impact of Improvisation Training on Service Employees in a European Airline: A Case Study," *European Journal of Marketing* 43 (2009): 459.

13. Paul Basken, "Actor Is Honored for Using Improv to Help Scientists Communicate," *Chronicle of Higher Education*, April 20, 2013, www.chronicle.com/article/Alan-Alda-Is-Honored-for-Using/138673; Kevin P. Boesen, Richard N. Herrier, David A. Apgar, and Rebekah M. Jackowski, "Improvisational Exercises to Improve Pharmacy Students' Professional Communication Skills," *American Journal of Pharmaceutical Education* 73, no. 2 (2009): 1–8; Melanie Leon, "Medically Relevant Improv: Using Improvisation to Teach Empathetic Communication to Medical Professionals" (honors thesis, Rollins College, 2014); Sarah Todd, "Practicing in the Uncertain: Reworking Standardized Clients as Improv Theatre," *Social Work Education* 31, no. 3 (2012): 302–315; Julie S. Huffaker and Ellen West, "Enhancing Learning in the Business Classroom: An Adventure with Improv Theater Techniques," *Journal of Management Education* 29 (2005): 852–869; Daly, Grove, Dorsch, and Fisk, "The Impact of Improvisation Training."

14. Paul Z. Jackson, "Applying Improvisation The Power of 'Yes, and' Paul Z Jackson at TEDxLSE," *Paul Z Jackson*, March 7, 2014, YouTube video, 13:19, www.youtube.com/watch?v=fr7jw8S6zqc.

15. Kelly Leonard and Tom Yorton, *Yes, and: How Improvisation Reverses "No, but" Thinking and Improves Creativity and Collaboration* (New York: Harper, 2015).

16. See, for example, Abigail Hess, "The 10 Most In-Demand Skills of 2019, According to LinkedIn," CNBC, January 6, 2019, www.cnbc.com/2019/01/04/the-30-most-in-demand-skills-in-2019-according-to-linkedin-.html; Alison Doyle, "Top Skills and Attributes Employers Look For," the balance careers, August 24, 2019, www.thebalancecareers.com/top-skills-employers-want-2062481; Hershey H. Friedman, Linda Weiser Friedman, and William Hampton-Sosa, "Is the Unidisciplinary College Major in Danger of Going the Way of Netscape, AOL, Myspace, Blockbuster, and the Blackberry?" SSRN, 2013, https://ssrn.com/abstract=2234498.

17. Graduate Management Admission Council, *Corporate Recruiters Survey: 2014 Survey Report*, 2014, www.gmac.com/-/media/files/gmac/research/employment-outlook/2014-corporaterecruiters-final-release-3.pdf, 4, 19–20.

18. Economist Intelligence Unit, "Organisational Agility: How Business can Survive and Thrive in Turbulent Times," *Economist*, March 2009, www.academia.edu/29130941/Organisational_agility_How_business_can_survive_and_thrive_in_turbulent_times.

19. IBM, "IBM 2010 Global CEO Study: Creativity Selected as Most Crucial Factor for Future Success," *IBM*, May 18, 2010, www-03.ibm.com/press/us/en/pressrelease/31670.wss.

20. Mark Stevens, cited in Rachel Zupek, "Top 10 Reasons Employers Want to Hire You," *Careerbuilder*, November 2, 2009, www.cnn.com/2009/LIVING/worklife/11/02/cb.hire.reasons.job/. See also Anil B. Jambekar and Karol I. Pelc, "Improvisation Model for Team Performance Enhancement in a Manufacturing Environment," *Team Performance Management: An International Journal* 13, no. 7 (2007): 259–274.

21. Paul Z. Jackson, *Easy: Your Lifepass to Creativity and Confidence* (London: The Solutions Focus, 2015), 73.

22. National Leadership Council for Liberal Education and America's Promise, *College Learning for the New Global Century* (Washington, DC: Association of American Colleges and Universities, 2007), www.aacu.org/sites/default/files/files/LEAP/GlobalCentury_final.pdf, 2–3.

23. Cited in Daniel H. Pink, *A Whole New Mind: Why Right-Brainers Will Rule the Future* (New York: Penguin, 2006), 56, 58.

24. Anthony P. Carnevale, Leila I. Gainer, and Ann S. Meltzer, *Workplace Basics Training Manual* (San Francisco: Jossey-Bass, 1990), 163–164.

25. Applied Improvisation Network, http://appliedimprovisation.network.

26. Barbara Tint and Adam Froerer, "Delphi Study Summary," Applied Improvisation Network, 2014, http://appliedimprovisation.network/wp-content/

uploads/2015/11/Delphi-Study-Summary.pdf, 2. See also Theresa Robbins Dudeck and Caitlin McClure, eds., *Applied Improvisation: Leading, Collaborating, and Creating Beyond the Theater* (London: Methuen, 2018), and Alan Alda, *If I Understood You, Would I Have This Look on My Face? My Adventures in the Art and Science of Relating and Communicating* (New York: Random House, 2018).

27. Jackson, *Easy*, 183–184.

28. Jill Bernard and Patrick Short, *Jill and Patrick's Small Book of Improv for Business* (Portland, OR: Viewers Like You, 2015), 7.

29. Paul Z. Jackson, "Wimbrovisers," *Paul Jackson Associates*, July 10, 2017, http://impro.org.uk/wimbrovisers/, par. 3.

30. Bob Kulhan, *Getting to "Yes, and": The Art of Business Improv* (Palo Alto, CA: Stanford University Press), 8, 47.

31. Charna Halpern, Del Close, and Kim Johnson, *Truth in Comedy: The Manual of Improvisation* (Colorado Springs: Meriwether 1994), 25–26. Other key figures in the improv world also note that, even in improv for comedy entertainment, "being a good improviser and being funny are not synonymous." The goal of improv has always been first and foremost "to build. Build relationships. Build solid scene work. Build a whole piece of theater with our partners." Jimmy Carrane and Elizabeth Allen, *Improvising Better: A Guide for the Working Improviser* (Portsmouth, NH: Heinemann, 2006), 51.

32. Chris Holcomb, " 'The Crown of All Our Study': Improvisation in Quintilian's Institutio Oratoria," *Rhetoric Society Quarterly* 31, no. 3 (2001): 53–72; Chris Kreiser, " 'I'm Not Just Making This Up as I Go Along': Reclaiming Theories of Improvisation for Discussions of College Writing," *Pedagogy* 14, no. 1 (2014): 81–106.

33. Don J. Waisanen and Rodney A. Reynolds, "Side-Coaching the Public Speech: Toward Improvisational Delivery Adjustments in the Moment," *Communication Teacher* 22, no. 1 (2008): 18–21.

34. W. Barnett Pearce, *Communication and the Human Condition* (Carbondale: Southern Illinois University Press, 1989); Pearce, *Making Social Worlds*.

35. Lipmanowicz and McCandless, *The Surprising Power*.

36. Deepak Malhotra and Max H. Bazerman, *Negotiation Genius* (New York: Bantam, 2008).

37. Pearce, *Making Social Worlds*, 9.

38. Theda Skocpol, *Diminished Democracy* (Norman: University of Oklahoma Press, 2003); Stephen Macedo, ed., *Democracy at Risk* (Washington, DC: Brookings, 2005); Jack M. McLeod, "When Democracy Failed: Can Political Communication Research Contribute to Civil Recovery," *Political Communication* 35, no. 4 (2018): 1–5.

39. Mark S. Pancer, *The Psychology of Citizenship and Civic Engagement* (New York: Oxford University Press, 2015), 3.

40. Thomas Ehrlich, ed., *Civic Responsibility and Higher Education* (Westport, CT: The American Council on Education and the Onyx Press, 2000), vi.

41. Jane Jacobs, *Dark Age Ahead* (New York: Random House, 2004), 35.

42. María José Canel and Vilma Luoma-aho, *Public Sector Communication: Closing Gaps between Citizens and Public Organizations* (Malden, MA: Wiley, 2019).

43. Silvio Waisbord, "Why Populism is Troubling for Democratic Communication," *Communication, Culture, & Critique* 11, no. 1 (2018): 21.

44. Harry Boyte, "How Can We Awaken Democracy? Groups Explore the Concept of Civic Muscle," *MinnPost*, September 26, 2018, www.minnpost.com/community-voices/2018/09/how-can-we-awaken-democracy-groups-explore-the-concept-of-civic-muscle/, par. 9.

45. James Lull, *Culture-on-Demand: Communication in a Crisis World* (Malden, MA: Blackwell), 2007.

46. Derek W. M. Barker, Noelle McAfee, and David W. McIvor, "Introduction: Democratizing Deliberation," in *Democratizing Deliberation—A Political Theory Anthology,* eds. David W. McIvor, Derek W. M. Barker, and Noëlle McAfee (Dayton, OH: Kettering Press, 2012), 7.

47. Meira Levinson, *No Citizen Left Behind* (Cambridge, MA: Harvard University Press, 2012), 286.

48. Stephen D. Brookfield and Stephen Preskill, *Discussion as a Way of Teaching: Tools and Techniques for Democratic Classrooms* (Hoboken, NJ: Wiley, 2012); Steven A. Beebe, Timothy P. Mottet, and K. David Roach, *Training and Development: Enhancing Communication and Leadership Skills* (Upper Saddle River, NJ: Pearson, 2013).

49. Although you wouldn't be the main audience for this book, you could also be an improv or theater teacher who'd like to bring more weight to your work or start an applied improv program by making connections with research and outside fields of practice.

50. In the arts, improvisation has remained a central part of other fields such as dance and musical forms like jazz. Nonetheless, this book draws on and extends the metaphor of improvisational theater as a better domain for the development of communication, leadership, and civic skills. With Aylesworth, I find that "theater is more accessible, transferable, and universal when compared to jazz"—with less specialized knowledge required and many of the same tools people use in their everyday talk and behaviors. It's also more accessible for students from different cultural traditions. Andy Aylesworth, "Improving Case Discussion with an Improv Mind-Set," *Journal of Marketing Education* 30, no. 2 (2008): 106–115, 107–108; Dusya Vera and Mary Crossan, "Theatrical Improvisation: Lessons for Organizations," *Organization Studies* 25, no. 5 (2004): 727–749.

51. I make every possible effort in this book to cite the exact sources where I learned particular ideas or exercises that are not my own. Yet it's worth noting up front that improv theater and applied improv are incredibly collaborative fields where ideas and exercises are freely shared in a way that's often impossible to trace original sources. After many years of doing this work, sometimes you'll even discover that what you thought was a new idea or exercise was actually formulated by

another individual or group further back in history. To the best of my knowledge, I'll always give credit where credit is due, but with a recognition that my sources may not always be acknowledging the histories that they themselves are building from—and through no fault of their own, since the background references may be too difficult to unearth. On another note, since contemporary culture tends to offer fragmentary "texts" and "contexts" regarding any topic, and that's especially the case with developments in improvisation around the world, in this book I use a methodology of weaving together extant data, ethnographic observations, and performance to construct a needed framework out of the many disparate fragments on this subject. For a call to use this approach, see Michael Calvin McGee, "Text, Context, and the Fragmentation of Contemporary Culture," *Western Journal of Communication* 54 (1990): 274–289.

52. Farnaz Tabaee, "Effects of Improvisation Techniques in Leadership Development" (PhD diss., Pepperdine University, 2013), 1.

53. Kevin W. Mossholder, Hettie A. Richardson, and Randall P. Settoon, "Human Resource Systems and Helping in Organizations: A Relational Perspective," *Academy of Management Review* 36, no. 1 (2011): 33.

54. Annette M. Holba, "Political Communication and Leisure," *The Review of Communication* 10, no. 1 (2010): 21, 24, 36.

55. Stephens, "Civics Lessons," par. 9.

56. Joshua A. Lerner, *Making Democracy Fun: How Game Design Can Empower Citizens and Transform Politics* (Cambridge, MA: MIT Press, 2014), 13, 15.

57. Ibid., 3.

58. Ibid., 5.

59. Common Craft, "Gamification," *Common Craft*, 2016, video, 2:27, www.commoncraft.com/video/gamification; Joseph Kahne, Ellen Middaugh, and Chris Evans, *The Civic Potential of Video Games* (Cambridge, MA: MIT Press, 2009). Relatedly, a long history of how fun has been employed in the service of serious public advocacy should be recognized here as well; for example, Adrienne Christiansen and Jeremy J. Hanson, "Comedy as Cure for Tragedy: ACT UP and the Rhetoric of AIDS," *Quarterly Journal of Speech* 82, no. 2 (1996): 157–170.

60. Augusto Boal, *Legislative Theater: Using Performance to Make Politics* (London: Routledge, 1998), 20.

61. Kettering Foundation, www.kettering.org.

62. Lois Holzman, *Vygotsky at Work and Play* (New York: Routledge, 2017).

63. Ibid., 19.

64. See "Improv for Humanity" at www.improvforhumanity.org and the group's Facebook page at www.facebook.com/Improv-for-Humanity-1325975384086386/.

65. Barbara S. Tint, Viv McWaters, and Raymond van Driel, "Applied Improvisation Training for Disaster Readiness and Response: Preparing Humanitarian Workers and Communities for the Unexpected," *Journal of Humanitarian Logistics and Supply Chain Management* 5, no. 1 (2015): 87.

66. Mary Tyszkiewicz, "Practicing for the Unimaginable: The Heroic Improv Cycle," in *Applied Improvisation*, eds. Theresa Robbins Dudeck and Caitlin McClure (London: Methuen, 2018), 117–132.

67. Embassy of the United States, Nicosia, Cyprus, "Improv Theatre Expert James Thomas Bailey Shares More Than Fun and Games on Return Visit to Cyprus," *Embassy of the United States, Nicosia, Cyprus*, May 4–16, 2009, https://cyprus.us embassy.gov/embatwork/improvmay09.html (site discontinued), par. 2; Embassy of the United States, Nicosia, Cyprus, "Improvisation Expert James Bailey Conducts Theatre Workshops with Local Educators and Artists," *Embassy of the United States, Nicosia, Cyprus*, September 29–October 28, 2008, https://cyprus.usembassy.gov/embatwork/improvoct08.html (site discontinued); Improv Resource Center Wiki, "IO West," *Improv Resource Center Wiki*, accessed April 16, 2020, http://wiki.improvresourcecenter.com/index.php/IO_West, par. 5.

68. Improv Resource Center Wiki, "IO West," par. 5.

69. Savannah Eadens, " 'Yes, and': Second City Behavioral Science Group Studies how Improv can Create Better Communication," *Chicago Tribune*, July 29, 2018, www.chicagotribune.com/entertainment/ct-ent-second-city-study-0725-story.html.

70. Don J. Waisanen, "Communication Training's Higher Calling: Using a Civic Frame to Promote Transparency and Elevate the Value of Services," in *Handbook of Communication Training*, eds. J. D. Wallace and Dennis Becker (New York: Routledge, 2018).

71. William C. Madsen and Kevin Gillespie, *Collaborative Helping: A Strengths Framework for Home-Based Services* (Hoboken, NJ: Wiley, 2014), 25.

Chapter 1

1. Vicki Salemi, "Good Grades Are Meaningless in the Modern Workplace," *New York Post*, March 21, 2016, http://nypost.com/2016/03/21/good-grades-are-meaningless-in-the-modern-workplace/.

2. Ibid., par. 9.

3. David J. Deming, "The Growing Importance of Social Skills in the Labor Market," *National Bureau of Economic Research*, December 8, 2017, www.nber.org/digest/nov15/w21473.html, par. 1.

4. Jean M. Twenge, *iGen: Why Today's Super-Connected Kids Are Growing Up Less Rebellious, More Tolerant, Less Happy—and Completely Unprepared for Adulthood—and What That Means for the Rest of Us* (New York: Simon and Schuster, 2017).

5. Credit for this quote goes to the late Carol Baker Tharpe, an inspirational thinker, activist, and advocate for democratic practices.

6. These metaphors are drawn from Ronald Heifetz, Alexander Grashow, and Marty Linsky, *The Practice of Adaptive Leadership: Tools and Tactics for Changing Your Organization and the World* (Cambridge, MA: Harvard University Press, 2010), 7.

7. Sharon Daloz Parks, *Leadership Can Be Taught: A Bold Approach for a Complex World* (Cambridge, MA: Harvard Business Review Press, 2005), 7.

8. Linda Weiser Friedman, Hershey H. Friedman, and Martin Frankel, "A New Mode of Learning in Higher Education: The Partnership Hybrid Class," SSRN, January 10, 2016, http://papers.ssrn.com/sol3/papers.cfm?abstract_id=2712763.

9. Ibid., 5.

10. Ralph G. Brocket, *Teaching Adults: A Practical Guide for New Teachers* (San Francisco: Jossey-Bass, 2016), 31–32.

11. Ken Robinson, "Do Schools Kill Creativity?" *TED*, February 2006, video, 19:13, www.ted.com/talks/ken_robinson_says_schools_kill_creativity?language=en.

12. Susan Engel, "Joy: A Subject Schools Lack," *The Atlantic*, January 26, 2015, www.theatlantic.com/education/archive/2015/01/joy-the-subject-schools-lack/384800/.

13. Bernard and Short, *Jill and Patrick's Small Book*, 14–15.

14. Alexander Grashow, "Adaptive Leadership Workshop," Coro New York Leadership Center, January 23, 2015; Ivan Illich, *Deschooling Society* (New York: Harper and Row), 1971.

15. Keith Johnstone, *Impro: Improvisation and the Theatre* (New York, Routledge, 1987), 15.

16. Ibid., 17. Those looking for more on improvisational theater's history (especially in the US) can now find many resources on this subject. A brief history of major figures and events includes the development of commedia dell'arte in 16th century Italy, which involved performances of stock characters and situations without any scripts. Viola Spolin's classic work developed in the 1930s as a way of training actors, eventually advancing the world-famous Second City theater in Chicago and offshoots like the Committee in San Francisco. In other countries, improvisational theater emerged parallel to these efforts. Keith Johnstone started using improvisation to counter Stanislavski's acting techniques, as a way to make actors less calculating and more spontaneous in their work. He developed Theatresports in Canada in the 1970s, a precursor to the type of *Whose Line is It Anyway* comedy performance games many audiences around the world have now seen on television. Figures like Augusto Boal used improv as a rehearsal tool for community theater and as a way of influencing politics in South America. Del Close and Charna Halpern developed what is now called "long-form improvisation" at the ImprovOlympic (or iO) Theater in Chicago, which moves beyond short games to improvising longer scenes or entire plays. Fast-forward to today, and almost all of the major improv theaters in the US have roots in one of these traditions, such as the Groundlings in Los Angeles (which stemmed from the Committee), the Upright Citizen's Brigade in Los Angeles and New York, and Comedysportz theaters all across the nation (which emerged from Johnstone's and others' Theatresports tradition). One of the biggest accomplishments of these simultaneous efforts has been to make improvisational theater its own stand-alone art form. See Bill Lynn, *Improvisation for Actors*

and Writers (Colorado Springs: Meriwether, 2004), 7; Tom Salinsky and Deborah Frances-White, *The Improv Handbook: The Ultimate Guide to Improvising in Comedy, Theatre, and Beyond* (New York: Methuen, 2013), 100, 2–4.

17. Tint, McWaters, and van Driel, "Applied Improvisation Training," 73–94; Curiosity Staff, "Improv Theater Was Invented to Help Immigrants Assimilate," Curiosity, September 20, 2016, https://m.curiosity.com/topics/improv-theater-was-invented-to-help-immigrants-assimilate-curiosity/ (site discontinued).

18. Esther Saxey, "Theatre Improvisation in Teaching," *Education Blog*, January 31, 2017, http://blogs.lse.ac.uk/education/2017/01/31/theatre-improvisation-in-teaching/.

19. Salinsky and Frances-White, *The Improv Handbook*, 40–41.

20. Ibid., 41.

21. Chip Heath and Dan Heath, *Switch: How to Change Things When Change Is Hard* (New York: Random House), 2010.

22. Rebecca Stockley, "UX Week 2013 | Rebecca Stockley | Visit Improv World Without Looking Like a Tourist," *adaptivepath*, December 9, 2013, YouTube video, 28:54, www.youtube.com/watch?v=ddEryrU0qRo.

23. I can't remember where I picked up this activity, but it's similar to Paul Z. Jackson's "Ping-Pong" exercise in Paul Z. Jackson, *58½ Ways to Improvise in Training* (London: Crown House, 2003).

24. See Heifetz, Grashow, and Linsky, *The Practice of Adaptive Leadership*, 178.

25. Cited in Jesse Singal, "The Bad Things that Happen When People Can't Deal with Ambiguous Situations," *NY Magazine*, October 19, 2015, http://nymag.com/scienceofus/2015/10/importance-of-dealing-with-ambiguity.html, par. 2.

26. Ibid., par. 4, 9.

27. Eli Pariser, "Beware Online 'Filter Bubbles,'" *TED Talks*, March 2011, video, 8:49, www.ted.com/talks/eli_pariser_beware_online_filter_bubbles?language=en.

28. Cathy Salit, *Performance Breakthrough: A Radical Approach to Work* (New York: Hachette, 2016), 17, xix, italics in original.

29. Andre P. Walton, "The Impact of Interpersonal Factors on Creativity," *International Journal of Entrepreneurial Behavior & Research* 9, no. 4 (2003): 146–162.

30. Carine Lewis and Peter J. Lovatt, "Breaking Away from Set Patterns of Thinking: Improvisation and Divergent Thinking," *Thinking Skills and Creativity* 9, no. 9 (2013): 46–58.

31. T. J. Jagodowski and David Pasquesi, *Improvisation at the Speed of Life* (Chicago: Sola Roma, 2015), xii.

32. Jackson, "Applying Improvisation."

33. Larry Gross, "Modes of Communication and the Acquisition of Symbolic Competence," in *Media and Symbols*, ed. David R. Olson (Chicago: University of Chicago Press, 1974), 58, 62.

34. John Greenwood, "Evidence Based Education: Active vs. Passive Learning," *The Teaching Course*, May 14, 2014, www.thetcblog.com/?p=2128 (site discontinued).

35. Ronald A. Berk and Rosalind H. Trieber, "Whose Classroom is it, Anyway? Improvisation as a Teaching Tool," *Journal on Excellence in College Teaching* 20, no. 3 (2009): 50–51. Howard Gardner has also written extensively about the "multiple intelligences" that contrast with a narrow, IQ-based view of intelligence, turning instead to "a pluralistic view of the mind" emerging from neuro- and cognitive science. There's musical, bodily-kinesthetic, logical-mathematical, linguistic, spatial, interpersonal, intrapersonal, and potentially naturalistic and spiritual intelligences. Gardner explains, "My research has suggested that any rich, nourishing topic—any topic worth teaching—can be approached in at least seven different ways that roughly speaking, map onto the multiple intelligences." Howard Gardner, *Multiple Intelligences* (New York: Basic Books, 2006), 5, 139.

36. Berk and Trieber, "Whose Classroom Is It, Anyway?, 35.

37. Mel Silberman, *Active Learning: 101 Strategies to Teach Any Subject* (San Francisco: Wiley, 2006), 1, 3, 7.

38. Donald L. Finkel, *Teaching with Your Mouth Shut* (Portsmouth, NH: Heinemann), 1999.

39. Andrew Tarvin, "What is Applied Improvisation?" *Humor that Works,* accessed April 20, 2020, www.humorthatworks.com/learning/what-is-applied-improvisation/.

40. Finkel, *Teaching*, 8, 9, 17, 33, 36, 41, 46–47.

41. Ibid., 54, 100–101.

42. Gerald Graff, *Clueless in Academe: How Schooling Obscures the Life of the Mind* (New Haven, CT: Yale University Press), 219.

43. Barnard College, "Reacting to the Past," Barnard College, 2016, https://reacting.barnard.edu/.

44. Silberman, *Active Learning*, 131.

45. Cited in Pink, *A Whole New Mind*, 191.

46. Jane McGonigal, *Reality Is Broken: Why Games Make Us Better and How They Can Change the World* (New York: Penguin, 2011), 3.

47. Ibid., 14, 127.

48. Dugan Laird, Elwood F. Holton, and Sharon Naquin, *Approaches to Training and Development* (New York: Basic Books, 2003).

49. Jonathan Keats, "Let's Play War," *Nautilus*, June 13, 2019, http://nautil.us/issue/73/play/lets-play-war-rp.

50. Carlos Diaz-Lazaro, Sandra Cordova, and Rosslyn Franklyn, "Experiential Activities for Teaching about Diversity," in *Getting Culture*, eds. Regan A. R. Gurung and Loreto R. Prieto (Sterling, VA: Stylus), 194; Bryan S. K. Kim and Heather Z. Lyons, "Experiential Activities and Multicultural Counseling Competence Training," *Journal of Counseling and Development: JCD* 81, no. 4 (2003): 400.

51. Eric Jensen, *Brain-Based Learning: The New Paradigm of Teaching* (Thousand Oaks, CA: SAGE, 2008), 5.

52. Ibid., 14, 5.

53. Ibid., 55.

54. Cited in Silberman, *Active Learning*, 1.

55. Will Thalheimer, "Debunk This: People Remember 10 Percent of What They Read," *ATD*, March 12, 2015, https://www.td.org/Publications/Blogs/Science-of-Learning-Blog/2015/03/Debunk-This-People-Remember-10-Percent-of-What-They-Read.

56. Arthur W. Chickering and Zelda F. Gamson, *Applying the Seven Principles for Good Practice in Undergraduate Education: New Directions for Teaching and Learning* (San Francisco: Jossey-Bass, 1991), 66.

57. Darin L. Garard, Lance Lippert, Stephen K. Hunt, and Scott T. Paynton, "Alternatives to Traditional Instruction: Using Games and Simulations to Increase Student Learning and Motivation," *Communication Research Reports* 15, no. 1 (1998): 36; Knut Aspegren, "BEME Guide No. 2: Teaching and Learning Communication Skills in Medicine: A Review with Quality Grading of Articles," *Medical Teacher* 21, no. 6 (1999): 563–570. See also David A. Kolb, *Experiential Learning: Experience as the Source of Learning and Development* (Upper Saddle River, NJ: FT Press, 2014).

58. Peter Gray, "The Decline of Play and Rise in Children's Mental Disorders," *Psychology Today*, January 26, 2010, www.psychologytoday.com/blog/freedom-learn/201001/the-decline-play-and-rise-in-childrens-mental-disorders.

59. Jensen, *Brain-Based*, 39.

60. Ori Brafman and Judah Pollack, *The Chaos Imperative* (New York: Crown Business, 2013), 68. See also David Brancaccio, "How Recess Can Make Students Better Job Candidates," Marketplace, December 19, 2017, www.marketplace.org/2017/12/19/education/recess-important-thriving-workplace-employers.

61. Antonio R. Damasio, *Descartes' Error: Emotion, Reason, and the Human Brain* (New York: Random House, 2006).

62. Jensen, *Brain-Based*, 38.

63. Additionally, "your learners' emotional state is at least as important as the intellectual–cognitive content of your presentation," so teachers and trainers should "elicit positive emotional states from learners with enjoyable activities, games, humor, personal attention, and acts of caring." Ibid., 37–39, 83.

64. Charna Halpern, *Art by Committee: A Guide to Advanced Improvisation* (Colorado Springs: Meriwether, 2006), 39.

65. Barbara Fredrickson, *Positivity* (New York: Random House, 2009).

66. Gordon Bermant, "Working With(out) a Net: Improvisational Theater and Enhanced Well-Being," *Frontiers in Psychology* 4 (December 2013): 929.

67. Barbara Fredrickson, "What Good are Positive Emotions?" *Review of General Psychology* 2, no. 3 (1998): 300.

68. Ellen Langer, *Mindfulness* (Philadelphia: De Capo Press, 2014).

69. Ellen J. Langer, "Mindfulness Forward and Back," in *The Wiley-Blackwell Handbook of Mindfulness*, eds. Amanda Ie, Christelle T. Ngnoumen, and Ellen J. Langer (Malden, MA: Blackwell, 2014), 11, italics added.

70. Ted DesMaisons, "Improv and Mindfulness," Applied Improvisation Network World Conference (preconference workshop, University of Oxford, Oxford, UK, August 11, 2016).

71. Caryn Musil, "Feminist Pedagogy: Setting the Standard for Engaged Learning," AAC&U 34 (2015): par. 1.

72. Halpern, *Art by Committee*, 55. This line of thought also stems from a growing recognition of the intersections between social causes and comedic forms of communication. One recent conference proposed that greater efforts should be made to bring "the organization power of social justice activism to comedy, and the persuasive power of comedy to social justice activism." Prateekshit Pandey, "Yes, and . . . Laughter Lab: Creating New Collaboration between Comedy and Social Justice," Center for Media & Social Impact, August 29, 2019, https://cmsimpact.org/comedy/yes-and-laughter-lab/, par. 2.

73. Ira Sharkansky and Yair Zalmanovitch, "Improvisation in Public Administration and Policy Making in Israel," *Public Administration Review* 60, no. 4 (2000): 321–329.

74. Doris A. Graber, *The Power of Communication: Managing Information in Public Organizations* (Thousand Oaks, CA: SAGE, 2002); Patricia C. Pitcher, *The Drama of Leadership* (New York: Wiley, 1997), 181, 226.

75. Michael Crozier, "Recursive Governance: Contemporary Political Communication and Public Policy," *Political Communication* 24, no. 1 (2007): 1, 4.

76. Susan FitzPatrick, "The Imaginary and Improvisation in Public Administration," *Administrative Theory & Praxis* 24, no. 4 (2002): 635–654.

77. Nick Horney, Bill Pasmore, and Tom O'Shea, "Leadership Agility: A Business Imperative for a VUCA World," *People & Strategy* 33, no. 4 (2010): 34.

78. Chris McDonald, "Crisis Management as Ethical Improvisation," *Critical Studies in Improvisation* 9, no. 1 (2013): par. 2, 7.

79. Lerner, *Making Democracy Fun*, 16.

80. Ibid.

81. Cited in Katherine S. McKnight and Mary Scruggs, *The Second City Guide to Improv in the Classroom* (San Francisco: Wiley, 2008), 3.

82. My thanks go to Gary Kramer at the National Comedy Theater for teaching me this practice.

83. There's a nuance here: we're not seeking to "celebrate" mistakes so much as find positive ways to quickly move beyond them *while* supporting successful behaviors. Paul Z. Jackson makes a great case that we don't want our dentist to embrace failure in the middle of dental surgery, we want them to get the behavior right the first time with pinpoint accuracy. Improv provides a different context where you can take more risks than scenarios like this, but the ultimate point shouldn't be lost: we're not embracing mistakes as ends in themselves, but rather so we can recalibrate quickly and emulate successful behaviors. See Paul Z. Jackson, "The

Mistakes Myth: Paul Z Jackson at TEDxRussellSquare," *TEDx Talks*, March 11, 2014, YouTube video, 14:26, www.youtube.com/watch?v=_o5beLKS5M4.

84. My understanding has been that this exercise or a variation of it goes back to Spolin, but I have seen "Zip Zap Zop" (its traditional name) and similar versions run by just about every improv instructor I have encountered. This may be the most co-created exercise in the improv world. For similar demonstrations of this exercise, see Patrick Reidy, "Improv Training Warm Up Game: Imaginary Balls Comedy," *lmaonyc*, May 20, 2012, YouTube video, 1:13, www.youtube.com/watch?v=6GxG4t1pW7M, and "Zip Zap Zop," *Laughter For A Change*, October 26, 2013, YouTube video, 1:19, www.youtube.com/watch?v=lyWKVGoXKak.

85. This exercise has a long history too, but for convenience I've adapted my way of teaching it from Val Gee and Sarah Gee's "Be in the Moment" activity. Val Gee and Sarah Gee, *Business Improv* (Columbus: McGraw Hill, 2011), 24–28. For a similar demonstration of this exercise, see Shana Merlin, "Improv Warm-Ups: Orange Ball, Thank You," *expertvillage*, October 3, 2008, YouTube video, 01:53, www.youtube.com/watch?v=x0noHPqyX00.

86. To stay current with state-of-the-art resources in this area, the Applied Improvisation Network now also maintains an online library that should prove helpful at http://appliedimprovisation.network/library/.

87. Katie Watson and Belinda Fu, "Medical Improv: A Novel Approach to Teaching Communication and Professionalism Skills," *Annals of Internal Medicine*, 165, no. 8 (2016): 591–592. See also Beth Boynton, "Launch into the Wonderland of Medical Improv with this Podcast Interview!" *Confident Voices in Healthcare*, June 7, 2016, www.confidentvoices.com/2016/06/07/launch-into-the-wonderland-of-medical-improv-with-this-podcast-interview/.

88. Ari Hoffman, Bryan Utley, and Dan Ciccarone, "Improving Medical Student Communication Skills through Improvisational Theater," *Medical Education* 42, no. 5 (2008): 537; Watson and Fu, "Medical Improv," 1; Neil Versal, "Improv Training helps Cleveland Clinic Improve MD Communications," *MedCity News*, April 14, 2016, http://medcitynews.com/2016/04/improv-training-helps-cleveland-clinic-improve-md-communications/.

89. Katie Watson, "Serious Play: Teaching Medical Skills with Improvisational Theater Techniques," *Academic Medicine* 86, no. 10 (2011): 1260.

90. Ibid., 1263; Jo Marie Reilly, Janet Trial, Debra E. Piver, and Pamela B. Schaff, "Using Theater to Increase Empathy Training in Medical Students," *Journal for Learning through the Arts* 8, no. 1 (2012): 1–8.

91. Krista Hoffmann-Longtin, Jason M. Organ, Jill V. Helphinstine, Deanna R. Reinoso, Zachary S. Morgan, and Elizabeth Weinstein, "Teaching Advocacy Communication to Pediatric Residents: The Efficacy of Applied Improvisational Theater (AIT) as an Instructional Tool," *Communication Education* 67, no. 4 (2018): 438.

92. Hoffman, Utley, and Ciccarone, "Improving Medical," 537–538.

93. Candace A. Campbell, "Improv to Improve Interprofessional Communication, Team Building, Patient Safety, and Patient Satisfaction (PhD diss., University of San Francisco, 2014).

94. Boesen, Herrier, Apgar, and Jackowski, "Improvisational Exercises," 1, 7.

95. See, for example, Mary Lorenz, "Employers Who Say 'Yes, and . . .' to Improv Comedy Gain Serious Benefits," *The Hiring Site,* February 4, 2010, http://thehiringsite.careerbuilder.com/2010/02/04/employers-who-say-yes-and-to-improv-comedy-gain-serious-benefits/ (site discontinued).

96. Huffaker and West, "Enhancing Learning," 855, 859, 861–862.

97. Wanda Orlikowski and J. Debra Hoffman, "An Improvisational Model for Change Management: The Case of Groupware Technologies," *Sloan Management Review* 38, no. 2 (1997): 11–21; Izzy Gesell, "Practiced Spontaneity: Using Improv Theater Skills to Help Teams Master Change," *The Journal for Quality and Participation* 28, no. 1 (2005): 4; Priya Nair Rajeev and Subramanian Kalpathi, "Let's Play: The Use of Improv Games in Change Management Training—A Case Study," *Industry and Higher Education* 30, no. 2 (2016): 149–154.

98. Dan Moshavi, " 'Yes and . . .': Introducing Improvisational Theatre Techniques to the Management Classroom," *Journal of Management Education* 25, no. 4 (2001): 437–449; Lakshmi Balachandra and Michael Wheeler, "What Negotiators can Learn from Improv Comedy," *Negotiation* 9, no. 8 (2008): 1–3.

99. David L. Corsun, Cheri A. Young, Amy McManus, and Mehmet Erdem, "Overcoming Managers' Perceptual Shortcuts through Improvisational Theater Games," *Journal of Management Development* 25, no. 4 (2006): 298.

100. Michael Wheeler, *The Art of Negotiation: How to Improvise Agreement in a Chaotic World* (New York: Simon and Schuster, 2013). See also Lakshmi Balachandra, Robert C. Bordone, Carrie Menkel-Meadow, Philip Ringstrom, and Edward Sarath, "Improvisation and Negotiation: Expecting the Unexpected," *Negotiation Journal* 21, no. 4 (2005): 415–423.

101. Leonard L. Riskin, "Beginning with Yes: A Review Essay on Michael Wheeler's *The Art of Negotiation: How to Improvise Agreement in a Chaotic World*," *Cardozo Journal of Conflict Resolution* 16, no. 605 (2015): 622–623.

102. Barbara Tint, "From Hell No to Yes And: Applied Improvisation for Training in Conflict Resolution, Mediation, and Law," in *Applied Improvisation*, eds. Theresa Robbins Dudeck and Caitlin McClure (London: Methuen, 2018), 212.

103. Lakshmi Balachandra, Frank Barrett, Howard Bellman, Colin Fisher, and Lawrence Susskind, "Improvisation and Mediation: Balancing Acts," *Negotiation Journal* 21, no. 4 (2005): 433.

104. Ilene C. Wasserman and Beth Fisher-Yoshida, *Communicating Possibilities: A Brief Introduction to the Coordinated Management of Meaning (CMM)* (Chagrin Falls, OH: Taos Institute Publications, 2017).

105. Richard A. Rocco and D. Joel Whalen, "Teaching Yes, and . . . Improv in Sales Classes Enhancing Student Adaptive Selling Skills, Sales Performance, and Teaching Evaluations," *Journal of Marketing Education* 36, no. 2 (2014): 197.

106. Karen Robson, Leyland Pitt, and Pierre R. Berthon, "'Yes, and . . .': What Improv Theater Can Teach Service Firms," *Business Horizons* 58, no. 4 (2015): 357.

107. Jörg Finsterwalder and Billy O'Steen, "Marketing Theatre Education: Using Improvisation for Teaching and Learning," *UC Research Repository* (2008): 1.

108. Carly Miller, "Why Improv Comedy Is the Next Big Marketing Trend," *The Content Strategist*, May 16, 2016, https://contently.com/strategist/2016/05/26/why-improv-comedy-is-the-next-big-marketing-trend/.

109. Vera and Crossan, "Theatrical Improvisation."

110. Ibid.

111. Jordana Cole, "I've Got Your Back: Utilizing Improv as a Tool to Enhance Workplace Relationships" (master's thesis, University of Pennsylvania, 2016), http://repository.upenn.edu/cgi/viewcontent.cgi?article=1096&context=mapp_capstone.

112. Karl Weick, "Introductory Essay—Improvisation as a Mindset for Organizational Analysis," *Organization Science* 9, no. 5 (1998): 551.

113. Leslie S. Jacques, "Borrowing from Professional Theatre Training to Build Essential Skills in Organization Development Consultants," *The Journal of Applied Behavioral Science* 49, no. 2 (2013): 246.

114. Ruth H. Yamamoto, "Serious Fun: The Perceived Influences of Improvisational Acting on Community College Students" (PhD diss., Walden University, 2015), 4.

115. Scott Jaschik, "Well Prepared in their Own Eyes," *Inside Higher Ed*, January 20, 2015, www.insidehighered.com/news/2015/01/20/study-finds-big-gaps-between-student-and-employer-perceptions.

116. National Leadership Council, *College Learning*, 5.

117. M. R. Diamond and M. H. Christensen, "Bravo! Do Acting Games Promote Learning in the College Classroom," *Journal on Excellence in College Teaching* 16, no. 2 (2005): 55–67; Anders Baerheim and Torild J. Alraek, "Utilizing Theatrical Tools in Consultation Training," *Medical Teacher* 27, no. 7 (2005): 652–654; Torild Jacobsen, Anders Baerheim, Margret Rose Lepp, and Edvin Schei, "Analysis of Role-Play in Medical Communication Training Using a Theatrical Device—The Fourth Wall," *Medical Education* 6, no. 1 (2006): 1–8; Johanna Shapiro and Lynn Hunt, "All the World's a Stage: The Use of Theatrical Performance in Medical Education," *Medical Education* 37 (2003): 922–927; Moshavi, "Yes and."

118. Theresa Becker, "Evaluating Improvisation as a Technique for Training Pre-service Teachers for Inclusive Classrooms" (PhD diss., University of Central Florida, 2012), iii–iv.

119. Ibid., iv.

120. Cassandra Kisiel, Margaret Blaustein, Joseph Spinazzola, Caren Swift Schmidt, Marla Zucker, and Bessel van der Kolk, "Evaluation of a Theater-Based Youth Violence Prevention Program for Elementary School Children," *Journal of School Violence* 5, no. 2 (2006): 32.

121. Todd, "Practicing in the Uncertain," 302.

122. Jonathan P. Rossing and Krista Hoffmann-Longtin, "Improv(ing) the Academy: Applied Improvisation as a Strategy for Educational Development," *To Improve the Academy* 35, no. 2 (2016): 303–325.

123. Anthony C. Stamatoplos, "Improvisational Theater as a tool for Enhancing Cooperation in Academic Libraries," in *Proceedings of the ACRL Fourteenth National Conference*, March 12–15, 2009, 65–70.

124. Vimal Patel, "Improv Helps Ph.D.'s Explain Their Work—and Loosen Up," *Chronicle of Higher Education*, November 10, 2014, www.chronicle.com/article/ Improv-Helps-PhDs-Explain/149887. See also Sara Castellanos, " 'Oh, My God, Where Is This Going?' When Computer-Science Majors Take Improv," *Wall Street Journal*, May 14, 2019, www.wsj.com/articles/oh-my-god-where-is-this-going-when-computer-science-majors-take-improv-11557846729.

125. Alan Alda Center for Communicating Science, "Improvisation for Scientists," The New York Academy of Sciences, December 16, 2011, www.nyas.org/ events/2011/improvisation-for-scientists/.

126. Alan Alda, "Improvisation for Scientists: Workshops by Alan Alda and the Center for Communicating Science," *SBUJournalism*, March 23, 2010, YouTube video, 9:18, www.youtube.com/watch?v=JtdyA7SibG8.

127. Joseph Holtgreive, "The Lessons of Engineering Improv," *InsideHigherEd*, January 11, 2018, pars. 8–9.

128. Mihaly Csikszentmihalyi, *Flow: The Psychology of Optimal Experience* (New York: Harper & Row, 1990), 33.

129. Holtgreive, "The Lessons of Engineering Improv," par. 15.

130. Bruce C. Ballon, Ivan Silver, and Donald Fidler, "Headspace Theater: An Innovative Method for Experiential Learning of Psychiatric Symptomatology using Modified Role-Playing and Improvisational Theater Techniques," *Academic Psychiatry* 31, no. 5 (2007): 380–387.

131. Clay Drinko, *Theatrical Improvisation, Consciousness, and Cognition* (New York: Palgrave Macmillan, 2013), 12.

132. Berman, "Working with(out) a Net."

133. Alison Phillips Sheesley, Mark Pfeffer, and Becca Barish, "Comedic Improv Therapy for the Treatment of Social Anxiety Disorder," *Journal of Creativity in Mental Health* 11, no. 2 (2016): 164, 166. See also Rachel Healy, " 'Improv Saved My Life': The Comedy Classes Helping People with Anxiety," *Guardian*, December 20, 2017, www.theguardian.com/stage/2017/dec/20/ comedy-improv-overcome-anxiety-depression.

134. Peter Balonon-Rosen, "Whose Line Is It Really? How Improv Benefits Children with Autism," *State Impact*, December 21, 2016, http://indianapublicmedia. org/stateimpact/2016/12/21/improv-autism-benefits/.

135. Lacy Alana and Jim Ansaldo, "The Connect Improv Curriculum: Supporting Youth on the Autism Spectrum and their Educators," in *Applied Improvisation*,

eds. Theresa Robbins Dudeck and Caitlin McClure (London: Methuen, 2018), 87.

136. Nancy E. Krusen, "Improvisation as an Adaptive Strategy for Occupational Therapy Practice." *Occupational Therapy in Health Care* 26 (2012): 64.

137. Danny Bega, Pamela Palmentera, Abby Wagner, Matt Hovde, Becca Barish, Mary J. Kwasny, and Tanya Simuni, "Laughter is the Best Medicine: The Second City® Improvisation as an Intervention for Parkinson's Disease," *Parkinsonism & Related Disorders* 34 (January 2017): 62–65.

138. Tint, McWaters, and van Driel, "Applied Improvisation Training," 73–78, 83.

139. Ibid., 78.

140. David Mendonça and Frank Fiedrich, "Training for Improvisation in Emergency Management: Opportunities and Limits for Information Technology," *International Journal of Emergency Management* 3, no. 3 (2006): 350–351.

141. Carrane and Allen, *Improvising Better*, 54.

142. This exercise can be located in many sources, but I have most used and adapted Alan Montague and Patrick Short's instructions here. Alan Montague and Patrick Short, "Intro to Applied Improvisation for Performers," Preconference workshop, Applied Improvisation Network World Conference, University of Oxford, Oxford, UK, August 11, 2016. For a similar demonstration of this exercise, see Matthew Milo, "Improvisational Warm Ups: Playing the 'Alien, Tiger, Cow' Improv Game," *expertvillage*, April 23, 2008, YouTube video, 1:30, www.youtube.com/watch?v=UeUUHd4bQBQ.

143. Jackson, *58½ Ways*, 79–80. For a similar demonstration of this exercise, see Glyn Trefor-Jones, "Theatre Game #5—Energy Circle. From Drama Menu—Drama Games & Ideas for Drama," *Drama Menu*, June 26, 2014, YouTube video, 01:28, www.youtube.com/watch?v=wWPiYksnKLI.

144. McKnight and Scruggs, *The Second City Guide*, 87.

145. I once heard the question of how one can graduate from old ways of being, thinking, and doing in a new world raised by Alexander Grashow, "Adaptive Leadership Workshop."

Chapter 2

1. For research and support for this idea, see Paul McGhee, *Humor as Survival Training for a Stressed-Out World: The 7 Humor Habits Program* (Bloomington, IN: Authorhouse), 2010.

2. Todd Zakrajsek, "Keep the Magic Alive," *NEA Higher Education Advocate* 28, no. 3 (2011): 5.

3. James Carse, *Finite and Infinite Games* (New York: Simon and Schuster, 2011), 15.

4. For an overview, see Lewis and Lovatt, "Breaking Away," 48.

5. Mark Gring and Jera W. Littlejohn, "Assessment of the Repeated Speech Performance as a Pedagogical Tool: A Pilot Study," *Basic Communication Course Annual* 12 (2000): 97–125. This need for repetition hearkens back to basic behaviorism; see B. F. Skinner, *About Behaviorism* (San Francisco: Knopf, 1974).

6. Lipmanowicz and McCandless, *The Surprising Power*. All 33 structures are explained at www.liberatingstructures.com.

7. Mick Napier, *Behind the Scenes: Improvising Long Form* (Englewood, CO: Meriwether, 2015), 108.

8. Richard M. Felder and Rebecca Brent, *Teaching and Learning STEM: A Practical Guide* (San Francisco: Jossey-Bass, 2016), 123. To get beyond typical debrief questions such as "How did that feel," Finest City Improv suggests drawing from this checklist of questions when designing debriefs: "What did you notice or observe during that activity?" "Did you notice . . . ? ('good' or 'bad' moments, moves, choices)," "What happened there . . . ? (if you pause a group and want them to describe and reflect on a specific moment)," "What did you experience?" "When did you feel the most at ease or the most joy?" "When did you feel tension or struggle?" "Why did that happen?" and "When else [in life] does that happen?" To observers you can also ask "What did they do well? (directly related to lesson goals—remind observers before the activity what to look for)" and "What did you enjoy about that?" Also, "with newer students, or reluctant students, it helps to ask for a specific number of responses such as 'I'd like to hear from *three* people—what's one thing you noticed worked well during that activity?' " and "How can you use that? (this is a great follow-up question in a discussion after someone has described something they learned. Always be looking for opportunities to connect lessons to future opportunities for growth!)." Finest City Improv, "How to Have Awesome Improv Classes by Posing Great Debriefing Questions," *Finest City Improv*, accessed April 23, 2020, www.finestcityimprov.com/great-debriefing-questions/.

9. Finkel, *Teaching*, 68–69, italics in original.

10. Ibid.

11. Ken Bain, *What the Best College Students Do* (Cambridge, MA: Harvard University Press, 2012), 44.

12. Tint, McWaters, and van Driel, "Applied Improvisation Training," 84.

13. Caitlin McClure, "Tiffany and Co. Says Yes, And," in *Applied Improvisation*, eds. Theresa Robbins Dudeck and Caitlin McClure (London: Methuen, 2018), 150.

14. See Waisanen and Reynolds, "Side-Coaching."

15. Viola Spolin, *Theater Games for the Classroom: A Teacher's Handbook* (Evanston, IL: Northwestern University Press, 1986), 5–6.

16. This advice is also supported by Tint and Froerer, "Delphi Study Summary," 3.

17. Felder and Brent, *Teaching and Learning STEM*.

18. Steve Roe, "How I Give Feedback When Teaching Improv," Hoopla, April 24, 2017, http://hooplaimpro.blogspot.com/2017/04/how-i-give-feedback-when-teaching-improv.html, pars. 4–9.

19. Huffaker and West, "Enhancing Learning."

20. Peter Seldin, cited in Christopher Lucas and John W. Murry, *New Faculty* (New York: Palgrave Macmillan, 2011), 44. Enthusiastic teaching also has an effect on students' cognitive and emotional engagement and is a catalyst for intrinsic motivation to learn. Qin Zhang, "Instructor's Corner #3: Teaching with Enthusiasm: Engaging Students, Sparking Curiosity, and Jumpstarting Motivation," *Communication Currents*, February 2014, www.natcom.org/communication-currents/instructors-corner-3-teaching-enthusiasm-engaging-students-sparking-curiosity. Citing research by Maryellen Weimer, Christopher Lucas and John W. Murry further say that good teachers consistently have "personal enthusiasm . . . clarity of discourse and presentation; preparedness and organization; an ability to stimulate and arouse interest from listeners; and knowledge . . . and an evident love of that subject matter." As part of this, "active learning activities" and "cooperative learning and collaboration among students in the pursuit of clearly defined tasks" are critical. Lucas and Murry, *New Faculty*, 43–44.

21. Zachary W. Goldman, Gregory A. Cranmer, Michael Sollitto, Sara Labelle, and Alexander L. Lancaster, "What do College Students Want? A Prioritization of Instructional Behaviors and Characteristics," *Communication Education* 66, no. 3 (2016): 1.

22. There's an entire field called "social marketing" that's dedicated to this critical difference between "awareness/education" and "behaviors." Most smokers, for example, know that smoking is bad for their health. They don't need to be made more *aware* that smoking is bad, they need initiatives that *help* them change their behavior. People who focus on behaviors can see and measure the results of their work. See Nancy R. Lee and Philip Kotler, *Social Marketing: Influencing Behaviors for Good* (Thousand Oaks, CA: SAGE, 2011).

23. This quote has been attributed to Del Close, cited in Salinsky and Frances-White, 61.

24. Ibid., 246–247. For further support for this concept in professional contexts, see Adam M. Grant, *Give and Take: Why Helping Others Drives Our Success* (New York: Penguin, 2014).

25. Lynn, *Improvisation*, 23–24.

26. Salinsky and Frances-White, *The Improv Handbook*, 45.

27. Lynn, *Improvisation*, 53, 138; Jack Hart, *Storycraft: The Complete Guide to Writing Narrative Nonfiction* (Chicago: University of Chicago Press, 2012).

28. Johnstone, *Impro*, 138, italics in original.

29. Salinsky and Frances-White, *The Improv Handbook*, 72.

30. Carrane and Allen, *Improvising Better*, 47, italics in original.

31. Salinsky and Frances-White, *The Improv Handbook*, 144, 273. In the improv comedy world, Matt Besser, Ian Roberts, and Matt Walsh also note how "in simplest terms, *commitment* is good acting," while "the antithesis of commitment is *detachment*"—so choices played halfheartedly will come across as bad acting. In essence, "*Ironic detachment* means consciously not committing to the reality of the scene in order to get a laugh. Again, this will take the audience out of the reality of the scene. This is also referred to as *commenting*." Matt Besser, Ian Roberts, and Matt Walsh, *The Upright Citizens Brigade Comedy Improvisation Manual* (New York: Comedy Council of Nicea, LLC, 2013), 48–49, italics in original.

32. Lynn, *Improvisation*, 49.

33. See Mike Bonifer, *Gamechangers: Improvisation for Business in the Networked World* (Los Angeles: Gamechangers, 2008), 163.

34. I have no idea where this exercise came from, but it's usually called "Crazy 8s" and I've seen it used in just about every improv theater I've visited. For a demonstration of this exercise, see Laughter For A Change, "Crazy 8s," *Laughter For A Change*, February 20, 2014, YouTube video, 0:56, www.youtube.com/watch?v=VEw7FidF61c.

35. This game has many variants; one explanation can be found here: *Improv Encyclopedia*, s.v. "Whoosh," accessed April 23, 2020, http://improvencyclopedia.org/games/Whoosh.html. For a similar demonstration of this exercise, see Melissa Kinsinger, "5C Improv Game—Whoosh!," *Melissa Kinsinger*, February 10, 2015, YouTube video, 0:52, www.youtube.com/watch?v=0N_-OtJBybU. Another, more advanced version that's played at the National Comedy Theater involves always starting with a "Zoom" (which is the same as the "tunnel" cue, but one rule is that you can never "zoom a zoom," i.e. there should never be two "zooms" passed in a row). You can also say "Pafegliano" (you pass the play to the person on your right or left only—it's a tongue twister that everyone will need to say a few times to get), "Schwartz" (which sends the play back to the person who just gave it to you; for example, if you say "Schwartz" after someone sends you a "Zoom," then the person sending the "Zoom" should send the next cue out again), "Bork" (which, like a bridge, skips over the person to the left or right, whichever direction you're facing), "Double bork" (which skips over four people to your left or right; the fifth person in said direction should pick up the cue), "Twizzler" (the play goes to the person behind you who you are not facing; tricky one this!), "Murph" (everyone puts their hands in their air and screams, play then returns to the same person who said this—basically, it's a freak out moment that still helps play continue), and finally "Warp" (in which the play can be picked up by any person who so chooses). For any mistakes, everyone should "Awooga"—see the Zip Zap Zop exercise from earlier.

36. Thanks to Peter McNerney at the Magnet Theater in New York for sharing this fun addition to the exercise during his class.

37. I drew these debrief questions from Jackson, *58½*, 56–57. For a similar demonstration of this exercise, see John Inchingham, "Improv Games: What Are

You Doing," *ShavaSue*, November 6, 2015, YouTube video, 3:56, www.youtube.com/watch?v=DGukly7CLrU.

38. I have run into this exercise in different forms at many improv theaters, but here I've mostly adapted it from "Last Letter First Letter" in Leonard and Yorton, *Yes, and*, 223. For a demonstration of this exercise, see Shana Merlin, "Improv Warm-Ups: Improv Warm-Ups: 1st Letter, Last Letter Word Association," *expertvillage*, October 3, 2008, YouTube video, 1:21, www.youtube.com/watch?v=VifzHThoMKc.

39. Stevie Ray, *Spontaneity Takes Practice* (Minneapolis: Punchline, 2005), 52–54.

40. I'm sure this exercise has a long history, but I'd like to credit Gary Kramer for first introducing it to me through the National Comedy Theater's WITS Teambuilding program.

41. I first encountered this exercise in the work of Keith Johnstone. See Keith Johnstone, *Impro for Storytellers* (New York: Routledge, 2014), 155. For a demonstration of this exercise, see Fred Gleeck and Avish Parashar, "Improv Exercise—Three Word Sentences," *Fred Gleeck*, December 5, 2009, YouTube video, 2:42, www.youtube.com/watch?v=AwuzruaJJ4Y.

42. I've adapted most of my explanation of this exercise from Salinsky and Frances-White, *The Improv Handbook*, 37–44.

43. Ibid., 39.

44. Ibid.

45. Stephen Nachmanovitch, *Free Play: Improvisation in Life and Art* (New York: Penguin, 1990), 10.

46. Napier, *Behind the Scenes*, 3, 5.

47. Paul Z. Jackson, *The Inspirational Trainer: Making Your Training Flexible, Spontaneous and Creative* (London: Kogan Page Publishers, 2001), 55.

48. Carse, *Finite*, 62.

49. Jackson, *The Inspirational Trainer*, 54.

50. I adapted and updated this exercise from a variation of the game "Create (And Sell) a Product That Can't Be Sold," Joseph A. Keefe, *Improv Yourself* (Hoboken: Wiley, 2002), 102, and the activity "Generate New Ideas," in Gee and Gee, *Business Improv*, 221–226.

51. This exercise was originally called "Bippity Bippity Bop." You can find many different explanations of it from a variety of sources, but I've most adapted my explanation here from McKnight and Scruggs, *The Second City Guide*. For a similar demonstration of this exercise, see Richard Silberg, "Bippity, bippity, bop," *Richard Silberg*, May 31, 2018, YouTube video, 2:47, www.youtube.com/watch?v=0yVjYUypP9I.

52. You can alternately work with "Hula," where a "student in the center does a hula dance; students on each side wave their arms like palm trees"; "Truck," where a "student in the center steers and honks the horn; students on each side show the circular motion of the wheels with their arms"; or even "Movie star," where

participants in "the center pose and blow kisses, with students on either side acting as camera-snapping paparazzi." McKnight and Scruggs, *The Second City Guide*, 56–57.

53. I drew these questions from Jackson, *58½*. For a similar demonstration of this exercise, see "Can you count from 1-20?," *Nicola Meg*, March 3, 2013, YouTube video, 2:22, www.youtube.com/watch?v=DKK5_I80i5Y.

Chapter 3

1. Scott Berkun, *Confessions of a Public Speaker* (Sebastopol, CA: O'Reilly, 2011), 141.

2. Sherwyn Morreale, Joseph Valenzano, and Janessa Bauer, "Why Communication Education is Important: A Third Study on the Centrality of the Discipline's Content and Pedagogy," *Communication Education* 66, no. 4 (2017): 402.

3. Ibid.

4. Linda B. Specht and Petrea K. Sandlin, "The Differential Effects of Experiential Learning Activities and Traditional Lecture Classes in Accounting," *Simulation & Gaming* 22, no. 2 (1991): 196–210.

5. San Bolkan, "Intellectually Stimulating Students' Intrinsic Motivation: The Mediating Influence of Affective Learning and Student Engagement," *Communication Reports* 28, no. 2 (2015): 80.

6. At least in the US. See William M. Keith, "We Are the Speech Teachers," *The Review of Communication* 11, no. 2 (2011): 88, italics in original.

7. Ibid., 87–89. Keith and Lundberg further invite those teaching communication to restore its civic and humanistic mission, finding that public speaking textbooks have become imitative of one another by emphasizing market success over civic engagement. William Keith and Christian Lundberg, "Creating a History for Public Speaking Instruction," *Rhetoric & Public Affairs* 17, no. 1 (2014): 139, 140, 144. The communication field also needs to connect performance and theory further—many scholars have called for the "importance of theorizing through experience or a theory of the flesh." Bernadette Marie Calafell, "The Future of Feminist Scholarship: Beyond the Politics of Inclusion," *Women's Studies in Communication* 37, no. 3 (2014): 266–270.

8. Celeste Condit, "You Can't Study and Improve Communication with a Telescope," *Communication Monographs* 76, no. 1 (2009): 6–7. By looking for the connections between improv and communication, this chapter also follows Barbara O'Keefe's call for "interconnections between previously separate disciplines . . . and projects that deliberately attempt to forge connections." Barbara J. O'Keefe, "Against Theory," *Journal of Communication* 43, no. 3 (1993): 75. See also Paul L. Witt, "The Future of Communication Education," *Communication Education* 61, no. 1 (2012): 1–3.

9. Isa N. Engleberg, Susan M. Ward, Lynn M. Disbrow, James A. Katt, Scott A. Myers, and Patricia O'Keefe, "The Development of a Set of Core Communication Competencies for Introductory Communication Courses," *Communication Education* 66, no. 1 (2016): 1–18.

10. John Shotter, cited in Robyn Penman, *Reconstructing Communication* (Mahwah, NJ: Lawrence Erlbaum, 2000), 47.

11. "Mansplaining" also invokes Deborah Tannen's classic gender communication distinctions between "report" talk (a masculine style) and "rapport" talk (a feminine style). Deborah Tannen, *You Just Don't Understand: Women and Men in Conversation* (London: Virago, 1991). To be clear, these are *behavioral* practices; although the concept concerns how men overwhelmingly tend to engage in this behavior, any person could "mansplain."

12. Kenneth Burke, *A Rhetoric of Motives* (Berkeley: University of California Press, 1950), 3–46.

13. Halpern, *Art by Committee*, 30, 52.

14. Judee K. Burgoon and Jerold L. Hale, "Nonverbal Expectancy Violations: Model Elaboration and Application to Immediacy Behaviors," *Communications Monographs* 55, no. 1 (1988): 58–79.

15. I have seen many variations of this exercise, but have adapted what follows from Ray, *Spontaneity*, 17.

16. See Chip Heath and Dan Heath, *Made to Stick: Why Some Ideas Survive and Others Die* (New York: Random House, 2007); Steven Pinker, *The Sense of Style* (New York: Penguin), 2015.

17. Ray, *Spontaneity*, 17. The "Physical Phone" exercise can also highlight the challenges of the curse of knowledge, moving participants beyond a one-to-one format to involve the whole group. See Beth Boynton, "A Medical Improv Activity: Breaking Tension & Improving Communication," *Nurse.org*, January 18, 2017, http://nurse.org/articles/medical-improv-activity-improving-communication/.

18. Credit for this adapted exercise, originally dubbed "Twittercore," goes to Cyriel Kortleven, as cited in Bernard and Short, *Jill and Patrick's Small Book*, 92, 95.

19. Leonard and Yorton, *Yes, and*, 22.

20. Mamet further writes that emotions only come about from the performance of outward actions—they're not worked up out of nowhere. David Mamet, *True and False: Heresy and Common Sense for the Actor* (New York: Vintage, 2011), 12–13, 95.

21. Bonifer, *Gamechangers*, 87.

22. As far I can tell, this exercise goes back to Spolin—but my adaptation here is from Leonard and Yorton, *Yes, and*, 22.

23. Martin McDermott, *Speak with Courage* (New York: Bedford/St. Martins, 2014).

24. Roderick P. Hart and Don M. Burks, "Rhetorical Sensitivity and Social Interaction," *Speech Monographs* 39, no. 2 (1972): 75–91.

25. Annette M. Holba, "In Defense of Leisure," *Communication Quarterly* 62, no. 2 (2014): 184.

26. I have adapted this part of the exercise from the "Confidence Party" activity in Jackson, *The Inspirational Trainer*, 77–78.

27. I base these cues on ones that I've learned across many improv theaters, but they also share connections with what Johnstone calls centering techniques in Johnstone, *Impro for Storytellers*.

28. These two cues are from Johnstone, *Impro for Storytellers*. To achieve similar effects, Johnstone provides other advanced cues, including imagining that there's a small steel ball located in different parts of the body, mixing adjectives and body parts (e.g., happy feet, angry chin), and an exercise that's used a lot in acting: channeling different animals. Johnstone gives the example of Anthony Hopkins adding some "snake" to his Hannibal Lecter character, or Lawrence Olivier using some of Disney's Big Bad Wolf with his Richard III. You want to emphasize that participants should use these subtly, as most people unwittingly do in their everyday lives. You can also implement this exercise through Jill Bernard's acronym "VAPAPO," which stands for voice, attitude, posture, animal, prop, and obsession. Although Bernard developed this as a way for improv comedians to create strong characters, cueing participants to change their voice, attitude, or posture in different ways also works well with the "Walk About" exercise. The latter three cues are better for more advanced students, using an animal (give participants cues to take on characteristics of certain animals), a prop (give participants random props to work with that change how they act and feel), and an obsession (give the participants an obsession to work with—obsessed with their smartphone, obsessed with a celebrity, etc.). Bernard emphasizes that when students pick one of these choices, they typically get the others at the same time; one physical change, for instance, will tend to put the voice into a different register. Jill Bernard, *Jill Bernard's Small Cute Book of Improv* (Minneapolis: Yes, and . . . , 2011).

29. Bonifer, *Gamechangers*, 95.

30. I have adapted this and the following parts of this exercise from gibberish trainings at many improv theaters, but also from the "Nonverbal Communication" activity in Gee and Gee, *Business Improv*. For a demonstration of gibberish, see Spolin Games Online, "Introduction to Gibberish," *Spolin Games Online*, accessed April 24, 2020, video, 5:23, https://spolingamesonline.org/introduction-to-gibberish/.

31. Cited in Anne Libera, *The Second City Almanac of Improvisation* (Evanston, IL: Northwestern University Press, 2004), 146.

32. This exercise is adapted from Spolin, *Theater Games*, 126–127.

33. Ibid.

34. Gee and Gee, *Business Improv*, 4.

35. Tony Schwartz and Catherine McCarthy, "Manage Your Energy, Not Your Time," *Harvard Business Review*, October 2017, https://hbr.org/2007/10/manage-your-energy-not-your-time.

36. Bonifer, *Gamechangers*, 140, italics removed.

37. Csikszentmihalyi, *Creativity*, 58.

38. Ori Brafman and Rom Brafman, *Sway: The Irresistible Pull of Irrational Behavior* (New York: Doubleday, 2008), 1–24. Michael Polanyi's famous phrase about the intuitive, tacit dimensions of human experience also comes to mind here: "we know more than we can tell." Michael Polanyi, *The Tacit Dimension* (Chicago: University of Chicago Press, 2009), 4.

39. Quentin Schultze, "Why Is So Much Public Communication Nasty?" *Quentin Schultze*, December 2, 2016, http://quentinschultze.com/civility-political-discourse/ (site discontinued).

40. Ibid., pars. 4, 8.

41. See Don J. Waisanen, "Arguments for Everybody: Social Media, Context Collapse, and the Universal Audience," in *Recovering Argument*, ed. Randall Lake (New York: Routledge, 2019), 264–269.

42. Peter L. Kranz, Sylvia Z. Ramirez, and Nick L. Lund, "The Use of Action Learning Techniques in a Race Relations Course," in *Getting Culture*, eds. Regan A. R. Gurung and Loreto R. Prieto (Sterling, VA: Stylus), 286–287.

43. Neil Postman, *Crazy Talk, Stupid Talk: How We Defeat Ourselves by the Way We Talk and What to Do About It* (New York: Delacorte Press, 1976), 117–118.

44. Don Waisanen, "Toward Robust Public Engagement: The Value of Deliberative Discourse for Civil Communication," *Rhetoric & Public Affairs* 17, no. 2 (2014): 287–322.

45. Paul Stob, "No Safe Space: James Arnt Aune and the Controversial Classroom," *Rhetoric & Public Affairs* 16, no. 3 (2013): 559.

46. Yehuda Baruch, "Role-Play Teaching: Acting in the Classroom," *Management Learning* 37, no. 1 (2006): 49, 51, 56.

47. Cited in Kenneth Burke, *Permanence and Change: An Anatomy of Purpose* (Berkeley: University of California Press, 1984), 7.

48. This exercise can be found in Sheesley, Pfeffer, and Barish, "Comedic Improv Therapy," 162–163. For a similar demonstration of this exercise, see Fred Gleeck and Avish Parashar, "Improv Exercise—Expert Interview," *Fred Gleeck*, December 6, 2009, YouTube video, 3:13, www.youtube.com/watch?v=gbpka36e-Xs.

49. Gordon Phillips, *Take it Personally: On the Art and Process of Personal Acting* (New York: Applause, 2000), 23.

50. Linda Flanagan, "How Improv Can Open up the Mind to Learning in the Classroom and Beyond," *KQED*, January 30, 2015, ww2.kqed.org/mindshift/2015/01/30/how-improv-can-open-up-the-mind-to-learning-in-the-classroom-and-beyond/.

51. Paul Watzlawick, Janet Beavin Bavelas, and Don Jackson, *Pragmatics of Human Communication* (New York: Norton, 1967), 1–5.

52. Libera, *The Second City Almanac*, 103. Bonifer similarly divides communication into three levels: cosmetic (the words), emotional (the subtext), and meta-communication (or "the way that a scene represents the issues, ideas and

concerns that exist on a societal or universal level, such as a global trend, widely held belief or aspect of the human condition"). Bonifer, *Gamechangers*, 79–81.

53. Carrane and Allen, *Improvising Better*, 41–42.

54. Jagodowski and Paquesi, *Improvisation*, 120.

55. This classic adage comes from Watzlawick, Bavelas, and Jackson, *Pragmatics*, 49.

56. Jagodowski and Paquesi, *Improvisation*, 49.

57. For a research-supported book on reading body language that still manages to stay humble about these matters, see Joe Navarro and Marvin Karlins, *What Every Body is Saying* (New York: Harper Collins, 2008).

58. I'm constructing part of my explanation for this exercise from Bill Lynn (who was also a student and performer at the Groundlings). See Lynn, *Improvisation*, 166.

59. Ibid., 166.

60. Mary Scruggs and Michael J. Gellman, *Process: An Improviser's Journey* (Evanston, IL: Northwestern University Press, 2008), 87.

61. I adapted this exercise from Johnstone, *Impro,* 265.

62. John A. Daly and Madeleine H. Redlick, "Handling Questions and Objections Affects Audience Judgments of Speakers," *Communication Education* 65, no. 2 (2016): 164–181.

63. Deanna P. Dannels, Ann Darling, Deanna L. Fassett, Jeff Kerssen-Griep, Derek Lane, Timothy P. Mottet, Keith Nainby, and Deanna Sellnow, "Inception: Beginning a New Conversation about Communication Pedagogy and Scholarship," *Communication Education* 63, no. 4 (2014): 366–382.

64. This phrase has been attributed to Del Close, cited in Halpern, *Art by Committee*, 45.

65. Ibid., 46.

66. Ibid.

67. Stephen Nachmanovitch, " 'Improvisation Is . . .'—Stephen Nachmanovitch," *Stephen Nachmanovitch*, December 10, 2010, YouTube video, 5:27, www.youtube.com/watch?v=6ZfgG8B0Y3Q.

68. Dannels et al., "Inception," 366–382. The updated version of Bloom's taxonomy can be found at Patricia Armstrong, "Bloom's Taxonomy," Vanderbilt University Center for Teaching, accessed April 27, 2020, https://cft.vanderbilt.edu/guides-sub-pages/blooms-taxonomy/.

69. Charlie Sweet, Hal Blythe, and Rusty Carpenter, "Why the Revised Bloom's Taxonomy is Essential to Creative Teaching," *The National Teaching & Learning Forum* 26, no. 1 (2016): 7–9.

70. Gardner, *Multiple Intelligences*, 177, 67.

71. Robert Sternberg, *Successful Intelligence: How Practical and Creative Intelligence Determine Success in Life* (New York: Plume, 1997).

72. Gardner, *Multiple Intelligences*, 180, 182.

73. Dannels et al., "Inception," 373, italics added.

74. Ibid., 375, 374.

75. Charles Kneupper and Floyd D. Anderson, "Uniting Wisdom and Eloquence: The Need for Rhetorical Invention," *Quarterly Journal of Speech* 66, no. 3 (1980): 313–326.

76. Johanna E. Hartelius, "Revisiting Vico's Pedagogy of Invention: The Intellectual Entrepreneurship Pre-Graduate School Internship," *Quarterly Journal of Speech* 98, no. 2 (2012): 171, 155–157, 169.

77. Halpern, Close, and Johnson, *Truth in Comedy*, 15.

78. Jagodowski and Paquesi, *Improvisation*, 94.

79. Libera, *The Second City Almanac*, 11.

80. Cited in Ibid., 16.

81. Johnstone, *Impro for Storytellers*, 59.

82. Mamet, 41, *True and False*, italics in original.

83. See chapter 6 on storytelling in Heath and Heath, *Made to Stick*.

84. Quentin J. Schultze, *Communicate Like a True Leader* (Grand Rapids, MI: Edenridge, 2017), 13.

85. Mamet, *True and False*, 66, 69, italics in original.

86. Thomas J. Socha and Gary A. Beck, "Positive Communication and Human Needs: A Review and Proposed Organizing Conceptual Framework," *Review of Communication* 15, no. 3 (2015): 173–199.

87. Julien Mirivel, *The Art of Positive Communication* (New York: Peter Lang, 2014), 7.

88. Sigal G. Barsade, "The Ripple Effect: Emotional Contagion and its Influence on Group Behavior," *Administrative Science Quarterly* 47, no. 4 (2002): 644. There's also a therapeutic aspect to such communication. See, for example, Jason Scott Quinn, "Improvising our Way through Tragedy: How an Improv Comedy Community Heals itself through Improvisation," *American Communication Journal* 9, no. 1 (2007), http://ac-journal.org/journal/2007/Spring/articles/tragedy.html.

89. Johnstone, *Impro for Storytellers*.

90. Carrane and Allen further share that in improv theater, you'll see over and over that "nice people + nice choices = boring scenes." Carrane and Allen, *Improvising Better*, 9. By caring and committing, an improviser's communication carries more water and becomes electrifying to watch.

91. Stephanie Kelly and Zachary Denton, "Instructor's Corner #3: For Math Anxiety, Actions (and Reactions) Speak Louder than Words," *Communication Currents*, June 2015, www.natcom.org/CommCurrentsArticle.aspx?id=6145, par 3.

92. For an excellent overview on the connections between communication and vulnerability, see Ori Brafman and Rom Brafman, *Click: The Forces Behind How We Fully Engage with People, Work, and Everything We Do* (New York: Crown Pub, 2010), 25–51. On "self-disclosure" and communication, see Amanda Carpenter and Kathryn Greene, "Social Penetration Theory," in The *International Encyclopedia of*

Interpersonal Communication, eds. Charles R. Berger and Michael E. Roloff (Hoboken, NJ: Wiley: 2016), 1670–1673.

93. Kelly and Denton, "Instructor's Corner #3," par. 7.

94. Thanks to Lisa Allison Pertoso for posting this exercise on the Applied Improvisation Network (AIN) Facebook page. Lisa Allison Pertoso, "One exercise that I love is having one person step on stage and have the audience clap and cheer for them. That person must stand there and breathe, not move or talk or react really. Only take," Facebook, October 4, 2016, www.facebook.com/groups/appliedimprov/?fref=nf.

95. Johnstone, *Impro for Storytellers,* 6.

96. I've adapted this exercise from Mick Napier, *Improvise: Scene from the Inside Out* (Portsmouth, NH: Heinemann, 2004), 125.

97. This variation can be found in Ray, *Spontaneity,* 50–51.

98. This exercise can be found in many different articles and books, but I'd like to thank Rachel Ben Hamou for bringing it back to my attention via the AIN Facebook page. Rachel Ben Hamou, "I like ones where people are given topics and asked to speak for 30 or 60 seconds without repetition or hesitation. Knowing you can speak on any subject is empowering," Facebook, October 4, 2016, www.facebook.com/groups/appliedimprov/?fref=nf.

99. Irving Janis, *Groupthink: Psychological Studies of Policy Decisions and Fiascoes,* 2nd ed. (Boston: Wadsworth, 1982); Robert B. Cialdini, *Influence: Science and Practice,* 5th ed. (New York: Allyn & Bacon, 2008).

100. Kenneth Burke, *Language as Symbolic Action: Essays on Life, Literature and Method* (Berkeley: University of California Press, 1966), 9.

101. Hartelius, "Revisiting Vico's," 155.

102. Cited in Salinsky and Frances-White, *The Improv Handbook,* 194.

103. Muzafer Sherif and Carl I. Hovland, *Social Judgment: Assimilation and Contrast Effects in Communication and Attitude Change* (Westport, CT: Greenwood Press, 1980). Rocco and Whalen also note how the "Yes, and . . ." principle works with Sherif's theories. Rocco and Whalen, "Teaching Yes, and," 201.

104. Alfonso Montuori, "Social Creativity, Academic Discourse, and the Improvisation of Inquiry," *ReVision* 20, no. 1 (1997): 34.

105. Isa N. Engleberg, "Learning to Speak," *Review of Communication* 14, no. 2 (2014): 183. The National Communication Association's communication competencies for teachers even listed "imaginative messages" that "speculate, theorize, or fantasize" as a goal for communication instruction. Cited in Sherwyn Morreale, Philip Backlund, and Leyla Sparks, "Communication Education and Instructional Communication: Genesis and Evolution as Fields of Inquiry," *Communication Education* 63, no. 4 (2014): 344–354.

106. Judi Brownell, "Elwood Murray: Pioneering Methodologist in Communication," *Communication Education* 63, no. 4 (2014): 331.

107. Lisbeth Lipari, "Rhetoric's Other," *Philosophy & Rhetoric* 45, no. 3 (2012): 227–245.

108. Brownell, "Elwood Murray," 331–332, 336.

109. Each of these teaching standards comes from Susan A. Ambrose, Michael W. Bridges, Michele DiPietro, Marsha C. Lovett, and Marie K. Norman, *How Learning Works: Seven Research-Based Principles for Smart Teaching* (San Francisco: Jossey-Bass, 2010).

Chapter 4

1. See Patricia Shaw and Ralph Stacey, eds., *Experiencing Spontaneity, Risk & Improvisation in Organizational Life: Working Live* (New York: Routledge, 2006); Daryl Conner, *Leading at the Edge of Chaos* (New York: Wiley, 1998).

2. Horney, Pasmore, and O'Shea, "Leadership Agility," 34.

3. Vivian Giang, "Why Top Companies and MBA Programs are Teaching Improv," *Fast Company*, January 13, 2016, www.fastcompany.com/3055380/why-top-companies-and-mba-programs-are-teaching-improv, par. 6.

4. Gagnon, Vough, and Nickerson, "Learning to Lead," 300.

5. Alfonso Montuori, "The Complexity of Improvisation and the Improvisation of Complexity: Social Science, Art and Creativity," *Human Relations* 56, no. 2 (2003): 237.

6. Tammy Tawadros, "Developing the Theater of Leadership: An Exploration of Practice and the Need for Research," *Advances in Developing Human Resources* 17, no. 3 (2015): 340.

7. Tabaee, "Effects of Improvisation," xvii.

8. Heifetz, Grashow, and Linsky, *The Practice of Adaptive Leadership*, 2–3. For a great video on many adaptive leadership fundamentals, see Marty Linsky, "TEDxStCharles—Marty Linsky—Adaptive Leadership—Leading Change," *TEDx Talks*, April 13, 2011, YouTube video, 21:00, www.youtube.com/watch?v=af-cSvnEExM.

9. Heifetz, Grashow, and Linsky, *The Practice of Adaptive Leadership*, 195, 275, 277.

10. Natalie Fratto, "Screw Emotional Intelligence—Here's The Key to the Future of Work," *Fast Company*, January 29, 2018, www.fastcompany.com/40522394/screw-emotional-intelligence-heres-the-real-key-to-the-future-of-work, "Why Adaptability," par. 1. Taking an adaptive perspective on leadership that's distinguished from psychological approaches also runs parallel to "discursive leadership," which focuses on distributing power across an organization and thinking in terms of broad influence. Discursive leadership positions coordinated action as more important than mental states, highlighting the socially constructed nature of working life rather than fixing essential selves and personalities as the locus of leadership. Gail T. Fairhurst,

"Discursive Leadership: A Communication Alternative to Leadership Psychology," *Management Communication Quarterly* 21, no. 4 (2008): 510–521.

11. John P. Kotter, cited in Peter G. Northouse, *Leadership: Theory and Practice* (Thousand Oaks, CA: SAGE, 2015), 13–14.

12. Joseph Rost, *Leadership for the Twenty-First Century* (New York: Praeger, 1991), 149–152.

13. Daloz Parks, *Leadership*, 109.

14. Ibid., 109–112.

15. Ibid., 116.

16. I learned this exercise and have adapted directions in this section from Montague and Short, "Intro to Applied Improvisation," 7–8. Montague and Short say that they originally learned this exercise from Adrian Jackson, a student of Augusto Boal. For a demonstration of this exercise, see Andrew Tarvin, "Walk/Stop—An Energizer Activity," *Humor That Works*, November 19, 2012, YouTube video, 3:18, www.youtube.com/watch?v=a72goyDtjeI. Regarding mistakes, Bernard and Short note that they once saw an improv teacher ask two people to get up and do the perfect improv scene. Everyone hesitated, two people got up and executed it half-heartedly. Then the teacher asked for two more people to do a horrible scene where all the rules would be broken. Everyone wanted to get on stage and this scene had many more laughs. This demonstrated that mistakes are often the source of creativity. They relate that "Ty Cobb has the best batting average in history at .366. That means out of every ten at-bats he 'screwed up' between six and seven times. . . . Mistakes hurt us when we spend a lot of time assigning blame and overreacting." Bernard and Short, *Jill and Patrick's Small Book*, 73, 74.

17. Heifetz, Grashow, and Linsky, *The Practice of Adaptive Leadership*, 7.

18. Mary Uhl-Bien, Russ Marion, and Bill McKelvey, "Complexity Leadership Theory: Shifting Leadership from the Industrial Age to the Knowledge Era," *The Leadership Quarterly* 18, no. 4 (2007): 298.

19. Michael P. Crozier, "Governing Codes: Information Dynamics and Contemporary Coordination Challenges," *Administration & Society* 47, no. 2 (2015): 151–152.

20. Weick and Sutcliffe further zero in on the common leadership mistake of assuming that "general expertise" can replace "situational knowledge." Karl E. Weick and Kathleen M. Sutcliffe, *Managing the Unexpected: Sustained Performance in a Complex World* (Hoboken, NJ: Wiley, 2015), 32, 120.

21. T. Bowell, "Feminist Standpoint Theory," *Internet Encyclopedia of Philosophy*, accessed April 28, 2020, www.iep.utm.edu/fem-stan/, par. 1.

22. This is often called the "Enemy/Defender" game. Molly Clare Wilson, "Improv Toolkit for Educators," The K12 Lab Wiki, June 22, 2012, https://dschool-old.stanford.edu/groups/k12/wiki/f8fb7/Improv_Toolkit_for_Educators.html. My basic description and adaptations for this exercise are drawn from the "Sun and Moon" exercise in Alan Montague and Izzy Gesell, "Level-Up Applied Improvisa-

tion: Intro to Applied Improvisation for Facilitators and Trainers," preconference handout, Applied Improvisation Network conference, Irvine, CA, August 2017, 10–11. The handout says that this exercise was learned from James Bailey. For a similar demonstration of this exercise, see Jenny Sauer-Klein, "Game #3 Enemy Defender," *Jenny Sauer-Klein*, July 6, 2013, YouTube video, 2:50, www.youtube.com/watch?v=zu31ZWtTRdw.

23. Viola Spolin, *Improvisation for the Theater* (Evanston, IL: Northwestern University Press, 1999), 22.

24. I've adapted this exercise from Beth Boynton, "De-Stress and Improve Communication with Medical Improv," *MedLine*, December 13, 2016, http://mkt.medline.com/advancing-blog/de-stress-and-improve-communication-with-medical-improv/ (site discontinued).

25. Johnstone, *Impro*, 35–37.

26. Ibid., 35–36.

27. Ibid., 33–74.

28. Watzlawick, Bavelas, and Jackson, *Pragmatics*.

29. Heifetz, Grashow, and Linsky, *The Practice of Adaptive Leadership*, 185, 209, 205.

30. Ibid., 211.

31. Ibid., 183–185.

32. Ibid., 213.

33. Keith Grint, *Leadership: A Very Short Introduction* (New York: Oxford University Press, 2010), 32.

34. See Erin Meyer, *The Culture Map: Decoding How People Think, Lead, and Get Things Done Across Cultures*, international edition (New York: PublicAffairs, 2016).

35. David Boromisza-Habashi, Jessica M. F. Hughes, and Jennifer A. Malkowski, "Public Speaking as Cultural Ideal: Internationalizing the Public Speaking Curriculum," *Journal of International and Intercultural Communication* 9, no. 1 (2016): 20–34.

36. Besser, Roberts, and Walsh, *The Upright Citizens Brigade*, 60.

37. Spolin, *Improvisation*, 11, 13, 44.

38. Bernard and Short, *Jill and Patrick's Small Book*, 36.

39. Robert Kegan and Lisa Laskow Lahey, *An Everyone Culture: Becoming a Deliberately Developmental Organization* (Boston: Harvard University Business Press, 2016), 1.

40. John Palfrey, *Safe Spaces, Brave Spaces: Diversity and Free Expression in Education* (Cambridge, MA: MIT Press, 2018).

41. Spolin, *Improvisation*, x, 7.

42. Daloz Parks, *Leadership*, 236.

43. Heifetz, Grashow, and Linsky, *The Practice of Adaptive Leadership*, 19–40.

44. I discovered and adapted this from a Second City exercise described in Sarah Fister Gale, "Live from Cigna, It's Improvisation," *Chief Learning Officer*,

June 25, 2015, www.clomedia.com/2015/06/25/live-from-cigna-its-improvisation/, "What Did We Learn Today," pars. 6–7.

45. I have adapted most components of this exercise from Johnstone, *Impro for Storytellers*, 221–224. For some demonstrations of status behaviors, see Mark Collard, "Group Energiser, Warm-Up, Fun Game—Jump In Jump Out," *Mark Collard*, September 16, 2012, YouTube video, 3:39, www.youtube.com/watch?v=k6bHltjIYzE, and Alison Goldie, "Status Exercise," *Improv Book*, September 23, 2015, YouTube video, 3:03, www.youtube.com/watch?v=UkBd3jrcvWc.

46. Salinsky and Frances-White, *The Improv Handbook*, 90–91.

47. Ibid.

48. Heifetz, Grashow, and Linsky, *The Practice of Adaptive Leadership*, 23.

49. Csikszentmihalyi, *Creativity*, 1.

50. Alfonso Montuori, "Beyond Postnormal Times: The Future of Creativity and the Creativity of the Future," *Futures* 43, no. 2 (2011): 221.

51. Joanna Levitt Cea and Jess Rimington, "Creating Breakout Innovation," *Stanford Social Innovation Review*, Summer 2017, https://ssir.org/articles/entry/creating_breakout_innovation.

52. Niklas K. Steffens, Frank Mols, S. Alexander Haslam, and Tyler G. Okimoto, "True to What We Stand For: Championing Collective Interests as a Path to Authentic Leadership," *The Leadership Quarterly* 27, no. 5 (2016): 726.

53. Weick and Sutcliffe, *Managing the Unexpected*, 34, italics in original.

54. Grint, *Leadership*, 116, 126.

55. Wei Gu, "Executive Talent Search Focuses on Adaptive Leadership," *The Wall Street Journal*, October 19, 2014, www.wsj.com/articles/boss-talk-asia-executive-talent-search-focuses-on-adaptive-leadership-1413751711, par. 2.

56. Tint, McWaters, and van Driel, "Applied Improvisation Training," 89.

57. Finkel, *Teaching*, 119–120, 123.

58. Arménio Rego, Bradley Owens, Susana Leal, Ana I. Melo, Miguel Pina e Cunha, Lurdes Gonçalves, and Paula Ribeiro, "How Leader Humility Helps Teams to be Humbler, Psychologically Stronger, and more Effective: A Moderated Mediation Model," *The Leadership Quarterly* 28, no. 5 (2017): 639–658.

59. Heifetz, Grashow, and Linsky, *The Practice of Adaptive Leadership*, 19.

60. Ibid., 119.

61. Grint, *Leadership*, 21.

62. Heifetz, Grashow, and Linsky, *The Practice of Adaptive Leadership*, 202–204, 161, 168.

63. Cited in George Cheney, Lars Thøger Christensen, Theodore E. Zorn Jr., and Shiv Ganesh, *Organizational Communication in an Age of Globalization* (Long Grove, IL: Waveland Press, 2010), 200.

64. Gamze Koseoglu, Yi Liu, and Christina E. Shalley, "Working with Creative Leaders: Exploring the Relationship between Supervisors' and Subordinates' Creativity," *The Leadership Quarterly* 28, no. 6 (2017): 798.

65. I adapted this exercise from Huffaker and West, "Enhancing Learning," 860.

66. Michele Williams (@MicheleWilliamz), "Erica Marx #P2P @ revithaca #coach 'Play when the stakes are low so you can perform when the stakes are high,'" Twitter, October 21, 2016, 7:49 p.m., https://twitter.com/MicheleWilliamz/status/789614512827662336.

67. Diane Coutu, "How Resilience Works," *Harvard Business Review*, May 2002, https://hbr.org/2002/05/how-resilience-works, "The Buzz," par. 8.

68. Weick and Sutcliffe, "Managing the Unexpected," 1–19, 79.

69. Ibid., 99, 69, italics in original.

70. Heifetz, Grashow, and Linsky, *The Practice of Adaptive Leadership*, 29–30. The productive zone of disequilibrium bears similarities to Vygotsky's concept of how human beings develop through a "Zone of Proximal Development," or "the distance between the actual development level as determined by independent problem solving, and the level of potential development as determined through problem solving, under guidance or in collaboration with more capable peers." And it is play that "creates a zone of proximal development. . . . in play a child always behaves beyond his average age, above his daily behavior; in play it is as though he were a head taller than himself." Cited in Holzman, *Vygotsky*, 27–28, 51.

71. Heifetz, Grashow, and Linsky, *The Practice of Adaptive Leadership*.

72. Ibid., 305.

73. Pearce, *Making Social Worlds*, 153.

74. P. D. Harms, Marcus Credé, Michael Tynan, Matthew Leon, and Wonho Jeung, "Leadership and Stress: A Meta-Analytic Review," *Leadership Quarterly* 28, no. 1 (2017): 178.

75. I originally came across this exercise in Ray, *Spontaneity*, 13. Over the years, I've adapted and updated it with the different variations reflected in this section.

76. Heifetz, Grashow, and Linsky, *The Practice of Adaptive Leadership*, 30.

77. Both the nonsensical and group delivery of bad news variations are from Ray, *Spontaneity*, 13.

78. I first learned this exercise from Patrick Short, who cites William Hall as its creator and Craig Klugman as the one who introduced the rule that the teams can shout their own commands. I draw the explanation for this exercise from Montague and Short, "Intro to Applied Improvisation," 16–17.

79. Northouse, *Leadership*, adapted from Peter W. Dorfman, Paul J. Hanges, and Felix C. Brodbeck, "Leadership and Cultural Variation: The Identification of Culturally Endorsed Leadership Profiles," in *Culture, Leadership, and Organizations: The GLOBE Study of 62 Societies*, eds. Robert J. House, Paul J. Hanges, Mansour Javidan, Peter W. Dorfman, and Vipin Gupta (Thousand Oaks, CA: SAGE, 2004), 669–719.

80. Mansour Javidan and Ali Dastmalchian, "Managerial Implications of the GLOBE Project: A Study of 62 Societies," *Asia Pacific Journal of Human Resources* 47, no. 1 (2009): 55.

81. John Antonakis, Marika Fenley, and Sue Liechti, "Can Charisma Be Taught? Tests of Two Interventions," *Academy of Management Learning & Education* 10, no. 3 (2011): 374–396.

82. Konstantin O. Tskhay, Rebecca Zhu, and Nicholas O. Rule, "Perceptions of Charisma from Thin Slices of Behavior Predict Leadership Prototypicality Judgments," *Leadership Quarterly* 28, no. 4 (2017): 555.

83. Olivia Fox Cabane, *The Charisma Myth* (New York: Penguin, 2013), 4, 6.

84. Amy Cuddy, Susan T. Fiske, and Peter Glick, "Warmth and Competence as Universal Dimensions of Social Perception: The Stereotype Content Model and the BIAS Map," *Advances in Experimental Social Psychology* 40 (2008): 61–149.

85. Anne Lamott, *Bird by Bird: Some Instructions on Writing and Life* (New York: Random House, 1994), 100–101.

86. Johnstone, *Impro*, 78, 87.

87. Alex Pentland, "Measuring the Impact of Charisma," *Psychology Today*, December 23, 2009, www.psychologytoday.com/us/blog/reality-mining/200912/measuring-the-impact-charisma, pars. 4–5.

88. Stephanie Vozza, "The One Thing You Need to Do to Become More Creative," *Fast Company*, April 24, 2017, www.fastcompany.com/40409481/the-one-thing-you-need-to-do-to-become-more-creativer.

89. Johnstone, *Impro for Storytellers*, 89.

90. Napier, *Improvise,* 4, 10, 14.

91. Yorton, "Using Improv Methods," 12.

92. Jackson, *Easy*, 14.

93. The Harnisch Foundation, "Funny Girls," *The Harnisch Foundation*, October 13, 2017, YouTube video, 2:38, www.youtube.com/watch?v=dmlSl6PGxFk. See also NBC News, "'Funny Girls' Non-Profit Teaches Girls to be Leaders through Improv," *NBC News*, March 13, 2018, www.nbcnews.com/nightly-news/video/-funny-girls-non-profit-teaches-girls-to-be-leaders-through-improv-1185114691950.

94. Roger Caillois, *Man, Play, and Games*, trans. Meyer Barash (Chicago: University of Illinois Press, 2001), 61, 76.

95. Lynn, *Improvisation*, 8.

96. Watzlawick, Bavelas, and Jackson, *Pragmatics*, 45.

97. Besser, Roberts, and Walsh, "*The Upright Citizens Brigade*," 114. One difference should be noted: according to Besser, Roberts, and Walsh, the Upright Citizens Brigade method for finding a comedic game involves attending to anything that strikes actors as unusual, weird, or funny in a scene and then exploring and heightening that focus. Applied improvisation isn't limited to this goal. I use "game" to refer to the rules, patterns, and habits that take place within any closed system, meaning those that always take place within situations where human beings are interacting.

98. Bonifer, *Gamechangers*, 46–48.

99. Ibid., 49.

100. Paul Watzlawick, *The Situation is Hopeless, but Not Serious (The Pursuit of Unhappiness)* (Norton: New York, 1993), 25, 30, 32.

101. Watzlawick, Bavelas, and Jackson, *Pragmatics*, 232–233.

102. Nachmanovitch, *Free Play*, 45, 84.

103. Bernard and Short, *Jill and Patrick's Small Book*, 19–20.

104. Rosamund S. Zander and Benjamin Zander, *The Art of Possibility* (Cambridge, MA: Harvard Business Press, 2000), 140–159.

105. John O. Burtis and Paul D. Turman, *Leadership Communication as Citizenship* (Thousand Oaks, CA: Sage, 2009), 187, 184.

106. Gregory Spencer, *Reframing the Soul* (Abilene, TX: Leafwood, 2018).

107. Weick and Sutcliffe, *Managing the Unexpected*, 110–111.

108. Heifetz, Grashow, and Linsky, *The Practice of Adaptive Leadership*, 120.

109. Henri Lipmanowicz and Keith McCandless, "Improv Prototyping," *Liberating Structures*, accessed April 28, 2020, www.liberatingstructures.com/15-improv-prototyping/, par. 2. I have adapted and shortened directions for this exercise in this section; for a fuller explanation visit the liberating structures site.

110. Lipmanowicz and McCandless, "Improv," par. 3.

111. Brafman and Pollack, *The Chaos Imperative*, ix, 15.

112. Lipmanowicz and McCandless, "Improv," par. 7.

113. Many concepts such as "situational leadership" theorize leadership along these axes. See Northouse, *Leadership*.

114. Peter Behrendt, Sandra Matz, and Anja S. Göritza, "An Integrative Model of Leadership Behavior," *The Leadership Quarterly* 28, no. 1 (2017): 29.

115. Grint, *Leadership*, 13.

116. Alan C. Mikkelson, Joy A. York, and Joshua Arritola, "Communication Competence, Leadership Behaviors, and Employee Outcomes in Supervisor-Employee Relationships," *Business and Professional Communication Quarterly* 78, no. 3 (2015): 336.

117. McClure, "Tiffany," 143–144.

118. I adapted this exercise from Gale, "Live from Cigna."

119. Ibid.

120. Csikszentmihalyi, *Creativity*, 63.

121. Peter Drucker, *Management* (New York: Collins, 2008), 288.

122. Paul M. Newton, "Leadership Lessons from Jazz Improvisation," *International Journal of Leadership in Education* 7, no. 1 (2004): 98.

123. George Shapiro, "How It's Done: Ideas for Ongoing Programs," in *The Cultivation of Leadership Roles, Methods and Responsibilities*, ed. Miriam B. Clark (Greensboro, NC: Center for Creative Leadership, 1987), 7.

124. Ken Robinson, *Out of Our Minds: Learning to Be Creative* (Chichester: Wiley, 2001), 107.

125. Peter A. Heslin and Lauren A. Keating, "In Learning Mode? The Role of Mindsets in Derailing and Enabling Experiential Leadership Development," *The*

Leadership Quarterly 28, no. 3 (2017): 367. On the difference between "fixed" and "growth" mindsets, see Carol S. Dweck, *Mindset: The New Psychology of Success* (New York: Random House, 2006).

126. Rick Reis, "Two Core Principles about Learning: What Every Teacher and Student Must Know about Education Theory," Stanford Tomorrow's Professor Postings, April 15, 2011, https://tomprof.stanford.edu/posting/1655.

127. Bain, *What the Best*, 37–38.

Chapter 5

1. The Detroit Creativity Project, "The 100% Model," *The Detroit Creativity Project*, 2015, http://detroitcreativityproject.org/annual-reports/. The video at "Why Improvise? Read on. Or watch the video" summarizes the program: http://detroit-creativityproject.org/the-improv-project/.

2. Jude Treder-Wolff, "How The Improv Project Helps Detroit Students Discover What's Possible," *Medium*, December 29, 2017, https://medium.com/@jude trederwolff/how-the-improv-project-helps-detroit-students-discover-whats-possible-98acedccea67, par. 6.

3. Rehearsal for Life, "The Urban Improv Method," *Rehearsal for Life*, accessed April 29, 2020, https://rehearsalforlife.org/urban-improv/method/, pars. 1–3.

4. Rehearsal for Life, "Urban Improv Program Impact," *Rehearsal for Life*, accessed April 29, 2020, https://rehearsalforlife.org/urban-improv/impact/, par. 4.

5. in2improv, "About in2improv," *in2improv*, accessed April 29, 2020, https://in2improv, www.in2improv.org/in2improv.html, par. 1. I highly recommend viewing the video "An in2improv documentary" about the institute and its programs at https://vimeo.com/197120806 (*ImprovISA*, 2017, Vimeo video, 16:24).

6. in2improv, "Testimonials," *in2improv*, accessed April 29, 2020, www.in2improv.org/testimonials.html, pars. 7–8.

7. Amanda T. Lago, "On the 45th Martial Law Anniversary, SPIT Manila Talks about the Value of Presence," *Rappler*, September 22, 2017, www.rappler.com/life-and-style/arts-and-culture/182992-spit-manila-improv-martial-law-45th-anniversary-show, pars. 15–16.

8. Martín Carcasson, "Beginning with the End in Mind: A Call for Goal-Driven Deliberative Practice," Occasional Paper 2, Public Agenda Center for Advances in Public Engagement, 2009, https://my.lwv.org/sites/default/files/carcasson.beginning_with_the_end_in_mind.pdf, 9.

9. William M. Keith, *Democracy as Discussion: Civic Education and the American Forum Movement* (Lanham, MD: Lexington, 2007), 83.

10. I first learned this exercise and have adapted it from watching John Windmueller's terrific workshop with the National Academy of Sciences. I retained all the essentials from Windmueller's description in this section. John Windmueller,

"The Science of Improv LIVE with Washington Improv Theater," Marian Koshland Science Museum of the National Academy of Sciences, February 15, 2017, https://facebook.com/story.php?story_fbid=10155749920736808&id=12496501807.

11. J. Marshall Shephard, "3 Kinds of Bias that Shape Your Worldview," *TED*, March 2018, video, 12:13, www.ted.com/talks/j_marshall_shepherd_3_kinds_bias_that_shape_your_worldview.

12. Omar Ali and Nadja Cech, " 'Yes, and' as Teaching-Learning Methodology," *Teaching & Learning in Higher Ed*, April 8, 2017, https://teachingandlearninginhighered.org/2017/04/08/yes-and-as-teaching-methodology/, "Yes, and," par. 15.

13. Benjamin Barber, *Strong Democracy: Participatory Politics for a New Age* (Berkeley: University of California Press, 2003), 173.

14. David Mathews, "Community Change through True Public Action," *National Civic Review* 83, no. 4 (1994): 400–404. Richard Palmer also writes that "creative thinking requires a special talent for listening and hearing, and these require a special openness, an openness difficult to achieve in the metaphors and framework of modern calculative consciousness." Richard E. Palmer, "What Hermeneutics Can Offer Rhetoric," in *Rhetoric and Hermeneutics in Our Time: A Reader,* eds. Walter Jost and Michael J. Hyde (New Haven, CT: Yale University Press, 1997), 123.

15. Salit, *Performance Breakthrough*, 81–82.

16. Jason Jay and Gabriel Grant. *Breaking Through Gridlock: The Power of Conversation in a Polarized World* (Oakland, CA: Berrett-Koehler Publishers, 2017), 31–33.

17. I came across and adapted this exercise from Yael Schy, "Improv to Bridge Divides," Presentation at the Applied Improvisation Network conference, Irvine, CA, August 2017.

18. Cited in Nassir Ghaemi, *A First-Rate Madness: Uncovering the Links between Leadership and Mental Illness* (New York: Penguin, 2011), 95.

19. Lerner, *Making Democracy Fun*, 130.

20. Scruggs and Gellman, *Process*, 55, 129.

21. See Waisanen, "Toward Robust Public Engagement."

22. Jonathan Haidt, *The Righteous Mind: Why Good People Are Divided by Politics and Religion* (New York: Vintage, 2012).

23. Arabella Lyon, *Deliberative Acts: Democracy, Rhetoric, and Rights* (University Park: Pennsylvania State University Press, 2013).

24. Jakob Svensson, "Expressive Rationality: A Different Approach for Understanding Participation in Municipal Deliberative Practices," *Communication, Culture & Critique* 1 (2008): 215.

25. Augusto Boal, *Theater of the Oppressed* (London: Pluto Press, 2000), ix, xx.

26. On Being Studios, "Greg Boyle—The Calling of Delight: Gangs, Service, and Kinship," *On Being Studios*, December 2017, Soundcloud podcast, 52:10, https://soundcloud.com/onbeing/greg-boyle-the-calling-of-delight-gangs-service-and-kinship-nov2017.

27. Jane McGonigal, "Gaming can Make a Better World," *TED*, February 2010, video, 19:49, www.ted.com/talks/jane_mcgonigal_gaming_can_make_a_better_world?language=en#t-28846.

28. Stuart Brown, *Play: How It Shapes the Brain, Opens the Imagination, and Invigorates the Soul* (New York: Penguin, 2009), 5.

29. Spolin, *Theater*, 3.

30. Wikipedia, s.v. "Flow (Psychology)," last modified 16 April 2020, 05:01, https://en.wikipedia.org/wiki/Flow_(psychology), par. 1.

31. Csikszentmihalyi, *Flow*, 80, 191.

32. Chris Barker and Brian Martin, "Participation: The Happiness Connection," *Journal of Public Deliberation* 7, no. 1 (2011): 12.

33. Carcasson, "Beginning," 2–3, 7–8.

34. Napier, *Behind the Scenes*, 3, 5.

35. Postman, *Crazy Talk*, 253.

36. Mary Kay Morrison, *Using Humor to Maximize Learning: The Links between Positive Emotions and Education* (Lanham, MD: Rowman & Littlefield, 2008), 57.

37. Ibid., 67.

38. Cited in Laura Black, "How People Communicate during Deliberative Events," in *Democracy in Motion,* eds. Tina Nabatchi and John Gastil (New York: Oxford University Press, 2012), 74.

39. Jonathan Crow, "John Cleese Explores the Health Benefits of Laughter," *Open Culture*, April 29, 2015, www.openculture.com/2015/04/john-cleese-explores-the-health-benefits-of-laughter-yoga.html, par. 3.

40. Heifetz, Grashow, and Linsky, *The Practice of Adaptive Leadership*, 137–138, 141.

41. I have paraphrased Lenski's complete explanation in this section, which I've found works well with just about any group. Tammy Lenski, "Conflict Resolution Activity: Demonstrate How Pushing Creates Pushback," *Tammy Lenski*, May 6, 2015, https://tammylenski.com/conflict-resolution-activities-fist-press/.

42. Ibid., par. 8.

43. I've experienced this exercise in many workshops across the US. I've adapted my explanation from Jude Treder-Wolff, "Gamechanger: Using Improv Games for Therapeutic Goals—Workshop Handout," *Medium*, February 22, 2017, https://medium.com/@judetrederwolff/gamechanger-using-improv-games-for-therapeutic-goals-workshop-handout-b4316b16d83d, "3 Line Obstacle Transformation," pars. 1–6.

44. Ibid., par. 5.

45. A host of research supports this conclusion. See, for example, George Gerbner's line of research described in Paul Bond, "Study: TV Violence Linked to 'Mean World Syndrome,'" *Hollywood Reporter*, June 18, 2014, www.hollywoodreporter.com/news/study-tv-violence-linked-mean-712890.

46. For more on this point, see Don Waisanen, *Political Conversion: Personal Transformation as Strategic Public Communication* (Lanham, MD: Lexington, 2018).

47. Barry Sanders, *A Is for Ox: The Collapse of Literacy and the Rise of Violence in an Electronic Age* (New York: Vintage, 1995).

48. See Thomas Kuhn, *The Structure of Scientific Revolutions* (Chicago: University of Chicago Press, 2012).

49. Burtis and Turman, *Leadership Communication*, 158.

50. Carse, *Finite*, 32–33; italics in original.

51. Jeff Katzman and Dan O'Connor, *Life Unscripted: Using Improv Principles to Get Unstuck, Boost Confidence, and Transform Your Life* (Berkeley, CA: North Atlantic Books, 2018).

52. Pearce, *Making Social Worlds*, 199.

53. FitzPatrick, "The Imaginary," 635; italics removed.

54. Brian McLaren, *Why Did Jesus, Moses, the Buddha and Mohammed Cross the Road? Christian Identity in a Multi-Faith World* (New York: Jericho, 2012).

55. Leslie Stager Jacques, "Borrowing from Professional Theatre Training to Build Essential Skills in Organization Development Consultants," *Journal of Applied Behavioral Science* 49, no. 2 (2012): 257.

56. Pearce, *Communication*, 202–203.

57. Salinsky and Frances-White, *The Improv Handbook*, 156.

58. Dorian Merina, "Comedy Improv Class Helps Veterans Deal with Civilian Life," *KPCC*, March 27, 2017, www.scpr.org/news/2017/03/27/70207/a-new-tool-for-vets-transitioning-to-civilian-life/, pars. 23–25.

59. Robert Asen, "A Discourse Theory of Citizenship," *Quarterly Journal of Speech* 90, no. 2 (2004): 189–211. See also Catherine Helen Palczewski, "Argument in an Off Key: Playing with the Productive Limits of Argument," in *Arguing Communication and Culture*, ed. G. Thomas Goodnight (Washington, DC: National Communication Association, 2002), 1–23.

60. Stephen T. Asma, "We Could All Do with Learning How to Improvise a Little Better," *Aeon*, May 29, 2017, https://aeon.co/ideas/we-could-all-do-with-learning-how-to-improvise-a-little-better, par. 5, 12. Gary Schwartz's eloquent formulation gets at a similar idea: "Judgment—using the past to measure the present, thus remaining uninvolved." Gary Schwartz, "What Does It Mean to Improvise?" *Improv Odyssey*, June 11, 2012, https://improv-odyssey.com/what-does-it-mean-to-improvise/.

61. I first came across this improv game at Comedysportz Buffalo in 2013. I'm not sure where it originated.

62. I have no idea where this exercise originated, but first learned it at Comedysportz Los Angeles, where it was called "Yay Boo." A student pointed out to me that it follows the "fortunately" and "unfortunately" structure of a popular children's book: Remy Charlip, *Fortunately* (New York: Simon & Schuster, 1964). For a similar demonstration of this exercise, see Chris Wade, "ComedySportz LA -

Boo! Yay!" *Chris Wade*, March 18, 2013, YouTube video, 4:33, www.youtube.com/watch?v=Fj20zcXUc4c.

63. I've come across this exercise at many improv theaters; instructions can be found here: *Improv Encyclopedia*, s.v. "Slide Show," accessed April 30, 2020, http://improvencyclopedia.org/games//Slide_Show.html.

64. See, for example, Kelly Happe, "The Body of Race: Toward a Rhetorical Understanding of Racial Ideology," *Quarterly Journal of Speech* 99, no. 2 (2013): 149.

65. All Stars Project, "Operation Conversation: Cops and Kids," *All Stars Project*, 2018, https://allstars.org/copsandkids/.

66. Johnstone, *Impro*, 133.

67. Haidt, *The Righteous Mind*, 277–278.

68. Meyer, *The Culture Map*.

69. This concept originated with Benjamin Broome, cited in James W. Neuliep, *Intercultural Communication: A Contextual Approach*, 7th ed. (Thousand Oaks, CA: SAGE, 2018), 310.

70. Rich Hollman, "How Improv Training Can Create Compassionate Behavior. | Rich Hollman | TEDxLincolnSquare," *TEDx Talks*, May 4, 2017, YouTube video, 14:03, www.youtube.com/watch?v=KcrbEQkTAvk.

71. This exercise is used all over the improv world; I've drawn my description from Kulhan, *Getting to "Yes, and,"* 88. A similar description can be found at William Hall, "1-2-3-Word," *Improv Games*, accessed April 30, 2020, www.improvgames.com/1-2-3-word-also-called-convergence/.

72. For more on this discussion, see Leonard and Yorton, *Yes, and*, 51–82.

73. Cited in Tina Nabatchi, "An Introduction to Deliberative Civic Engagement," in *Democracy in Motion,* eds. Tina Nabatchi and John Gastil (New York: Oxford University Press, 2012), 1.

74. Stephen Gencarella Olbrys, "Dissoi Logoi, Civic Friendship, and the Politics of Education," *Communication Education* 55, no. 4 (2006): 355, 354.

75. Sara M. Evans and Harry C. Boyte, *Free Spaces: The Sources of Democratic Change in America* (Chicago: University of Chicago Press, 1992), 17–18.

76. Albert Weale, Aude Bicquelet, and Judith Bara, "Debating Abortion, Deliberative Reciprocity and Parliamentary Advocacy," *Political Studies* 60, no. 3 (2012): 643.

77. Angus Chen, "Loneliness May Warp Our Genes, and Our Immune Systems," *NPR*, November 29, 2015, www.npr.org/sections/health-shots/2015/11/29/457255876/loneliness-may-warp-our-genes-and-our-immune-systems, par. 1.

78. Amy Edmondson, cited in Charles Duhigg, "What Google Learned from Its Quest to Build the Perfect Team," *New York Times Magazine*, February 25, 2016, https://mobile.nytimes.com/2016/02/28/magazine/what-google-learned-from-its-quest-to-build-the-perfect-team.html, par. 34.

79. I have drawn my explanation of this exercise from Tint, McWaters, and van Driel, "Applied Improvisation Training," 85. For a demonstration of this exercise, see Huge Improve Theater, "Huge Improve Theater: 'I Am a Tree,'" *MN Original*, June 23, 2011, YouTube video, 2:35, www.youtube.com/watch?v=D_4KacJam5c.

80. Tint, McWaters, and van Driel, "Applied Improvisation Training,"85.

81. John Hanson, Rob Alesiani, and Steve Ayscue, "Improv Everything 103," *Improv Everything*, November 1, 2017, podcast, 45:41, http://pca.st/Vv48.

82. Victor Turner, *The Ritual Process* (New York: Routledge, 1969).

83. Cited in Leslie Becker-Phelps, "Don't Just React: Choose Your Response," *Psychology Today,* July 23, 2013, www.psychologytoday.com/blog/making-change/201307/dont-just-react-choose-your-response.

84. Leslie A. Baxter and Barbara M. Montgomery, *Relating: Dialogues and Dialectics* (New York: Guilford, 1996).

85. Lois Holzman, *The Overweight Brain* (New York: East Side Institute Press, 2018), 1–2, italics in original. Gerard Hauser further argues that "capacitating students to be competent citizens is our birthright. It has been ours since antiquity," but "modern education has stripped us of it." Gerard Hauser, cited in William Keith and Roxanne Mountford, "The Mt. Oread Manifesto on Rhetorical Education 2013," *Rhetoric Society Quarterly* 44, no. 1 (2014): 1.

86. Holzman, *The Overweight Brain*, 3.

87. Cited in Stephen Nachmanovitch, "Stephen Nachmanovitch—Stamping Out Nouns," *Stephen Nachmanovitch*, September 16, 2013, YouTube video, 7:33, www.youtube.com/watch?v=gWJCAilAxXw.

88. The Hideout Theater, "Building Connections," *The Hideout Theater*, June 17, 2016, Vimeo video, 5:49, https://vimeo.com/171129826; Michael Schulman, "Improv for Cops," *The New Yorker*, July 2, 2016, http://www.newyorker.com/culture/culture-desk/improv-for-cops.

89. Alan Alda, *Things I Overheard While Talking to Myself* (New York: Random House, 2007), 17.

90. Marianne Williamson, *A Return to Love: Reflections on the Principles of A Course in Miracles* (New York: Harper Collins, 1992), 190–191, italics in original.

Conclusion

1. Michael Schulman, "Improv for Cops," *New Yorker*, July 2, 2016, www.newyorker.com/culture/culture-desk/improv-for-cops, par. 1.

2. Ibid., par. 2.

3. Mickey Rapkin, "Tim Robbins's Prison Improv Classes Make Inmates Less Likely to Re-Offend," *New York Magazine*, November 14, 2016, http://nymag.com/vindicated/2016/11/tim-robbins-proves-acting-classes-for-inmates-work.html, par. 6.

4. Ibid., par. 19.

5. Ibid., pars. 19, 15. For a similar project, see Matt Weinstein, "Playfair at the Prison Entrepreneurship Program," *Matt Weinstein*, December 17, 2013, Vimeo video, 3:24, https://vimeo.com/82117818.

6. Kwame Anthony Appiah, *Cosmopolitanism: Ethics in a World of Strangers* (New York: Norton, 2007), xv.

7. Cited in Zander and Zander, *The Art of Possibility*, 197.

8. Arthur Jensen, *A Cosmopolitan Future: Enacting Mystery and Using Cosmopolitan Communication to Meet the 21st Century Head On* (unpublished manuscript, forthcoming), 2. See also Celeste Condit, "You Can't Study and Improve Communication with a Telescope," *Communication Monographs* 76 (2010): 3–12.

9. Bruce Gronbeck, "Rhetorical Criticism in the Liberal Arts Curriculum," *Communication Education* 38, no. 3 (1989): 185.

10. Jagodowski and Paquesi, *Improvisation*, 56.

11. Pearce, *Communication*, 199.

12. Jesse Sostrin, *Re-Making Communication at Work* (New York: Palgrave Macmillan), 2013, 46–47.

13. Ernest Wilson, "5 Skills Employers Want That You Won't See in a Job Ad," *Fortune*, June 10, 2015, http://fortune.com/2015/06/10/5-skills-employers-want-that-you-wont-see-in-a-job-ad/ pars. 1–9.

14. Quintilian, cited in Kreiser, "I'm Not," 81.

15. Peter Sloterdijk, *Critique of Cynical Reason* (Minneapolis: University of Minnesota Press, 1987), 124.

16. Coonoor Behal, "Organizational Improv: A Creative Approach to Corporate Training," *Mindhatch*, June 14, 2017, www.mindhatchllc.com/insights/organizational-improv-creative-corporate-training/.

17. Brian Caplan, "What Students Know that Experts Don't: School Is All About Signaling, Not Skill-Building," *Los Angeles Times*, February 11, 2018, www.latimes.com/opinion/op-ed/la-oe-caplan-education-credentials-20180211-story.html, par. 4.

18. Cited in Kevin L. Jones, "An Upright Citizen's Podcast Demonstrates Improv at its Best," *KZED Arts*, February 6, 2015, https://ww2.kqed.org/arts/2015/02/06/ucb-co-founders-podcast-demonstrates-improv-at-its-best/, "So you're," par. 2.

19. Cited in Andis Robecnieks, "Actor Alan Alda Advises AAMC Attendees on How to Talk about Medical Science," *Modern Healthcare*, November 8, 2014, www.modernhealthcare.com/article/20141108/blog/311089936, par. 7.

20. Cited in Berkun, *Confessions*, 132.

21. Jackson, *Easy*, 138.

22. Adam Blatner, "Psychodrama," in *Play Therapy with Adults*, ed. Charles E. Schaefer (Hoboken, NJ: Wiley, 2003), 35.

23. Holzman, *Vygotsky*, 9.

24. Ibid., 62.

25. Ibid., 32.

26. Ibid., 84–85, 95.

27. In tune with the idea of cultivating broader experiences, Dias also highlights Augusto Boal's use of "jokers," or "the neutral, flexible figure who changes suits and therefore fit[s] into any hand," whose "goal is principally to upset or destabilize any normative reality and point out multiple interpretations of any singular event

or situation." Annalisa Dias, "Decolonizing 'Diversity' on Campus Using Applied Improvisation," in *Applied Improvisation*, eds. Theresa Robbins Dudeck and Caitlin McClure (London: Methuen, 2018), 229, 238.

28. Michael Golding, "Guns, Education and Improv," All Things Michael, February 28, 2018, https://improvisliving.blogspot.com/2018/02/guns-education-and-improv-by-michael.html.

29. Simon Worrall, "Why the Brain-Body Connection Is More Important than We Think," *National Geographic*, March 17, 2018, https://news.nationalgeographic.com/2018/03/why-the-brain-body-connection-is-more-important-than-we-think/.

30. See Dweck, *Mindset*.

31. Penelope Brown and Stephen C. Levinson, *Politeness: Some Universals in Language Usage* (New York: Cambridge University Press, 1987).

32. The authors further write that "Learning that is driven by passion and play is poised to significantly alter and extend our ability to think, innovate, and discover in ways that have not previously been possible." Douglas Thomas and John Seely Brown, *A New Culture of Learning: Cultivating the Imagination for a World of Constant Change* (Lexington, KY: CreateSpace, 2011), 114, 89.

33. Bernard and Short, *Jill and Patrick's Small Book*, 75.

34. Jackson, *Easy*, 17.

35. Lipmanowicz and McCandless, *The Surprising Power*.

36. Kevin Loria, "Something Weird Happens to Your Brain When You Start Improvising," *Business Insider*, April 18, 2015, https://www.businessinsider.com/what-creativity-looks-like-in-the-brain-2015-4.

37. Darrah Brustein, "6 Tips from the Improv Stage You Can Apply to Your Business," *Entrepreneur*, July 1, 2016, www.entrepreneur.com/article/277707.

38. Cited in Janice Taylor, "The 9 DO NOTS of Active Listening," *HuffPost*, September 19, 2014, www.huffingtonpost.com/janice-taylor/the-9-do-nots-of-active-l_b_5852646.

39. Adam Frank, "Science's Journey from Data to Truth," *NPR*, December 11, 2017, www.npr.org/sections/13.7/2017/12/11/569907969/sciences-journey-from-data-to-truth.

40. Sara Bender, "Forever Applaud: A Look at How 'YES Activism' can Help Us Live Our Wild and Precious Life," *Medium*, February 25, 2018, https://medium.com/@sarabender/forever-applaud-a-look-at-how-yes-activism-can-help-us-live-our-wild-and-precious-life-6ff3ebca9073, "Finding the Offer in Everything," par. 1.

41. See, for example, Ray Oldenburg, *The Great Good Place: Cafes, Coffee Shops, Bookstores, Bars, Hair Salons, and Other Hangouts at the Heart of a Community* (New York: Marlowe & Company: 1999); Robert D. Putnam, *Bowling Alone: The Collapse and Revival of American Community* (New York: Simon and Schuster: 2000).

42. John B. Horrigan, "Americans' Attitudes Toward Public Libraries," *Pew Research Center*, September 9, 2016, www.pewinternet.org/2016/09/09/americans-attitudes-toward-public-libraries/.

43. See Toastmasters International, www.toastmasters.org.

44. See National Issues Forums, www.nifi.org.

45. In particular, see the Applied Improvisation Network (AIN) (http://appliedimprovisation.network/) and all its offshoots to continue reading about the incredible number of new advances many members are making in areas from therapy to healthcare. I especially recommend joining the AIN's public Facebook group (www.facebook.com/groups/appliedimprov/) for the sharing and development of new games and exercises that many members contribute to the forum on a weekly, if not daily, basis.

46. Oldenberg, *The Great Good Place*, xxii, italics in original.

47. Mary Parker Follett, *The New State: Group Organization, the Solution of Popular Government* (Manfield Centre, CT: Martino, 1918), 363.

48. Finkel, *Teaching*, 115–116, italics in original.

49. For many more improvisational exercises to use in teaching or training, see Improv Encyclopedia, improvencyclopedia.org; improwiki, improwiki.com; and Spolin Games Online, spolingamesonline.org.

Bibliography

Alan Alda Center for Communicating Science. "Improvisation for Scientists." The New York Academy of Sciences, December 16, 2011. www.nyas.org/events/2011/improvisation-for-scientists/.

Alana, Lacy, and Jim Ansaldo. "The Connect Improv Curriculum: Supporting Youth on the Autism Spectrum and their Educators." In *Applied Improvisation*, edited by Theresa Robbins Dudeck and Caitlin McClure, 79–98. London: Methuen, 2018.

Alda, Alan. *If I Understood You, Would I Have This Look on My Face? My Adventures in the Art and Science of Relating and Communicating*. New York: Random House, 2018.

———. "Improvisation for Scientists: Workshops by Alan Alda and the Center for Communicating Science." *SBUJournalism*, March 23, 2010. YouTube video, 9:18. www.youtube.com/watch?v=JtdyA7SibG8.

———. *Things I Overheard While Talking to Myself*. New York: Random House, 2007.

Ali, Omar, and Nadja Cech. "'Yes, and' as Teaching-Learning Methodology." *Teaching & Learning in Higher Ed*, April 8, 2017. https://teachingandlearninginhighered.org/2017/04/08/yes-and-as-teaching-methodology/.

Allcott, Hunt, and Matthew Gentzkow. "Social Media and Fake News in the 2016 Election." *Journal of Economic Perspectives* 31, no. 2 (2017): 211–236.

All Stars Project. "Operation Conversation: Cops and Kids." *All Stars Project*, 2018. https://allstars.org/copsandkids/.

Ambrose, Susan A., Michael W. Bridges, Michele DiPietro, Marsha C. Lovett, and Marie K. Norman. *How Learning Works: Seven Research-Based Principles for Smart Teaching*. San Francisco: Jossey-Bass, 2010.

Antonakis, John, Marika Fenley, and Sue Liechti. "Can Charisma Be Taught? Tests of Two Interventions." *Academy of Management Learning & Education* 10, no. 3 (2011): 374–396.

Appiah, Kwame Anthony. *Cosmopolitanism: Ethics in a World of Strangers*. New York: Norton, 2007.

Armstrong, Patricia. "Bloom's Taxonomy." Vanderbilt University Center for Teaching, accessed April 27, 2020. https://cft.vanderbilt.edu/guides-sub-pages/blooms-taxonomy/.

Asen, Robert. "A Discourse Theory of Citizenship." *Quarterly Journal of Speech* 90, no. 2 (2004): 189–211.

Asma, Stephen T. "We Could All Do with Learning How to Improvise a Little Better." *Aeon*, May 29, 2017. https://aeon.co/ideas/we-could-all-do-with-learning-how-to-improvise-a-little-better.

Aspegren, Knut. "BEME Guide No. 2: Teaching and Learning Communication Skills in Medicine: A Review with Quality Grading of Articles." *Medical Teacher* 21, no. 6 (1999): 563–570.

Aylesworth, Andy. "Improving Case Discussion with an Improv Mindset." *Journal of Marketing Education* 30, no. 2 (2008): 106–115.

Baerheim, Anders, and Torild J. Alraek, "Utilizing Theatrical Tools in Consultation Training." *Medical Teacher* 27, no. 7 (2005): 652–654.

Bain, Ken. *What the Best College Students Do*. Cambridge, MA: Harvard University Press, 2012.

Balachandra, Lakshmi, Frank Barrett, Howard Bellman, Colin Fisher, and Lawrence Susskind. "Improvisation and Mediation: Balancing Acts." *Negotiation Journal* 21, no. 4 (2005): 425–434.

Balachandra, Lakshmi, and Michael Wheeler. "What Negotiators can Learn from Improv Comedy." *Negotiation* 9, no. 8 (2008): 1–3.

Balachandra, Lakshmi, Robert C. Bordone, Carrie Menkel-Meadow, Philip Ringstrom, and Edward Sarath. "Improvisation and Negotiation: Expecting the Unexpected." *Negotiation Journal* 21, no. 4 (2005): 415–423.

Ballon, Bruce C., Ivan Silver, and Donald Fidler. "Headspace Theater: An Innovative Method for Experiential Learning of Psychiatric Symptomatology Using Modified Role-Playing and Improvisational Theater Techniques." *Academic Psychiatry* 31, no. 5 (2007): 380–387.

Balonon-Rosen, Peter. "Whose Line Is It Really? How Improv Benefits Children with Autism." *State Impact*, December 21, 2016. indianapublicmedia.org/stateimpact/2016/12/21/improv-autism-benefits.

Barber, Benjamin. *Strong Democracy: Participatory Politics for a New Age*. Berkeley: University of California Press, 2003.

Barker, Chris, and Brian Martin. "Participation: The Happiness Connection." *Journal of Public Deliberation* 7, no. 1 (2011): 12.

Barker, Derek W. M., Noelle McAfee, and David W. McIvor. "Introduction: Democratizing Deliberation." In *Democratizing Deliberation—A Political Theory Anthology*, edited by David W. McIvor, Derek W. M. Barker, and Noëlle McAfee. Dayton, OH: Kettering Press, 2012.

Barnard College. "Reacting to the Past." Barnard College, 2016. https://reacting.barnard.edu/.

Barsade, Sigal G. "The Ripple Effect: Emotional Contagion and its Influence on Group Behavior." *Administrative Science Quarterly* 47, no. 4 (2002): 644–675.

Baruch, Yehuda. "Role-Play Teaching: Acting in the Classroom." *Management Learning* 37, no. 1 (2006): 43–61.

Basken, Paul. "Actor Is Honored for Using Improv to Help Scientists Communicate." *Chronicle of Higher Education*, April 20, 2013. www.chronicle.com/article/Alan-Alda-Is-Honored-for-Using/138673.

Baxter, Leslie A., and Barbara M. Montgomery. *Relating: Dialogues and Dialectics.* New York: Guilford, 1996.

Becker, Theresa. "Evaluating Improvisation as a Technique for Training Pre-service Teachers for Inclusive Classrooms." PhD diss., University of Central Florida, 2012.

Becker-Phelps, Leslie. "Don't Just React: Choose Your Response." *Psychology Today,* July 23, 2013. www.psychologytoday.com/blog/making-change/201307/dont-just-react-choose-your-response.

Beebe, Steven A., Timothy P. Mottet, and K. David Roach. *Training and Development: Enhancing Communication and Leadership Skills.* Upper Saddle River, NJ: Pearson, 2013.

Bega, Danny, Pamela Palmentera, Abby Wagner, Matt Hovde, Becca Barish, Mary J. Kwasny, and Tanya Simuni. "Laughter Is the Best Medicine: The Second City® Improvisation as an Intervention for Parkinson's Disease." *Parkinsonism & Related Disorders* 34 (January 2017): 62–65.

Behal, Coonoor. "Organizational Improv: A Creative Approach to Corporate Training." *Mindhatch*, June 14, 2017. www.mindhatchllc.com/insights/organizational-improv-creative-corporate-training/.

Behrendt, Peter, Sandra Matz, and Anja S. Göritza. "An Integrative Model of Leadership Behavior." *The Leadership Quarterly* 28, no. 1 (2017): 229–244.

Bender, Sara. "Forever Applaud: A Look at How 'YES Activism' Can Help Us Live Our Wild and Precious Life." *Medium*, February 25, 2018. https://medium.com/@sarabender/forever-applaud-a-look-at-how-yes-activism-can-help-us-live-our-wild-and-precious-life-6ff3ebca9073.

Berk, Ronald A., and Rosalind H. Trieber. "Whose Classroom Is It, Anyway? Improvisation as a Teaching Tool." *Journal on Excellence in College Teaching* 20, no. 3 (2009): 29–60.

Berkun, Scott. *Confessions of a Public Speaker.* Sebastopol, CA: O'Reilly, 2011.

Bermant, Gordon. "Working with(out) a Net: Improvisational Theater and Enhanced Well-Being." *Frontiers in Psychology* 4 (December 2013): 929.

Bernard, Jill. *Jill Bernard's Small Cute Book of Improv.* Minneapolis: Yes, and . . . , 2011.

Bernard, Jill, and Patrick Short. *Jill and Patrick's Small Book of Improv for Business.* Portland, OR: Viewers Like You, 2015.

Besser, Matt, Ian Roberts, and Matt Walsh. *The Upright Citizens Brigade Comedy Improvisation Manual*. New York: Comedy Council of Nicea, LLC, 2013.

Black, Laura. "How People Communicate During Deliberative Events." In *Democracy in Motion,* edited by Tina Nabatchi and John Gastil, 59–82. New York: Oxford University Press, 2012.

Blatner, Adam. "Psychodrama." In *Play Therapy with Adults*, edited by Charles E. Schaefer, 34–61. Hoboken, NJ: Wiley, 2003.

Boal, Augusto. *Legislative Theater: Using Performance to Make Politics*. London: Routledge, 1998.

———. *Theater of the Oppressed*. London: Pluto Press, 2000.

Boesen, Kevin P., Richard N. Herrier, David A. Apgar, and Rebekah M. Jackowski. "Improvisational Exercises to Improve Pharmacy Students' Professional Communication Skills." *American Journal of Pharmaceutical Education* 73, no. 2 (2009): 1–8.

Bolkan, San. "Intellectually Stimulating Students' Intrinsic Motivation: The Mediating Influence of Affective Learning and Student Engagement." *Communication Reports* 28, no. 2 (2015): 80–91.

Bond, Paul. "Study: TV Violence Linked to 'Mean World Syndrome.'" *Hollywood Reporter*, June 18, 2014. www.hollywoodreporter.com/news/study-tv-violence-linked-mean-712890.

Bonifer, Mike. *Gamechangers: Improvisation for Business in the Networked World*. Los Angeles: Gamechangers, 2008.

Booth, Wayne C. *The Rhetoric of Rhetoric: The Quest for Effective Communication*. Malden, MA: Blackwell, 2009.

Boromisza-Habashi, David, Jessica, M. F. Hughes, and Jennifer A. Malkowski. "Public Speaking as Cultural Ideal: Internationalizing the Public Speaking Curriculum." *Journal of International and Intercultural Communication* 9, no. 1 (2016): 20–34.

Bowell, T. "Feminist Standpoint Theory," *Internet Encyclopedia of Philosophy*, accessed April 28, 2020. www.iep.utm.edu/fem-stan/.

Boynton, Beth. "De-Stress and Improve Communication with Medical Improv." *MedLine*, December 13, 2016. http://mkt.medline.com/advancing-blog/de-stress-and-improve-communication-with-medical-improv/ (site discontinued).

———. "Launch into the Wonderland of Medical Improv with this Podcast Interview!" *Confident Voices in Healthcare*, June 7, 2016. www.confidentvoices.com/2016/06/07/launch-into-the-wonderland-of-medical-improv-with-this-podcast-interview/.

———. "A Medical Improv Activity: Breaking Tension & Improving Communication." *Nurse.org*, January 18, 2017. http://nurse.org/articles/medical-improv-activity-improving-communication/.

Boyte, Harry. "How Can We Awaken Democracy? Groups Explore the Concept of Civic Muscle." *MinnPost*, September 26, 2018. www.minnpost.com/community-voices/2018/09/how-can-we-awaken-democracy-groups-explore-the-concept-of-civic-muscle/.

Brafman, Ori, and Judah Pollack. *The Chaos Imperative*. New York: Crown Business, 2013.

Brafman, Ori, and Rom Brafman. *Click: The Forces Behind How We Fully Engage with People, Work, and Everything We Do*. New York: Crown, 2010.

———. *Sway: The Irresistible Pull of Irrational Behavior*. New York: Doubleday, 2008.

Brancaccio, David. "How Recess Can Make Students Better Job Candidates." *Marketplace*, December 19, 2017. www.marketplace.org/2017/12/19/education/recess-important-thriving-workplace-employers.

Brocket, Ralph G. *Teaching Adults: A Practical Guide for New Teachers*. San Francisco: Jossey-Bass, 2016.

Brookfield, Stephen D., and Stephen Preskill. *Discussion as a Way of Teaching: Tools and Techniques for Democratic Classrooms*. Hoboken, NJ: Wiley, 2012.

Brown, Penelope, and Stephen C. Levinson. *Politeness: Some Universals in Language Usage*. New York: Cambridge University Press, 1987.

Brown, Stuart. *Play: How It Shapes the Brain, Opens the Imagination, and Invigorates the Soul*. New York: Penguin, 2009.

Brownell, Judi. "Elwood Murray: Pioneering Methodologist in Communication." *Communication Education* 63, no. 4 (2014): 329–343.

Brustein, Darrah. "6 Tips from the Improv Stage You Can Apply to Your Business." *Entrepreneur*, July 1, 2016. www.entrepreneur.com/article/277707.

Burgoon Judee, K., and Jerold L. Hale. "Nonverbal Expectancy Violations: Model Elaboration and Application to Immediacy Behaviors." *Communications Monographs* 55, no. 1 (1988): 58–79.

Burke, Kenneth. *Language as Symbolic Action: Essays on Life, Literature and Method*. Berkeley: University of California Press, 1966.

———. *Permanence and Change: An Anatomy of Purpose*. Berkeley: University of California Press, 1984.

———. *A Rhetoric of Motives*. Berkeley: University of California Press, 1950.

Burtis, John O., and Paul D. Turman. *Leadership Communication as Citizenship*. Thousand Oaks, CA: SAGE, 2009.

Caillois, Roger. *Man, Play, and Games*. Translated by Meyer Barash. Chicago: University of Illinois Press, 2001.

Calafell, Bernadette Marie. "The Future of Feminist Scholarship: Beyond the Politics of Inclusion." *Women's Studies in Communication* 37, no. 3 (2014): 266–270.

Campbell, Candace A. "Improv to Improve Interprofessional Communication, Team Building, Patient Safety, and Patient Satisfaction." PhD diss., University of San Francisco, 2014.

Canel, María José and Vilma Luoma-aho. *Public Sector Communication: Closing Gaps Between Citizens and Public Organizations*. Malden, MA: Wiley, 2019.

Caplan, Brian. "What Students Know that Experts Don't: School Is All About Signaling, Not Skill-Building." *Los Angeles Times*, February 11, 2018. www.latimes. com/opinion/op-ed/la-oe-caplan-education-credentials-20180211-story.html.

Carcasson, Martín. "Beginning with the End in Mind: A Call for Goal-Driven Deliberative Practice." Occasional Paper 2, Public Agenda Center for Advances in Public Engagement, 2009. https://my.lwv.org/sites/default/files/carcasson. beginning_with_the_end_in_mind.pdf.

Carnevale, Anthony P., Leila I. Gainer, and Ann S. Meltzer. *Workplace Basics Training Manual.* San Francisco: Jossey-Bass, 1990.

Carpenter, Amanda, and Kathryn Greene. "Social Penetration Theory." In *The International Encyclopedia of Interpersonal Communication,* edited by Charles R. Berger and Michael E. Roloff, 1670–1673. Hoboken, NJ: Wiley, 2016.

Carrane, Jimmy, and Elizabeth Allen. *Improvising Better: A Guide for the Working Improviser.* Portsmouth, NH: Heinemann, 2006.

Carse, James. *Finite and Infinite Games.* New York: Simon and Schuster, 2011.

Castellanos, Sara. "'Oh, My God, Where Is This Going?' When Computer-Science Majors Take Improv." *Wall Street Journal,* May 14, 2019. www.wsj.com/articles/ oh-my-god-where-is-this-going-when-computer-science-majors-take-improv-11557846729.

Cea, Joanna Levitt, and Jess Rimington. "Creating Breakout Innovation." *Stanford Social Innovation Review*, Summer 2017. ssir.org/articles/entry/creating_breakout_innovation.

Charlip, Remy. *Fortunately.* New York: Simon & Schuster, 1964.

Chen, Angus. "Loneliness May Warp Our Genes, and Our Immune Systems." *NPR*, November 29, 2015. www.npr.org/sections/health-shots/2015/11/29/457 255876/loneliness-may-warp-our-genes-and-our-immune-systems.

Cheney, George, Lars Thøger Christensen, Theodore E. Zorn Jr., and Shiv Ganesh. *Organizational Communication in an Age of Globalization.* Long Grove, IL: Waveland Press, 2010.

Chickering, Arthur W., and Zelda F. Gamson. *Applying the Seven Principles for Good Practice in Undergraduate Education: New Directions for Teaching and Learning.* San Francisco: Jossey-Bass, 1991.

Christiansen, Adrienne, and Jeremy J. Hanson. "Comedy as Cure for Tragedy: ACT UP and the Rhetoric of AIDS." *Quarterly Journal of Speech* 82, no. 2 (1996): 157–170.

Cialdini, Robert B. *Influence: Science and Practice.* 5th ed. New York: Allyn & Bacon, 2008.

Cole, Jordana. "I've Got Your Back: Utilizing Improv as a Tool to Enhance Workplace Relationships." Master's thesis, University of Pennsylvania, 2016. http://repository. upenn.edu/cgi/viewcontent.cgi?article=1096&context=mapp_capstone.

Collard, Mark. "Group Energiser, Warm-Up, Fun Game—Jump In Jump Out." *Mark Collard*, September 16, 2012. YouTube video, 3:39. www.youtube.com/ watch?v=k6bHltjIYzE.

Common Craft. "Gamification." *Common Craft*, 2016. Video, 2:27. www.common craft.com/video/gamification.

Condit, Celeste. "You Can't Study and Improve Communication with a Telescope," *Communication Monographs* 76, no. 1 (2009): 3–12.

Conner, Daryl. *Leading at the Edge of Chaos*. New York: Wiley, 1998.

Corsun, David L., Cheri A. Young, Amy McManus, and Mehmet Erdem. "Overcoming Managers' Perceptual Shortcuts through Improvisational Theater Games." *Journal of Management Development* 25, no. 4 (2006): 298–315.

Coutu, Diane. "How Resilience Works." *Harvard Business Review*, May 2002. https://hbr.org/2002/05/how-resilience-works.

Crow, Jonathan. "John Cleese Explores the Health Benefits of Laughter." *Open Culture*, April 29, 2015. www.openculture.com/2015/04/john-cleese-explores-the-health-benefits-of-laughter-yoga.html.

Crozier, Michael P. "Governing Codes: Information Dynamics and Contemporary Coordination Challenges." *Administration & Society* 47, no. 2 (2015): 151–170.

———. "Recursive Governance: Contemporary Political Communication and Public Policy." *Political Communication* 24, no. 1 (2007): 1–18.

Csikszentmihalyi, Mihaly. *Creativity: Flow and the Psychology of Discovery and Invention*. New York: Harper & Row, 1990.

———. *Flow: The Psychology of Optimal Experience*. New York: Harper & Row, 1990.

Cuddy, Amy, Susan T. Fiske, and Peter Glick. "Warmth and Competence as Universal Dimensions of Social Perception: The Stereotype Content Model and the BIAS Map." *Advances in Experimental Social Psychology* 40 (2008): 61–149.

Curiosity Staff. "Improv Theater Was Invented to Help Immigrants Assimilate." *Curiosity*, September 20, 2016. https://m.curiosity.com/topics/improv-theater-was-invented-to-help-immigrants-assimilate-curiosity/ (site discontinued).

Daloz Parks, Sharon. *Leadership Can Be Taught: A Bold Approach for a Complex World*. Cambridge, MA: Harvard Business Review Press, 2005.

Daly, Aiden, Stephen J. Grove, Michael J. Dorsch, and Raymond P. Fisk. "The Impact of Improvisation Training on Service Employees in a European Airline: A Case Study." *European Journal of Marketing* 43, no. 3–4 (2009): 459–472.

Daly, John A., and Madeleine H. Redlick. "Handling Questions and Objections Affects Audience Judgments of Speakers." *Communication Education* 65, no. 2 (2016): 164–181.

Damasio, Antonio R. *Descartes' Error: Emotion, Reason, and the Human Brain*. New York: Random House, 2006.

Dannels, Deanna P., Ann Darling, Deanna L. Fassett, Jeff Kerssen-Griep, Derek Lane, Timothy P. Mottet, Keith Nainby, and Deanna Sellnow. "Inception: Beginning a New Conversation about Communication Pedagogy and Scholarship." *Communication Education* 63, no. 4 (2014): 366–382.

Deming, David J. "The Growing Importance of Social Skills in the Labor Market." *National Bureau of Economic Research*, December 8, 2017. http://www.nber.org/digest/nov15.

DesMaisons, Ted. "Improv and Mindfulness." Preconference workshop, Applied Improvisation Network World Conference, University of Oxford, Oxford, UK, August 11, 2016.

The Detroit Creativity Project. "The 100% Model." *The Detroit Creativity Project*, 2015. http://detroitcreativityproject.org/annual-reports/.

———. "Why Improvise? Read on. Or watch the video." *The Detroit Creativity Project*, 2015. http://detroitcreativityproject.org/the-improv-project/.

Diamond, M. R., and M. H. Christensen. "Bravo! Do Acting Games Promote Learning in the College Classroom?" *Journal on Excellence in College Teaching* 16, no. 2 (2005): 55–67.

Dias, Annalisa. "Decolonizing 'Diversity' on Campus Using Applied Improvisation." In *Applied Improvisation*, edited by Theresa Robbins Dudeck and Caitlin McClure, 221–244. London: Methuen, 2018.

Diaz-Lazaro, Carlos, Sandra Cordova, and Rosslyn Franklyn. "Experiential Activities for Teaching about Diversity." In *Getting Culture*, edited by Regan A. R. Gurung and Loreto R. Prieto, 191–200. Sterling, VA: Stylus, 2009.

Dorfman, Peter W., Paul J. Hanges, and Felix C. Brodbeck. "Leadership and Cultural Variation: The Identification of Culturally Endorsed Leadership Profiles." In *Culture, Leadership, and Organizations: The GLOBE Study of 62 Societies*, edited by Robert J. House, Paul J. Hanges, Mansour Javidan, Peter W. Dorfman, and Vipin Gupta, 669–720. Thousand Oaks, CA: SAGE, 2004.

Doyle, Alison. "Top Skills and Attributes Employers Look For." *the balance careers*, August 24, 2019. www.thebalancecareers.com/top-skills-employers-want-2062481.

Drinko, Clay. *Theatrical Improvisation, Consciousness, and Cognition*. New York: Palgrave Macmillan, 2013.

Drucker, Peter. *Management*. New York: Collins, 2008.

Dudeck, Theresa Robbins, and Caitlin McClure, eds. *Applied Improvisation: Leading, Collaborating, and Creating Beyond the Theater*. London: Methuen, 2018.

Duhigg, Charles. "What Google Learned from Its Quest to Build the Perfect Team." *New York Times Magazine*, February 25, 2016. https://mobile.nytimes.com/2016/02/28/magazine/what-google-learned-from-its-quest-to-build-the-perfect-team.html.

Dweck, Carol S. *Mindset: The New Psychology of Success*. New York: Random House, 2006.

Eadens, Savannah. " 'Yes, and': Second City Behavioral Science Group Studies How Improv Can Create Better Communication." *Chicago Tribune*, July 29, 2018. www.chicagotribune.com/entertainment/ct-ent-second-city-study-0725-story.html.

Economist Intelligence Unit. "Organisational Agility: How Business Can Survive and Thrive in Turbulent Times." *Economist*, March 2009. http://static1.1.sqspcdn.com/static/f/447037/22518673/1366674874460/TheEconomist_organisational_agility.pdf.

Ehrlich, Thomas. *Civic Responsibility and Higher Education*. Westport, CT: The American Council on Education and the Onyx Press, 2000.

Embassy of the United States, Nicosia, Cyprus. "Improvisation Expert James Bailey Conducts Theatre Workshops with Local Educators and Artists." *Embassy of the United States, Nicosia, Cyprus*, September 29–October 28, 2008, https://cyprus.usembassy.gov/embatwork/improvoct08.html (site discontinued).

———. "Improv Theatre Expert James Thomas Bailey Shares More Than Fun and Games on Return Visit to Cyprus." *Embassy of the United States, Nicosia, Cyprus*, May 4–16, 2009, https://cyprus.usembassy.gov/embatwork/improvmay09.html (site discontinued).

Engel, Susan. "Joy: A Subject Schools Lack." *The Atlantic*, January 26, 2015. www.theatlantic.com/education/archive/2015/01/joy-the-subject-schools-lack/384800/.

Engleberg, Isa N. "Learning to Speak." *Review of Communication* 14, no. 2 (2014): 182–190.

Engleberg, Isa N., Susan M. Ward, Lynn M. Disbrow, James A. Katt, Scott A. Myers, and Patricia O'Keefe. "The Development of a Set of Core Communication Competencies for Introductory Communication Courses." *Communication Education* 66, no. 1 (2016): 1–18.

Evans, Sara M., and Harry C. Boyte. *Free Spaces: The Sources of Democratic Change in America*. Chicago: University of Chicago Press, 1992.

Fairhurst, T. "Discursive Leadership: A Communication Alternative to Leadership Psychology." *Management Communication Quarterly* 21, no. 4 (2008): 510–521.

Felder, Richard M., and Rebecca Brent. *Teaching and Learning STEM: A Practical Guide*. San Francisco: Jossey-Bass, 2016.

Finest City Improv. "How to Have Awesome Improv Classes by Posing Great Debriefing Questions." *Finest City Improv*, accessed April 23, 2020. www.finestcityimprov.com/great-debriefing-questions/.

Finkel, Donald L. *Teaching with Your Mouth Shut*. Portsmouth, NH: Heinemann, 1999.

Finsterwalder, Jörg, and Billy O'Steen. "Marketing Theatre Education: Using Improvisation for Teaching and Learning." *UC Research Repository* (2008): 1–10.

FitzPatrick, Susan. "The Imaginary and Improvisation in Public Administration." *Administrative Theory & Praxis* 24, no. 4 (2002): 635–654.

Flanagan, Linda. "How Improv Can Open up the Mind to Learning in the Classroom and Beyond." *KQED*, January 30, 2015. ww2.kqed.org/mindshift/2015/01/30/how-improv-can-open-up-the-mind-to-learning-in-the-classroom-and-beyond/.

Fox Cabane, Olivia. *The Charisma Myth*. New York: Penguin, 2013.

Frank, Adam. "Science's Journey from Data to Truth." *NPR*, December 11, 2017. www.npr.org/sections/13.7/2017/12/11/569907969/sciences-journey-from-data-to-truth.

Fratto, Natalie. "Screw Emotional Intelligence—Here's The Key to the Future of Work." *Fast Company*, January 29, 2018. www.fastcompany.com/40522394/screw-emotional-intelligence-heres-the-real-key-to-the-future-of-work.

Fredrickson, Barbara. *Positivity*. New York: Random House, 2009.

———. "What Good Are Positive Emotions?" *Review of General Psychology* 2, no. 3 (1998): 300–319.

Friedman, Hershey H., Linda Weiser Friedman, and William Hampton-Sosa. "Is the Unidisciplinary College Major in Danger of Going the Way of Netscape, AOL, Myspace, Blockbuster, and the Blackberry?" SSRN, March 16, 2013. https://ssrn.com/abstract=2234498.

Friedman, Linda Weiser, Hershey H. Friedman, and Martin Frankel. "A New Mode of Learning in Higher Education: The Partnership Hybrid Class." SSRN, January 10, 2016. http://papers.ssrn.com/sol3/papers.cfm?abstract_id=2712763.

Gabor, Andrea. "Bring Back High School Civics (With a Twist)." *Bloomberg*, September 17, 2019. www.bloomberg.com/opinion/articles/2019-09-17/high-school-civics-is-on-the-way-back-with-a-twist?srnd=opinion.

Gagnon, Suzanne, Heather C. Vough, and Robert Nickerson. "Learning to Lead, Unscripted: Developing Affiliative Leadership through Improvisational Theatre." *Human Resource Development Review* 11, no. 3 (2012): 299–325.

Gale, Sarah Fister. "Live from Cigna, It's Improvisation." *Chief Learning Officer*, June 25, 2015. www.clomedia.com/2015/06/25/live-from-cigna-its-improvisation/.

Garard, Darin L., Lance Lippert, Stephen K. Hunt, and Scott T. Paynton. "Alternatives to Traditional Instruction: Using Games and Simulations to Increase Student Learning and Motivation." *Communication Research Reports* 15, no. 1 (1998): 36–44.

Gardner, Howard. *Multiple Intelligences*. New York: Basic Books, 2006.

Gee, Val, and Sarah Gee. *Business Improv*. Columbus: McGraw Hill, 2011.

Gencarella Olbrys, Stephen. "Dissoi Logoi, Civic Friendship, and the Politics of Education." *Communication Education* 55, no. 4 (2006): 353–369.

Gesell, Izzy. "Practiced Spontaneity: Using Improv Theater Skills to Help Teams Master Change." *The Journal for Quality and Participation* 28, no. 1 (2005): 4–7.

Ghaemi, Nassir. *A First-Rate Madness: Uncovering the Links between Leadership and Mental Illness*. New York: Penguin, 2011.

Giang, Vivian. "Why Top Companies and MBA Programs are Teaching Improv." *Fast Company*, January 13, 2016. www.fastcompany.com/3055380/why-top-companies-and-mba-programs-are-teaching-improv.

Gladstone, Brooke, William Gibson, David Brin, and Anne Simon. "The Science in Science Fiction." *NPR*, October 22, 2018. Radio program, 50:23. www.npr.org/2018/10/22/1067220/the-science-in-science-fiction.

Gleeck, Fred, and Avish Parashar. "Improv Exercise—Expert Interview." *Fred Gleeck*, December 6, 2009. YouTube video, 3:13. www.youtube.com/watch?v=gbpka36e-Xs.

———. "Improv Exercise—Three Word Sentences." *Fred Gleeck*, December 5, 2009. YouTube video, 2:42. www.youtube.com/watch?v=AwuzruaJJ4Y.

Goldie, Alison. "Status Exercise." *Improv Book*, September 23, 2015. YouTube video, 3:03. www.youtube.com/watch?v=UkBd3jrcvWc.

Golding, Michael. "Guns, Education and Improv." All Things Michael, February 28, 2018. https://improvisliving.blogspot.com/2018/02/guns-education-and-improv-by-michael.html.

Goldman, Zachary W., Gregory A. Cranmer, Michael Sollitto, Sara Labelle, and Alexander L. Lancaster. "What do College Students Want? A Prioritization of Instructional Behaviors and Characteristics." *Communication Education* 66, no. 3 (2016): 280–298.

Graber, Doris A. *The Power of Communication: Managing Information in Public Organizations*. Thousand Oaks, CA: SAGE, 2002.

Graduate Management Admission Council. *Corporate Recruiters Survey: 2014 Survey Report*. Graduate Management Admission Council, 2014. www.gmac.com/-/media/files/gmac/research/employment-outlook/2014-corporaterecruiters-final-release-3.pdf.

Graff, Gerald. *Clueless in Academe: How Schooling Obscures the Life of the Mind*. New Haven, CT: Yale University Press, 2003.

Grant, Adam M. *Give and Take: Why Helping Others Drives Our Success*. New York: Penguin, 2014.

Grashow, Alexander. "Adaptive Leadership Workshop." Coro New York Leadership Center, January 23, 2015.

Gray, Peter. "The Decline of Play and Rise in Children's Mental Disorders." *Psychology Today*, January 26, 2010. www.psychologytoday.com/blog/freedom-learn/201001/the-decline-play-and-rise-in-childrens-mental-disorders.

Greenwood, John. "Evidence Based Education: Active vs. Passive Learning." *The Teaching Course*, May 14, 2014. www.thetcblog.com/?p=2128 (site discontinued).

Gring, Mark, and Jera W. Littlejohn. "Assessment of the Repeated Speech Performance as a Pedagogical Tool: A Pilot Study." *Basic Communication Course Annual* 12 (2000): 97–125.

Grint, Keith. *Leadership: A Very Short Introduction*. New York: Oxford University Press, 2010.

Gronbeck, Bruce. "Rhetorical Criticism in the Liberal Arts Curriculum." *Communication Education* 38, no. 3 (1989): 184–190.

Gross, Larry. "Modes of Communication and the Acquisition of Symbolic Competence." In *Media and Symbols*, edited by David R. Olson, 58–62. Chicago: University of Chicago Press, 1974.

Gu, Wei. "Executive Talent Search Focuses on Adaptive Leadership." *The Wall Street Journal*, October 19, 2014. www.wsj.com/articles/boss-talk-asia-executive-talent-search-focuses-on-adaptive-leadership-1413751711.

Haidt, Jonathan. *The Righteous Mind: Why Good People Are Divided by Politics and Religion*. New York: Vintage, 2012.

Hall, William. "1-2-3-Word." *Improv Games*, accessed April 30, 2020. www.improv-games.com/1-2-3-word-also-called-convergence/.

Halpern, Charna. *Art by Committee: A Guide to Advanced Improvisation*. Colorado Springs: Meriwether, 2006.

Halpern, Charna, Del Close, and Kim Johnson. *Truth in Comedy: The Manual of Improvisation*. Colorado Springs: Meriwether, 1994.

Hanson, John, Rob Alesiani, and Steve Ayscue. "Improv Everything 103." *Improv Everything*, November 1, 2017. Podcast, 45:41. http://pca.st/Vv48.

Happe, Kelly. "The Body of Race: Toward a Rhetorical Understanding of Racial Ideology." *Quarterly Journal of Speech*, 99, no. 2 (2013): 131–155.

Harms, P. D., Marcus Credé, Michael Tynan, Matthew Leon, and Wonho Jeung. "Leadership and Stress: A Meta-Analytic Review." *Leadership Quarterly* 28, no. 1 (2017): 178–194.

The Harnisch Foundation. "Funny Girls." *The Harnisch Foundation*, October 13, 2017. YouTube video, 2:38. www.youtube.com/watch?v=dmlSl6PGxFk.

Hart, Jack. *Storycraft: The Complete Guide to Writing Narrative Nonfiction*. Chicago: University of Chicago Press, 2012.

Hart, Roderick P., and Don M. Burks. "Rhetorical Sensitivity and Social Interaction." *Speech Monographs* 39, no. 2 (1972): 75–91.

Hartelius, Johanna E. "Revisiting Vico's Pedagogy of Invention: The Intellectual Entrepreneurship Pre-Graduate School Internship." *Quarterly Journal of Speech* 98, no. 2 (2012): 153–177.

Healy, Rachel. " 'Improv Saved My Life': The Comedy Classes Helping People with Anxiety." *Guardian*, December 20, 2017. www.theguardian.com/stage/2017/dec/20/comedy-improv-overcome-anxiety-depression.

Heath, Chip, and Dan Heath. *Made to Stick: Why some Ideas Survive and Others Die*. New York: Random House, 2007.

———. *Switch: How to Change Things When Change Is Hard*. New York: Random House, 2010.

Heifetz, Ronald, Alexander Grashow, and Marty Linsky. *The Practice of Adaptive Leadership: Tools and Tactics for Changing Your Organization and the World*. Cambridge, MA: Harvard University Press, 2010.

Heslin, Paul A., and Lauren A. Keating. "In Learning Mode? The Role of Mind-sets in Derailing and Enabling Experiential Leadership Development." *The Leadership Quarterly* 28, no. 3 (2017): 367–384.

Hess, Abigail. "The 10 Most In-Demand Skills of 2019, According to LinkedIn." CNBC, January 6, 2019. www.cnbc.com/2019/01/04/the-30-most-in-demand-skills-in-2019-according-to-linkedin-.html.

The Hideout Theater. "Building Connections." *The Hideout Theater*, June 17, 2016. Vimeo video, 5:49. https://vimeo.com/171129826.

Hoffman, Ari, Bryan Utley, and Dan Ciccarone. "Improving Medical Student Communication Skills through Improvisational Theater." *Medical Education* 42, no. 5 (2008): 537–538.

Hoffmann-Longtin, Krista, Jason M. Organ, Jill V. Helphinstine, Deanna R. Reinoso, Zachary S. Morgan, and Elizabeth Weinstein. "Teaching Advocacy Communication to Pediatric Residents: The Efficacy of Applied Improvisational Theater (AIT) as an Instructional Tool." *Communication Education* 67, no. 4 (2018): 438–459.

Hogan, J. Michael, Jeffrey A. Kurr, Jeremy D. Johnson, and Michael J. Bergmaier. "Speech and Debate as Civic Education." *Communication Education* 65, no. 4 (2016): 377–381.

Holba, Annette M. "In Defense of Leisure." *Communication Quarterly* 62, no. 2 (2014): 179–192.

———. "Political Communication and Leisure." *The Review of Communication* 10, no. 1 (2010): 20–37.

Holcomb, Chris. " 'The Crown of All Our Study': Improvisation in Quintilian's Institutio Oratoria." *Rhetoric Society Quarterly* 31, no. 3 (2001): 53–72.

Hollman, Rich. "How Improv Training Can Create Compassionate Behavior. | Rich Hollman | TEDxLincolnSquare." *TEDx Talks*, May 4, 2017. YouTube video, 14:03. www.youtube.com/watch?v=KcrbEQkTAvk.

Holtgreive, Joseph. "The Lessons of Engineering Improv." *InsideHigherEd*, January 11, 2018. www.insidehighered.com/views/2018/01/11/how-engineering-students-can-learn-through-improvisational-theater-opinion.

Holzman, Lois. *The Overweight Brain.* New York: East Side Institute Press, 2018.

———. *Vygotsky at Work and Play.* New York: Routledge, 2017.

Horney, Nick, Bill Pasmore, and Tom O'Shea. "Leadership Agility: A Business Imperative for a VUCA World." *People & Strategy* 33, no. 4 (2010): 34–42.

Horrigan, John B. "Americans' Attitudes Toward Public Libraries." *Pew Research Center,* September 9, 2016. www.pewinternet.org/2016/09/09/americans-attitudes-toward-public-libraries/.

Huffaker, Julie S., and Ellen West. "Enhancing Learning in the Business Classroom: An Adventure with Improv Theater Techniques." *Journal of Management Education* 29, no. 6 (2005): 852–886.

Huge Improve Theater. "Huge Improve Theater: 'I Am a Tree.' " *MN Original*, June 23, 2011. YouTube video, 2:35. www.youtube.com/watch?v=D_4KacJam5c.

IBM. "IBM 2010 Global CEO Study: Creativity Selected as Most Crucial Factor for Future Success." *IBM*, May 18, 2010, www-03.ibm.com/press/us/en/pressrelease/31670.wss.

iDebate NL. "Second Wave 'My City Real World' in Gouda." *IDEA Debate Exchange*, August 26, 2015. YouTube video, 8:02. www.youtube.com/watch?v=6NTThMO2ufo.

Illich, Ivan. *Deschooling Society.* New York: Harper and Row, 1971.

Improv Encyclopedia. s.v. "Slide Show." Accessed April 30, 2020. http://improvencyclopedia.org/games//Slide_Show.html.

———. s.v. "Whoosh." Accessed April 23, 2020. http://improvencyclopedia.org/games/Whoosh.html.

Improv Resource Center Wiki, "IO West," *Improv Resource Center Wiki*, accessed April 16, 2020. http://wiki.improvresourcecenter.com/index.php/IO_West.

Inchingham, John. "Improv Games: What Are You Doing." *ShavaSue*, November 6, 2015. YouTube video, 3:56. www.youtube.com/watch?v=DGukly7CLrU.

in2improv. "About in2improv." *in2improv*, accessed April 29, 2020. https://in2improv, www.in2improv.org/in2improv.html.

———. "An in2improv documentary." *ImprovISA*, 2017. Vimeo video, 16:24. https://vimeo.com/197120806.

———. "Testimonials," *in2improv*, accessed April 29, 2020. www.in2improv.org/testimonials.html.

Jackson, Paul Z. "Applying Improvisation The Power of 'Yes, and' Paul Z Jackson at TEDxLSE." *Paul Z Jackson*, March 7, 2014. YouTube video, 13:19. www.youtube.com/watch?v=fr7jw8S6zqc.

———. *Easy: Your Lifepass to Creativity and Confidence*. London: The Solutions Focus, 2015.

———. *58½ Ways to Improvise in Training*. London: Crown House, 2003.

———. *The Inspirational Trainer: Making Your Training Flexible, Spontaneous and Creative*. London: Kogan Page Publishers, 2001.

———. "The Mistakes Myth: Paul Z Jackson at TEDxRussellSquare." *TEDx Talks*, March 11, 2014. YouTube video, 14:26. www.youtube.com/watch?v=_o5beLKS5M4.

———. "Wimbrovisers." *Paul Jackson Associates*, July 10, 2017. http://impro.org.uk/wimbrovisers/.

Jacobs, Jane. *Dark Age Ahead*. New York: Random House, 2004.

Jacobsen, Torild, Anders Baerheim, Margaret Rose Lepp, and Edvin Schei. "Analysis of Role-Play in Medical Communication Training Using a Theatrical Device—The Fourth Wall." *Medical Education* 6, no. 1 (2006): 1–8.

Jacques, Leslie S. "Borrowing from Professional Theatre Training to Build Essential Skills in Organization Development Consultants." *Journal of Applied Behavioral Science* 49, no. 2 (2013): 246–262.

Jagodowski, T. J., and David Pasquesi. *Improvisation at the Speed of Life*. Chicago: Sola Roma, 2015.

Jambekar, Anil B., and Karol I. Pelc. "Improvisation Model for Team Performance Enhancement in a Manufacturing Environment." *Team Performance Management: An International Journal* 13, no. 7 (2007): 259–274.

Janis, Irving. *Groupthink: Psychological Studies of Policy Decisions and Fiascoes*. 2nd ed. Boston: Wadsworth, 1982.

Jaschik, Scott. "Well Prepared in their Own Eyes." *Inside Higher Ed*, January 20, 2015. www.insidehighered.com/news/2015/01/20/study-finds-big-gaps-between-student-and-employer-perceptions.

Javidan, Mansour, and Ali Dastmalchian. "Managerial Implications of the GLOBE Project: A Study of 62 Societies." *Asia Pacific Journal of Human Resources* 47, no. 1 (2009): 541–558.

Jay, Jason, and Gabriel Grant. *Breaking Through Gridlock: The Power of Conversation in a Polarized World*. Oakland, CA: Berrett-Koehler Publishers, 2017.

Jensen, Arthur. *A Cosmopolitan Future: Enacting Mystery and Using Cosmopolitan Communication to Meet the 21st Century Head On*. Unpublished manuscript, forthcoming.

Jensen, Eric. *Brain-Based Learning: The New Paradigm of Teaching*. Thousand Oaks, CA: SAGE, 2008.

Johnstone, Keith. *Impro for Storytellers*. New York: Routledge, 2014.

———. *Impro: Improvisation and the Theatre*. New York: Routledge, 1987.

Jones, Kevin L. "An Upright Citizen's Podcast Demonstrates Improv at its Best." *KZED Arts*, February 6, 2015. https://ww2.kqed.org/arts/2015/02/06/ucb-co-founders-podcast-demonstrates-improv-at-its-best/.

Kahne, Joseph, Ellen Middaugh, and Chris Evans. *The Civic Potential of Video Games*. Cambridge, MA: MIT Press, 2009.

Katzman, Jeff, and Dan O'Connor. *Life Unscripted: Using Improv Principles to Get Unstuck, Boost Confidence, and Transform Your Life*. Berkeley, CA: North Atlantic Books, 2018.

Keats, Jonathan. "Let's Play War." *Nautilus*, June 13, 2019. http://nautil.us/issue/73/play/lets-play-war-rp.

Keefe, Joseph A. *Improv Yourself*. Hoboken: Wiley, 2002.

Kegan, Robert, and Lisa Laskow Lahey. *An Everyone Culture: Becoming a Deliberately Developmental Organization*. Boston: Harvard University Business Press, 2016.

Keith, William M. *Democracy as Discussion: Civic Education and the American Forum Movement*. Lanham, MD: Lexington, 2007.

———. "We Are the Speech Teachers." *The Review of Communication* 11, no. 2 (2011): 83–92.

Keith, William M., and Christian Lundberg. "Creating a History for Public Speaking Instruction." *Rhetoric & Public Affairs* 17, no. 1 (2014): 139–146.

Keith, William, and Roxanne Mountford. "The Mt. Oread Manifesto on Rhetorical Education 2013." *Rhetoric Society Quarterly* 44, no. 1 (2014): 1–5.

Kelly, Stephanie, and Zachary Denton. "Instructor's Corner #3: For Math Anxiety, Actions (and Reactions) Speak Louder than Words." *Communication Currents*, June 2015. www.natcom.org/CommCurrentsArticle.aspx?id=6145.

Kim, Bryan S. K., and Heather Z. Lyons. "Experiential Activities and Multicultural Counseling Competence Training." *Journal of Counseling and Development: JCD* 81, no. 4 (2003): 400–408.

Kinsinger, Melissa. "5C Improv Game—Whoosh!" *Melissa Kinsinger*, February 10, 2015. YouTube video, 0:52. www.youtube.com/watch?v=0N_-OtJBybU.

Kisiel, Cassandra, Margaret Blaustein, Joseph Spinazzola, Caren Swift Schmidt, Marla Zucker, and Bessel van der Kolk. "Evaluation of a Theater-Based Youth Violence Prevention Program for Elementary School Children." *Journal of School Violence* 5, no. 2 (2006): 19–36.

Kneupper, Charles, and Floyd D. Anderson. "Uniting Wisdom and Eloquence: The Need for Rhetorical Invention." *Quarterly Journal of Speech* 66, no. 3 (1980): 313–326.

Kolb, David A. *Experiential Learning: Experience as the Source of Learning and Development.* Upper Saddle River, NJ: FT Press, 2014.

Koseoglu, Gamze, Yi Liu, and Christina E. Shalley. "Working with Creative Leaders: Exploring the Relationship between Supervisors' and Subordinates' Creativity." *The Leadership Quarterly* 28, no. 6 (2017): 798–811.

Kranz, Peter L., Sylvia Z. Ramirez, and Nick L. Lund. "The Use of Action Learning Techniques in a Race Relations Course." In *Getting Culture,* edited by Regan A. R. Gurung and Loreto R. Prieto, 286–287. Sterling, VA: Stylus, 2010.

Kreiser, Chris. " 'I'm Not Just Making This Up as I Go Along': Reclaiming Theories of Improvisation for Discussions of College Writing." *Pedagogy* 14, no. 1 (2014): 81–106.

Krusen, Nancy E. "Improvisation as an Adaptive Strategy for Occupational Therapy Practice." *Occupational Therapy in Health Care* 26, no. 1 (2012): 64–73.

Kuhn, Thomas. *The Structure of Scientific Revolutions.* Chicago: University of Chicago Press, 2012.

Kulhan, Bob. *Getting to "Yes, and": The Art of Business Improv.* Palo Alto, CA: Stanford University Press, 2017.

Lago, Amanda T. "On the 45th Martial Law Anniversary, SPIT Manila Talks about the Value of Presence." *Rappler*, September 22, 2017. www.rappler.com/life-and-style/arts-and-culture/182992-spit-manila-improv-martial-law-45th-anniversary-show.

Laird, Dugan, Elwood F. Holton, and Sharon Naquin. *Approaches to Training and Development.* New York: Basic Books, 2003.

Lamott, Anne. *Bird by Bird: Some Instructions on Writing and Life.* New York: Random House, 1994.

Langer, Ellen J. *Mindfulness.* Philadelphia: Da Capo Press, 2014.

———. "Mindfulness Forward and Back." In *The Wiley-Blackwell Handbook of Mindfulness*, edited by Amanda Ie, Christelle T. Ngnoumen, and Ellen J. Langer, 7–20. Malden, MA: Blackwell, 2014.

Laughter For A Change. "Crazy 8s." *Laughter For A Change*, February 20, 2014. YouTube video, 0:56. www.youtube.com/watch?v=VEw7FidF61c.

Lee, Nancy R., and Philip Kotler. *Social Marketing: Influencing Behaviors for Good.* Thousand Oaks, CA: SAGE, 2011.

Lenski, Tammy. "Conflict Resolution Activity: Demonstrate How Pushing Creates Pushback." *Tammy Lenski*, May 6, 2015. https://tammylenski.com/conflict-resolution-activities-fist-press/.

Leon, Melanie. "Medically Relevant Improv: Using Improvisation to Teach Empathetic Communication to Medical Professionals." Honors thesis, Rollins College, 2014.

Leonard, Kelly, and Tom Yorton. *Yes, and: How Improvisation Reverses "No, but" Thinking and Improves Creativity and Collaboration*. New York: Harper, 2015.

Lerner, Joshua A. *Making Democracy Fun: How Game Design Can Empower Citizens and Transform Politics*. Cambridge, MA: MIT Press, 2014.

Levinson, Meira. *No Citizen Left Behind*. Cambridge, MA: Harvard University Press, 2012.

Lewis, Carine, and Peter J. Lovatt. "Breaking Away from Set Patterns of Thinking: Improvisation and Divergent Thinking." *Thinking Skills and Creativity* 9, no. 9 (2013): 46–58.

Libera, Anne. *The Second City Almanac of Improvisation*. Evanston, IL: Northwestern University Press, 2004.

Linsky, Marty. "TEDxStCharles—Marty Linsky—Adaptive Leadership—Leading Change." *TEDx Talks*, April 13, 2011. YouTube video, 21:00. www.youtube.com/watch?v=af-cSvnEExM.

Lipari, Lisbeth. "Rhetoric's Other." *Philosophy & Rhetoric* 45, no. 3 (2012): 227–245.

Lipmanowicz, Henri, and Keith McCandless. "Improv Prototyping." *Liberating Structures*, accessed April 28, 2020. www.liberatingstructures.com/15-improv-prototyping/.

———. *The Surprising Power of Liberating Structures*. New York: Liberating Structures Press, 2013.

Lorenz, Mary. "Employers Who Say 'Yes, and . . .' to Improv Comedy Gain Serious Benefits." *The Hiring Site,* February 4, 2010. http://thehiringsite.careerbuilder.com/2010/02/04/employers-who-say-yes-and-to-improv-comedy-gain-serious-benefits/ (site discontinued).

Loria, Kevin. "Something Weird Happens to Your Brain When You Start Improvising." *Business Insider*, April 18, 2015. www.businessinsider.com/what-creativity-looks-like-in-the-brain-2015-4.

Lucas, Christopher, and John W. Murry. *New Faculty*. New York: Palgrave, 2011.

Lull, James. *Culture-on-Demand: Communication in a Crisis World*. Malden, MA: Blackwell, 2007.

Lynn, Bill. *Improvisation for Actors and Writers*. Colorado Springs: Meriwether, 2004.

Lyon, Arabella. *Deliberative Acts: Democracy, Rhetoric, and Rights*. University Park: Pennsylvania State University Press, 2013.

Macedo, Stephen, ed. *Democracy at Risk*. Washington, DC: Brookings, 2005.

Madsen, William C., and Kevin Gillespie. *Collaborative Helping: A Strengths Framework for Home-Based Services*. Hoboken, NJ: Wiley, 2014.

Malhotra, Deepak, and Max H. Bazerman. *Negotiation Genius*. New York: Bantam, 2008.

Mamet, David. *True and False: Heresy and Common Sense for the Actor*. New York: Vintage, 2011.

Marino, Claudia, Gianluca Gini, Alessio Vieno, and Marcantonio M. Spada. "The Associations between Problematic Facebook Use, Psychological Distress and Well-Being among Adolescents and Young Adults: A Systematic Review and Meta-Analysis." *Journal of Affective Disorders* 226 (2018): 274–281.

Mathews, David. "Community Change through True Public Action." *National Civic Review* 83, no. 4 (1994): 400–404.

McClure, Caitlin. "Tiffany & Co. Says Yes, And." In *Applied Improvisation*, edited by Theresa Robbins Dudeck and Caitlin McClure, 141–162. London: Methuen, 2018.

McDermott, Martin. *Speak with Courage*. New York: Bedford/St. Martins, 2014.

McDonald, Chris. "Crisis Management as Ethical Improvisation." *Critical Studies in Improvisation* 9, no. 1 (2013): 1–3.

McGee, Michael Calvin. "Text, Context, and the Fragmentation of Contemporary Culture." *Western Journal of Communication* 54 (1990): 274–289.

McGhee, Paul. *Humor as Survival Training for a Stressed-Out World: The 7 Humor Habits Program*. Bloomington, IN: Authorhouse, 2010.

McGonigal, Jane. "Gaming can Make a Better World." *TED*, February 2010. Video, 19:49. www.ted.com/talks/jane_mcgonigal_gaming_can_make_a_better_world?language=en#t-28846.

———. *Reality is Broken: Why Games Make Us Better and How They Can Change the World*. New York: Penguin, 2011.

McKnight, Katherine S., and Mary Scruggs. *The Second City Guide to Improv in the Classroom*. San Francisco: Wiley, 2008.

McLaren, Brian. *Why Did Jesus, Moses, the Buddha and Mohammed Cross the Road? Christian Identity in a Multi-Faith World*. New York: Jericho, 2012.

McLeod, Jack M. "When Democracy Failed: Can Political Communication Research Contribute to Civil Recovery." *Political Communication* 35, no. 4 (2018): 1–5.

Meg, Nicola. "Can You Count from 1–20?" *Nicola Meg*, March 3, 2013. YouTube video, 2:22. www.youtube.com/watch?v=DKK5_I80i5Y.

Mendonça, David, and Frank Fiedrich. "Training for Improvisation in Emergency Management: Opportunities and Limits for Information Technology." *International Journal of Emergency Management* 3, no. 3 (2006): 348–363.

Merina, Dorian. "Comedy Improv Class Helps Veterans Deal with Civilian Life." *KPCC*, March 27, 2017. www.scpr.org/news/2017/03/27/70207/a-new-tool-for-vets-transitioning-to-civilian-life/.

Merlin, Shana. "Improv Warm-Ups: Improv Warm-Ups: 1st Letter, Last Letter Word Association." *expertvillage*, October 3, 2008. YouTube vidco, 1:21. www.youtube.com/watch?v=VifzHThoMKc.

———. "Improv Warm-Ups: Orange Ball, Thank You." *expertvillage*, October 3, 2008. YouTube video, 01:53. www.youtube.com/watch?v=x0noHPqyX00.

Meyer, Erin. *The Culture Map: Decoding How People Think, Lead, and Get Things Done Across Cultures*, international edition. New York: PublicAffairs, 2016.

Mikkelson, Alan C., Joy A. York, and Joshua Arritola. "Communication Competence, Leadership Behaviors, and Employee Outcomes in Supervisor-Employee Relationships." *Business and Professional Communication Quarterly* 78, no. 3 (2015): 336–354.

Miller, Carly. "Why Improv Comedy Is the Next Big Marketing Trend." *The Content Strategist*, May 16, 2016. https://contently.com/strategist/2016/05/26/why-improv-comedy-is-the-next-big-marketing-trend/.

Milo, Matthew. "Improvisational Warm Ups: Playing the 'Alien, Tiger, Cow' Improv Game." *expertvillage*, April 23, 2008. YouTube video, 1:30. www.youtube.com/watch?v=UeUUHd4bQBQ.

Mirivel, Julien. *The Art of Positive Communication*. New York: Peter Lang, 2014.

Montague, Alan, and Izzy Gesell. "Level-Up Applied Improvisation: Intro to Applied Improvisation for Facilitators and Trainers." Preconference handout, Applied Improvisation Network conference, Irvine, CA, August 2017.

Montague, Alan, and Patrick Short. "Intro to Applied Improvisation for Performers." Preconference workshop, Applied Improvisation Network World Conference, University of Oxford, Oxford, UK, August 11, 2016.

Montuori, Alfonso. "Beyond Postnormal Times: The Future of Creativity and the Creativity of the Future." *Futures* 43, no. 2 (2011): 221–227.

———. "The Complexity of Improvisation and the Improvisation of Complexity: Social Science, Art and Creativity." *Human Relations* 56, no. 2 (2003): 237–255.

———. "Social Creativity, Academic Discourse, and the Improvisation of Inquiry." *ReVision* 20, no 1 (1997): 34–36.

Morreale, Sherwyn, Joseph Valenzano, and Janessa Bauer. "Why Communication Education is Important: A Third Study on the Centrality of the Discipline's Content and Pedagogy." *Communication Education* 66, no. 4 (2017): 402–422.

Morreale, Sherwyn, Philip Backlund, and Leyla Sparks. "Communication Education and Instructional Communication: Genesis and Evolution as Fields of Inquiry." *Communication Education* 63, no. 4 (2014): 344–354.

Morrison, Mary Kay. *Using Humor to Maximize Learning: The Links between Positive Emotions and Education*. Lanham, MD: Rowman & Littlefield, 2008.

Moshavi, Dan. " 'Yes and . . .': Introducing Improvisational Theatre Techniques to the Management Classroom." *Journal of Management Education* 25, no. 4 (2001): 437–449.

Mossholder, Hettie A. Richardson, and Randall P. Settoon. "Human Resource Systems and Helping in Organizations: A Relational Perspective." *Academy of Management Review* 36, no. 1 (2011): 33–52.

Musil, Caryn. "Feminist Pedagogy: Setting the Standard for Engaged Learning." AAC&U, 34 (2015).

Nabatchi, Tina. "An Introduction to Deliberative Civic Engagement." In *Democracy in Motion,* edited by Tina Nabatchi and John Gastil, 3–18. New York: Oxford University Press, 2012.

Nachmanovitch, Stephen. *Free Play: Improvisation in Life and Art.* New York: Penguin, 1990.

———. "'Improvisation is . . .'—Stephen Nachmanovitch." *Stephen Nachmanovitch*, December 10, 2010. YouTube video, 5:27. www.youtube.com/watch?v=6Zfg G8B0Y3Q.

———. "Stephen Nachmanovitch—Stamping Out Nouns," *Stephen Nachmanovitch*, September 16, 2013, YouTube video, 7:33, www.youtube.com/watch?v=gWJC AilAxXw.

Napier, Mick. *Behind the Scenes: Improvising Long Form.* Englewood, CO: Meriwether, 2015.

———. *Improvise: Scene from the Inside Out.* Portsmouth, NH: Heinemann, 2004.

National Leadership Council for Liberal Education and America's Promise. *College Learning for the New Global Century.* Washington, DC: Association of American Colleges and Universities, 2007. www.aacu.org/sites/default/files/files/LEAP/GlobalCentury_final.pdf.

National Task Force on Civic Learning and Democratic Engagement. *A Crucible Moment: College Learning and Democracy's Future.* Washington, DC: AAC&U, 2012. aacu.org/sites/default/files/files/crucible/Crucible_508F.pdf.

Navarro, Joe, and Marvin Karlins. *What Every Body is Saying.* New York: Harper Collins, 2008.

NBC News. "'Funny Girls' non-profit teaches girls to be leaders through improv." *NBC News*, March 13, 2018. www.nbcnews.com/nightly-news/video/-funny-girls-non-profit-teaches-girls-to-be-leaders-through-improv-1185114691950.

Neuliep, James W. *Intercultural Communication: A Contextual Approach.* 7th ed. Thousand Oaks, CA: SAGE, 2018.

Newton, Paul M. "Leadership Lessons from Jazz Improvisation." *International Journal of Leadership in Education* 7, no. 1 (2004): 83–99.

Northouse, Peter G. *Leadership: Theory and Practice.* Thousand Oaks, CA: SAGE, 2015.

O'Keefe, Barbara J. "Against Theory," *Journal of Communication* 43, no. 3 (1993): 75–82.

Oldenburg, Ray. *The Great Good Place: Cafes, Coffee Shops, Bookstores, Bars, Hair Salons, and Other Hangouts at the Heart of a Community.* New York: Marlowe & Company, 1999.

On Being Studios. "Greg Boyle—The Calling of Delight: Gangs, Service, and Kinship." *On Being Studios*, December 2017. Soundcloud podcast, 52:10. https://soundcloud.com/onbeing/greg-boyle-the-calling-of-delight-gangs-service-and-kinship-nov2017.

Orlikowski, Wanda, and J. Debra Hoffman. "An Improvisational Model for Change Management: The Case of Groupware Technologies." *Sloan Management Review* 38, no. 2 (1997): 11–21.

Palczewski, Catherine Helen. "Argument in an Off Key: Playing with the Productive Limits of Argument." In *Arguing Communication and Culture*, edited by G. Thomas Goodnight, 1–23. Washington, DC: National Communication Association, 2002.

Palfrey, John. *Safe Spaces, Brave Spaces: Diversity and Free Expression in Education*. Cambridge, MA: MIT Press, 2018.

Palmer, Richard E. "What Hermeneutics Can Offer Rhetoric." In *Rhetoric and Hermeneutics in Our Time: A Reader,* edited by Walter Jost and Michael J. Hyde, 108–131. New Haven, CT: Yale University Press, 1997.

Pancer, Mark S. *The Psychology of Citizenship and Civic Engagement*. New York: Oxford University Press, 2015.

Pandey, Prateekshit. "Yes, and . . . Laughter Lab: Creating New Collaboration between Comedy and Social Justice." Center for Media & Social Impact, August 29, 2019, https://cmsimpact.org/comedy/yes-and-laughter-lab/.

Pariser, Eli. "Beware Online 'Filter Bubbles.'" *TED Talks*, March 2011. Video, 8:49. www.ted.com/talks/eli_pariser_beware_online_filter_bubbles?language=en.

Parker Follett, Mary. *The New State: Group Organization, The Solution of Popular Government*. Manfield Centre, CT: Martino, 1918.

Patel, Vimal. "Improv Helps Ph.D.'s Explain Their Work—and Loosen Up." *Chronicle of Higher Education*, November 10, 2014. www.chronicle.com/article/Improv-Helps-PhDs-Explain/149887.

Pearce, W. Barnett. *Making Social Worlds: A Communication Perspective*. Malden, MA: Blackwell, 2009.

———. *Communication and the Human Condition*. Carbondale: Southern Illinois University Press, 1989.

Penman, Robyn. *Reconstructing Communication*. Mahwah, NJ: Lawrence Erlbaum, 2000.

Pentland, Alex. "Measuring the Impact of Charisma." *Psychology Today*, December 23, 2009. www.psychologytoday.com/us/blog/reality-mining/200912/measuring-the-impact-charisma.

Phillips, Gordon. *Take It Personally: On the Art and Process of Personal Acting*. New York: Applause, 2000.

Phillips Sheesley, Alison, Mark Pfeffer, and Becca Barish. "Comedic Improv Therapy for the Treatment of Social Anxiety Disorder." *Journal of Creativity in Mental Health* 11, no. 2 (2016): 157–169.

Pink, Daniel H. *A Whole New Mind: Why Right-Brainers Will Rule the Future*. New York: Penguin, 2006.

Pinker, Steven. *The Sense of Style*. New York: Penguin, 2015.

Pitcher, Patricia C. *The Drama of Leadership*. New York: Wiley, 1997.

Polanyi, Michael. *The Tacit Dimension*. Chicago: University of Chicago Press, 2009.

Postman, Neil. *Crazy Talk, Stupid Talk: How We Defeat Ourselves by the Way We Talk and What to Do About It*. New York: Delacorte Press, 1976.

Putnam, Robert D. *Bowling Alone: The Collapse and Revival of American Community*. New York: Simon and Schuster, 2000.

Quinn, Jason Scott. "Improvising our Way through Tragedy: How an Improv Comedy Community Heals Itself through Improvisation." *American Communication Journal* 9, no. 1 (2007). http://ac-journal.org/journal/2007/Spring/articles/tragedy.html.

Rajeev, Priya Nair, and Subramanian Kalpathi. "Let's Play: The Use of Improv Games in Change Management Training—A Case Study." *Industry and Higher Education* 30, no. 2 (2016): 149–154.

Rapkin, Mickey. "Tim Robbins's Prison Improv Classes Make Inmates Less Likely to Re-Offend." *New York Magazine*, November 14, 2016. http://nymag.com/vindicated/2016/11/tim-robbins-proves-acting-classes-for-inmates-work.

Ray, Stevie. *Spontaneity Takes Practice*. Minneapolis: Punchline, 2005.

Rego, Arménio, Bradley Owens, Susana Leal, Ana I. Melo, Miguel Pina e Cunha, Lurdes Gonçalves, and Paula Ribeiro. "How Leader Humility Helps Teams to be Humbler, Psychologically Stronger, and More Effective: A Moderated Mediation Model." *The Leadership Quarterly* 28, no. 5 (2017): 639–658.

Rehearsal for Life. "The Urban Improv Method." *Rehearsal for Life*, accessed April 29, 2020. https://rehearsalforlife.org/urban-improv/method/.

———. "Urban Improv Program Impact." *Rehearsal for Life*, accessed April 29, 2020. https://rehearsalforlife.org/urban-improv/impact/.

Reidy, Patrick. "Improv Training Warm Up Game: Imaginary Balls Comedy." *lmaonyc*, May 20, 2012. YouTube video, 1:13. www.youtube.com/watch?v=6GxG4t1pW7M.

———. "Zip Zap Zop." *Laughter For A Change*, October 26, 2013. YouTube video, 1:19. www.youtube.com/watch?v=lyWKVGoXKak.

Reis, Rick. "Two Core Principles about Learning: What Every Teacher and Student Must Know about Education Theory." Stanford Tomorrow's Professor Postings, April 15, 2011. https://tomprof.stanford.edu/posting/1655.

Reilly, Jo Marie, Janet Trial, Debra E. Piver, and Pamela B. Schaff. "Using Theater to Increase Empathy Training in Medical Students." *Journal for Learning through the Arts* 8, no. 1 (2012): 1–8.

Riskin, Leonard L. "Beginning with Yes: A Review Essay on Michael Wheeler's *The Art of Negotiation: How to Improvise Agreement in a Chaotic World*." *Cardozo Journal of Conflict Resolution* 16, no. 605 (2015): 622–623.

Robecnieks, Andis. "Actor Alan Alda Advises AAMC Attendees on How to Talk about Medical Science." *Modern Healthcare*, November 8, 2014. www.modernhealthcare.com/article/20141108/blog/311089936.

Robinson, Ken. "Do Schools Kill Creativity?" *TED*, February 2006. Video, 19:13. www.ted.com/talks/ken_robinson_says_schools_kill_creativity?language=en.

———. *Out of Our Minds: Learning to Be Creative*. Chichester: Wiley, 2001.

Robson, Karen, Leyland Pitt, and Pierre R. Berthon. " 'Yes, and . . .' What Improv Theater Can Teach Service Firms." *Business Horizons* 58, no. 4 (2015): 357–362.

Rocco, Richard A., and D. Joel Whalen. "Teaching Yes, and . . . Improv in Sales Classes Enhancing Student Adaptive Selling Skills, Sales Performance, and Teaching Evaluations." *Journal of Marketing Education* 36, no. 2 (2014): 197–208.

Roe, Steve. "How I Give Feedback When Teaching Improv." Hoopla, April 24, 2017. http://hooplaimpro.blogspot.com/2017/04/how-i-give-feedback-when-teaching-improv.html.

Rossing, Jonathan P., and Krista Hoffmann-Longtin. "Improv(ing) the Academy: Applied Improvisation as a Strategy for Educational Development." *To Improve the Academy* 35, no. 2 (2016): 303–325.

Rost, Joseph. *Leadership for the Twenty-First Century*. New York: Praeger, 1991.

Salemi, Vicki. "Good Grades Are Meaningless in the Modern Workplace." *New York Post*, March 21, 2016. http://nypost.com/2016/03/21/good-grades-are-meaningless-in-the-modern-workplace/.

Salinsky, Tom, and Deborah Frances-White. *The Improv Handbook: The Ultimate Guide to Improvising in Comedy, Theatre, and Beyond*. New York: Methuen, 2013.

Salit, Cathy. *Performance Breakthrough: A Radical Approach to Work*. New York: Hachette, 2016.

Sanders, Barry. *A Is for Ox: The Collapse of Literacy and the Rise of Violence in an Electronic Age*. New York: Vintage, 1995.

Sauer-Klein, Jenny. "Game #3 Enemy Defender." *Jenny Sauer-Klein*, July 6, 2013. YouTube video, 2:50. www.youtube.com/watch?v=zu31ZWtTRdw.

Saxey, Esther. "Theatre Improvisation in Teaching." *Education Blog*, January 31, 2017. http://blogs.lse.ac.uk/education/2017/01/31/theatre-improvisation-in-teaching/.

Schulman, Michael. "Improv for Cops." *New Yorker*, July 2, 2016. www.newyorker.com/culture/culture-desk/improv-for-cops.

Schultze, Quentin J. *Communicate Like a True Leader*. Grand Rapids, MI: Edenridge, 2017.

———. "Why Is So Much Public Communication Nasty?" *Quentin Schultze*, December 2, 2016. http://quentinschultze.com/civility-political-discourse/ (site discontinued).

Schwartz, Gary. "What Does It Mean to Improvise?" *Improv Odyssey*, June 11, 2012. https://improv-odyssey.com/what-does-it-mean-to-improvise/.

Schwartz, Tony, and Catherine McCarthy. "Manage Your Energy, Not Your Time." *Harvard Business Review*, October 2017. https://hbr.org/2007/10/manage-your-energy-not-your-time.

Schy, Yael. "Improv to Bridge Divides." Presentation at the Applied Improvisation Network conference, Irvine, CA, August 2017.

Scruggs, Mary, and Michael J. Gellman. *Process: An Improviser's Journey*. Evanston, IL: Northwestern University Press, 2008.

Shapiro, George. "How It's Done: Ideas for Ongoing Programs." In *Cultivation of Leadership Roles, Methods and Responsibilities*, edited by Miriam B. Clark, 75–83. Greensboro, NC: Center for Creative Leadership, 1987.

Shapiro, Johanna, and Lynn E. Hunt. "All the World's a Stage: The Use of Theatrical Performance in Medical Education." *Medical Education* 37 (2003): 922–927.

Sharkansky, Ira, and Yair Zalmanovitch. "Improvisation in Public Administration and Policy Making in Israel." *Public Administration Review* 60, no. 4 (2000): 321–329.

Shaw, Patricia, and Ralph Stacey, eds. *Experiencing Spontaneity, Risk & Improvisation in Organizational Life: Working Live*. New York: Routledge, 2006.

Shephard, J. Marshall. "3 Kinds of Bias that Shape Your Worldview." *TED*, March 2018. Video, 12:13. www.ted.com/talks/j_marshall_shepherd_3_kinds_bias_that_shape_your_worldview.

Sherif, Muzafer, and Carl I. Hovland. *Social Judgment: Assimilation and Contrast Effects in Communication and Attitude Change*. Westport, CT: Greenwood Press, 1980.

Silberg, Richard. "Bippity, bippity, bop." *Richard Silberg*, May 31, 2018. YouTube video, 2:47. www.youtube.com/watch?v=0yVjYUypP9I.

Silberman, Mel. *Active Learning: 101 Strategies to Teach Any Subject*. San Francisco: Wiley, 2006.

Singal, Jesse. "The Bad Things that Happen When People Can't Deal with Ambiguous Situations." *NY Magazine*, October 19, 2015. www.thecut.com/2015/10/importance-of-dealing-with-ambiguity.html.

Skinner, B. F. *About Behaviorism*. San Francisco: Knopf, 1974.

Skocpol, Theda. *Diminished Democracy*. Norman: University of Oklahoma Press, 2003.

Sloterdijk, Peter. *Critique of Cynical Reason*. Minneapolis: University of Minnesota Press, 1987.

Socha, Thomas J. and Gary A. Beck. "Positive Communication and Human Needs: A Review and Proposed Organizing Conceptual Framework." *Review of Communication* 15, no. 3 (2015): 173–199.

Sostrin, Jesse. *Re-Making Communication at Work*. New York: Palgrave Macmillan, 2013.

Specht, Linda B., and Petrea K. Sandlin. "The Differential Effects of Experiential Learning Activities and Traditional Lecture Classes in Accounting." *Simulation & Gaming* 22, no. 2 (1991): 196–210.

Spencer, Gregory. *Reframing the Soul*. Abilene, TX: Leafwood, 2018.

Spolin, Viola. *Theater Games for the Classroom: A Teacher's Handbook*. Evanston, IL: Northwestern University Press, 1986.

———. *Improvisation for the Theater*. Evanston, IL: Northwestern University Press, 1999.

Spolin Games Online. "Introduction to Gibberish." *Spolin Games Online*, accessed April 24, 2020. Video, 5:23. https://spolingamesonline.org/introduction-to-gibberish/.

Stager Jacques, Leslie. "Borrowing from Professional Theatre Training to Build Essential Skills in Organization Development Consultants." *Journal of Applied Behavioral Science* 49, no. 2 (2012): 246–262.

Stamatoplos, Anthony C. "Improvisational Theater as a Tool for Enhancing Cooperation in Academic Libraries." In *Proceedings of the ACRL Fourteenth National Conference*, Seattle, March 12–15, 2009, 65–70.

Steffens, Niklas K., Frank Mols, S. Alexander Haslam, and Tyler G. Okimoto. "True to What We Stand For: Championing Collective Interests as a Path to Authentic Leadership." *The Leadership Quarterly* 27, no. 5 (2016): 726–744.

Stephens, Dustin. "Civics Lessons: Justices Sonia Sotomayor, Neil Gorsuch on Promoting Education in Citizenship." *CBS News*, November 4, 2018. www.cbsnews.com/news/supreme-court-justices-sonia-sotomayor-and-neil-gorsuch-promote-civics-education/.

Sternberg, Robert. *Successful Intelligence: How Practical and Creative Intelligence Determine Success in Life*. New York: Plume, 1997.

Stob, Paul. "No Safe Space: James Arnt Aune and the Controversial Classroom." *Rhetoric & Public Affairs* 16, no. 3 (2013): 555–566.

Stockley, Rebecca. "UX Week 2013 | Rebecca Stockley | Visit Improv World Without Looking Like a Tourist." *adaptivepath*, December 9, 2013. YouTube video, 28:54. www.youtube.com/watch?v=ddEryrU0qRo.

Sunstein, Cass R. *#Republic: Divided Democracy in the Age of Social Media*. Princeton, NJ: Princeton University Press, 2018.

Suspitsyna, Tatiana. "Higher Education for Economic Advancement and Engaged Citizenship: An Analysis of the U.S. Department of Education Discourse." *The Journal of Higher Education* 83, no. 1 (2012): 49–72.

Svensson, Jacob. "Expressive Rationality: A Different Approach for Understanding Participation in Municipal Deliberative Practices." *Communication, Culture & Critique* 1 (2008): 203–221.

Sweet, Charlie, Hal Blythe, and Rusty Carpenter. "Why the Revised Bloom's Taxonomy is Essential to Creative Teaching." *The National Teaching & Learning Forum* 26, no. 1 (2016): 7–9.

Tabaee, Farnaz. "Effects of Improvisation Techniques in Leadership Development." PhD diss., Pepperdine University, 2013.

Tannen, Deborah. *You Just Don't Understand: Women and Men in Conversation*. London: Virago, 1991.

Tarvin, Andrew. "Walk/Stop—An Energizer Activity." *Humor That Works*, November 19, 2012. YouTube video, 3:18. www.youtube.com/watch?v=a72goyDtjeI.

———. "What is Applied Improvisation?" *Humor That Works,* accessed April 20, 2020, www.humorthatworks.com/learning/what-is-applied-improvisation/.

Tawadros, Tammy. "Developing the Theater of Leadership: An Exploration of Practice and the Need for Research." *Advances in Developing Human Resources* 17, no. 3 (2015): 337–347.

Taylor, Janice. "The 9 DO NOTS of Active Listening." *HuffPost*, September 19, 2014. www.huffingtonpost.com/janice-taylor/the-9-do-nots-of-active-l_b_5852646.

Thalheimer, Will. "Debunk This: People Remember 10 Percent of What They Read." *ATD*, March 12, 2015. https://www.td.org/Publications/Blogs/Science-of-Learning-Blog/2015/03/Debunk-This-People-Remember-10-Percent-of-What-They-Read.

Thomas, Douglas, and John Seely Brown. *A New Culture of Learning: Cultivating the Imagination for a World of Constant Change*. Lexington, KY: CreateSpace, 2011.

Tint, Barbara. "From Hell No to Yes And: Applied Improvisation for Training in Conflict Resolution, Mediation, and Law." In *Applied Improvisation*, edited by Theresa Robbins Dudeck and Caitlin McClure, 199–220. London: Methuen, 2018.

Tint, Barbara, and Adam Froerer. "Delphi Study Summary." Applied Improvisation Network, 2014. http://appliedimprovisation.network/wp-content/uploads/2015/11/Delphi-Study-Summary.pdf.

Tint, Barbara S., Viv McWaters, and Raymond van Driel. "Applied Improvisation Training for Disaster Readiness and Response: Preparing Humanitarian Workers and Communities for the Unexpected." *Journal of Humanitarian Logistics and Supply Chain Management* 5, no. 1 (2015): 73–94.

Todd, Sarah. "Practicing in the Uncertain: Reworking Standardized Clients as Improv Theatre." *Social Work Education* 31, no. 3 (2012): 302–315.

Treder-Wolff, Jude. "Gamechanger: Using Improv Games for Therapeutic Goals—Workshop Handout." *Medium*, February 22, 2017. https://medium.com/@judetrederwolff/gamechanger-using-improv-games-for-therapeutic-goals-workshop-handout-b4316b16d83d.

———. "How The Improv Project Helps Detroit Students Discover What's Possible." *Medium*, December 29, 2017. https://medium.com/@judetrederwolff/how-the-improv-project-helps-detroit-students-discover-whats-possible-98aedccea67.

Trefor-Jones, Glyn. "Theatre Game #5—Energy Circle. From Drama Menu—Drama Games & Ideas for Drama." *Drama Menu*, June 26, 2014. YouTube video, 01:28. www.youtube.com/watch?v=wWPiYksnKLI.

Tskhay, Konstantin O., Rebecca Zhu, and Nicholas O. Rule. "Perceptions of Charisma from Thin Slices of Behavior Predict Leadership Prototypicality Judgments." *Leadership Quarterly* 28, no. 4 (2017): 555–562.

Turner, Victor. *The Ritual Process*. New York: Routledge, 1969.

Twenge, Jean M. *iGen: Why Today's Super-Connected Kids Are Growing Up Less Rebellious, More Tolerant, Less Happy—and Completely Unprepared for Adulthood—and What That Means for the Rest of Us*. New York: Simon and Schuster, 2017.

Tyszkiewicz, Mary. "Practicing for the Unimaginable: The Heroic Improv Cycle." In *Applied Improvisation*, edited by Theresa Robbins Dudeck and Caitlin McClure, 117–140. London: Methuen, 2018.

Uhl-Bien, Mary, Russ Marion, and Bill McKelvey. "Complexity Leadership Theory: Shifting Leadership from the Industrial Age to the Knowledge Era." *The Leadership Quarterly* 18, no. 4 (2007): 298–318.

Vera, Dusya, and Mary Crossan. "Theatrical Improvisation: Lessons for Organizations." *Organization Studies* 25, no. 5 (2004): 727–749.

Versal, Neil. "Improv Training Helps Cleveland Clinic Improve MD Communications." *MedCity News*, April 14, 2016. http://medcitynews.com/2016/04/improv-training-helps-cleveland-clinic-improve-md-communications/.

Vozza, Stephanie. "The One Thing You Need to Do to Become More Creative." *Fast Company*, April 24, 2017. www.fastcompany.com/40409481/the-one-thing-you-need-to-do-to-become-more-creative.

Wade, Chris. "ComedySportz LA—Boo! Yay!" *Chris Wade*, March 18, 2013. YouTube video, 4:33. www.youtube.com/watch?v=Fj20zcXUc4c.

Waisanen, Don J. "Arguments for Everybody: Social Media, Context Collapse, and the Universal Audience." In *Recovering Argument,* edited by Randall Lake, 264–269. New York: Routledge, 2019.

———. "Communication Training's Higher Calling: Using a Civic Frame to Promote Transparency and Elevate the Value of Our Services." In *Handbook of Communication Training,* edited by J. D. Wallace and Dennis Becker, 21–35. New York: Routledge, 2018.

———. *Political Conversion: Personal Transformation as Strategic Public Communication.* Lanham, MD: Lexington, 2018.

———. "Toward Robust Public Engagement: The Value of Deliberative Discourse for Civil Communication." *Rhetoric & Public Affairs* 17, no. 2 (2014): 287–322.

Waisanen, Don J., and Rodney A. Reynolds. "Side-Coaching the Public Speech: Toward Improvisational Delivery Adjustments in the Moment." *Communication Teacher* 22, no. 1 (2008): 18–21.

Waisbord, Silvio. "Why Populism is Troubling for Democratic Communication." *Communication, Culture, & Critique* 11, no. 1 (2018): 21–34.

Walton, Andre P. "The Impact of Interpersonal Factors on Creativity." *International Journal of Entrepreneurial Behavior & Research* 9, no. 4 (2003): 146–162.

Wasserman, Ilene C., and Beth Fisher-Yoshida. *Communicating Possibilities: A Brief Introduction to the Coordinated Management of Meaning (CMM).* Chagrin Falls, OH: Taos Institute Publications, 2017.

Watson, Katie. "Serious Play: Teaching Medical Skills with Improvisational Theater Techniques." *Academic Medicine* 86, no. 10 (2011): 1260–1265.

Watson, Katie, and Belinda Fu. "Medical Improv: A Novel Approach to Teaching Communication and Professionalism Skills." *Annals of Internal Medicine*, 165, no. 8 (2016): 591–592.

Watzlawick, Paul. *The Situation is Hopeless, but Not Serious (The Pursuit of Unhappiness)*. New York: Norton, 1993.

Watzlawick, Paul, Janet Beavin Bavelas, and Don Jackson. *Pragmatics of Human Communication*. New York: Norton, 1967.

Weale, Albert, Aude Bicquelet, and Judith Bara. "Debating Abortion, Deliberative Reciprocity and Parliamentary Advocacy." *Political Studies* 60, no. 3 (2012): 643–667.

Weick, Karl E. "Introductory Essay—Improvisation as a Mindset for Organizational Analysis." *Organization Science* 9, no. 5 (1998): 543–555.

Weick, Karl E., and Kathleen M. Sutcliffe. *Managing the Unexpected: Sustained Performance in a Complex World*. Hoboken, NJ: Wiley, 2015.

Weinstein, Matt. "Playfair at the Prison Entrepreneurship Program." *Matt Weinstein*, December 17, 2013. Vimeo video, 3:24. https://vimeo.com/82117818.

Wheeler, Michael. *The Art of Negotiation: How to Improvise Agreement in a Chaotic World*. New York: Simon and Schuster, 2013.

Wikipedia. s.v. "Flow (Psychology)." Last modified 16 April 2020, 05:01. https://en.wikipedia.org/wiki/Flow_(psychology).

Williams, Michele (@MicheleWilliamz). "Erica Marx #P2P @ revithaca #coach 'Play when the stakes are low so you can perform when the stakes are high.'" Twitter, October 21, 2016, 7:49 p.m. https://twitter.com/MicheleWilliamz/status/789614512827662336.

Williamson, Marianne. *A Return to Love: Reflections on the Principles of A Course in Miracles*. New York: Harper Collins, 1992.

Wilson, Ernest. "5 Skills Employers Want That You Won't See in a Job Ad." *Fortune*, June 10, 2015. http://fortune.com/2015/06/10/5-skills-employers-want-that-you-wont-see-in-a-job-ad/.

Wilson, Molly Clare. "Improv Toolkit for Educators." *The K12 Lab Wiki*, June 22, 2012. https://dschool-old.stanford.edu/groups/k12/wiki/f8fb7/Improv_Toolkit_for_Educators.html.

Windmueller, John. "The Science of Improv LIVE with Washington Improv Theater." Marian Koshland Science Museum of the National Academy of Sciences, February 15, 2017. https://facebook.com/story.php?story_fbid=10155749920736808&id=12496501807.

Witt, Paul L. "The Future of Communication Education." *Communication Education* 61, no. 1 (2012): 1–3.

Worrall, Simon. "Why the Brain-Body Connection Is More Important than We Think." *National Geographic*, March 17, 2018. https://news.nationalgeographic.com/2018/03/why-the-brain-body-connection-is-more-important-than-we-think.

Yamamoto, Ruth H. "Serious Fun: The Perceived Influences of Improvisational Acting on Community College Students." PhD diss., Walden University, 2015.

Yorton, Tom. "Using Improv Methods to Overcome the Fear Factor." *Employment Relations Today* 31, no. 4 (2005): 7–13.

Zakrajsek, Todd. "Keep the Magic Alive." *NEA Higher Education Advocate* 28, no. 3 (2011): 5–8.

Zander, Rosamund S., and Benjamin Zander. *The Art of Possibility*. Cambridge, MA: Harvard Business Press, 2000.

Zhang, Qin. "Instructor's Corner #3: Teaching with Enthusiasm: Engaging Students, Sparking Curiosity, and Jumpstarting Motivation." *Communication Currents*, February 1, 2014. www.natcom.org/communication-currents/instructors-corner-3-teaching-enthusiasm-engaging-students-sparking-curiosity.

Zupek, Rachel. "Top 10 Reasons Employers Want to Hire You." *Careerbuilder*, November 2, 2009. www.cnn.com/2009/LIVING/worklife/11/02/cb.hire.reasons.job.

Index

Printed in Great Britain
by Amazon